中

Red China today

共

現

在

HUGO PORTISCH

Red China today

TRANSLATED FROM
THE GERMAN BY
**Heinz von
Koschembahr**

CHICAGO
**Quadrangle
Books · 1966**

Library of Congress Catalog Card Number: 66-11872

DESIGNED BY LAWRENCE LEVY

Second Printing

Preface

On October 16, 1964, somewhere in the wasteland of Sinkiang Province, Chinese scientists exploded an atomic bomb. The mushroom cloud above China, and the radioactive fallout spreading around the world in the stratosphere, gave proof that the second great communist power on earth had penetrated the secret of the atom.

By the evening of that October 16 the world was no longer the same. The explosion which a nameless Chinese scientist had set off by merely pushing a button had changed it. Now we must reckon with the fact that the most populous nation on earth, under perhaps the most stringent dictatorship in the history of mankind, would soon know how to apply this secret to the production of military weapons—weapons which constitute the main threat to peace in our time.

Until that October day, the military might of China was considered in terms of mere numbers. Even the largest army in the world, which the Chinese undoubtedly have at their disposal, had little power to intimidate so long as it lacked modern means of mass destruction. Now it is not only probable but virtually certain that this gigantic army will be equipped with nuclear weapons.

On that same day, millions of people must have wondered whether our fathers' and grandfathers' bugaboo, "the Yellow Peril," had become reality.

To dismiss this question with a flat "no" would be rash and unrealistic. Nor should we, at this time, answer with an emphatic "yes" merely because China shows the first signs of becoming able eventually to join the atomic bomb club; other powers, with infinitely greater industrial capacity, have had this potential for some time and to a high degree.

Nonetheless, the political power structure of the world has been altered drastically by the event of October 16, 1964. Fear of and respect for the giant Red nation have grown. Concomitantly, so has China's potential ability to influence world affairs, especially in Asia, Africa, and South America.

All the more reason why it is imperative to discover what goes on in China under the mushroom cloud.

No other country has posed, or continues to pose, greater riddles for the statesmen, economists, and sociologists of the West than that nation in the Far East which the Chinese themselves continue to call the "Middle Kingdom" (Chung Kuo). Even the population figure of China is a secret. Are there 700 or perhaps 750 million Chinese? To what extent and at what rate does the Chinese population grow?

There are no reliable current statistics today.

Is the population pressure so strong that China must seek new territory to provide for its people? Or is its virgin land sufficient — in a country that covers an area of nearly three and three-quarter million square miles — to sustain further hundreds of millions?

Quite a few state departments in both the West and the East take it for granted that an answer to these questions would indicate whether China will pursue a peaceful or warlike policy.

But is that true? May not China's policy depend rather on what answers the makers of Chinese policy give themselves on these questions, or wish to give? Possibly more can be learned about that than about China's population surplus, if a surplus really exists. Furthermore, are the decisions of the Chinese leaders governed by considerations of national interest or by communist ideology?

It is not easy to fathom the communism practiced today in Peking. Is it the communism of Lenin, or that of Stalin? Or is it a

Chinese communism, a "sinocized" variant of Marxism-Leninism, which it would be better to term Maoism? If so, what is the core of its policies, both domestic and foreign?

And then, what about the Chinese people? What do they think? Have they submitted to communism? Have they adopted the mode of life dictated to them by the communist leaders? Have they forgotten four thousand years of independent and outstanding ways of thinking? Have they given up their equally ancient culture? Have they sacrificed practical wisdom to collectivist catch phrases? Are they enthusiastically following their new leaders, or are they unwillingly enduring the new regime? Do they even dare to resist?

An answer to these questions would be easier to come by if we knew whether the communist government is successfully solving the country's basic problem—feeding the nation—and, in connection with that, the living conditions of the 600 to 650 million Chinese who are still engaged exclusively in agriculture.

And that leads to the next question: How strong is China's industry? How fast or how slow is its growth? How much, if any, surplus has the nation been able to produce over and above the demands of its rising birth rate?

Despite these many unknown facts, or perhaps because of them, many reports about China have been published. No other country seems to be scrutinized as closely as China—mainly from outside, but also by travelers, scientists, economists, and to a lesser extent journalists, who now and then get a permit to visit the Middle Kingdom.

How their reports contradict each other! On one side are those who see a powerfully entrenched China, an impressive China dominated by one strong resolve; on the other side are those who see a weak, backward, unprogressive China, a China where conditions have hardly changed in a hundred — or a thousand — years.

Overestimation, underestimation — what is the truth?

In the first place, the reason for these contradictory reports seems simple: they do not depend solely on the traveler but, above all, on what he is shown, what he is permitted to see and hear, and how it is presented to him.

A businessman who is allowed to see two or three model establishments where his contacts are only highly competent people, well-versed in the latest developments, will get a different impression of China than a tourist who is shepherded from attraction to attraction; a sociologist who knows how to differentiate very well between the old and the new China; or a journalist who tries for as all-encompassing a picture as possible.

But even the attempts of the journalist depend on the willingness of the Chinese authorities to show him all, or on the efforts of these authorities to make a part seem to be all. This attitude of the functionaries is in turn influenced by what sort of journalist is visiting: a friend, a foe, or a neutral observer. Or at what particular time the visit takes place; whether Peking just then deems it necessary or inadvisable to let the world know the truth about China.

I do not know how they had classified me. I had not been invited by the Chinese authorities. It took me two and a half years to get my entry permit to China. I traveled alone, and my newspaper paid all the travel costs.

Yet, like all foreigners, I could only hope that I would be allowed to see the cities, factories, people's communes, universities, residential sections, markets—in short, the entire gamut of life in China. Wherever and however it was possible I tried, by questioning and through personal inspection, to discover more, to see more than what, under the circumstances, the officials who were involved intended me to hear and see.

What is offered here is a report of what I experienced and was able to absorb in China. From my vantage point I tried to delve as much as possible into many of the open questions about China. My account is as objective as I know how to be and as subjective as it has to be, for all the reasons I have stated.

Contents

Red China today

1

Border control with tea

Until recently, China was considered to be one of the most tightly closed-off countries in the East communist bloc. Not only was an entry permit difficult or impossible to obtain, it was not even easy to get to China by modern means of transportation. For almost fifteen years, from the founding of the Communist People's Republic of China, only one airline maintained a regular schedule of traffic with China: the Soviet Aeroflot, flying its four-motored Ilyushin 18 turboprop "Moscow" or the twin-jet Tupolev 104 from Moscow via Irkutsk and Ulan Bator to Peking.

Since that was the only airline connection between China and the rest of the world, all passenger traffic was filtered through a Soviet screen. Anyone who wanted to travel on the Aeroflot planes could do so only out of Moscow, and to get to Moscow it was necessary to apply for a Soviet transit permit. This enabled the Soviet authorities to maintain a register of all air travelers to China; they knew quite accurately from the information on the transit-permit applications who sought contact with Peking and whom the Chinese asked to visit their country. This transit permit also made it easy for the Soviets, if they wished, to exercise a strict control over China's political and economic connections with the other East bloc countries as well as with the nations of the West.

As long as relations between Peking and Moscow were cordial, the Chinese did not seem to object particularly to this arrangement. But when the conflict between China and the Soviet Union became pronounced, when the two socialist brother countries began to keep secrets from each other, Peking became very eager to break through its isolation. It no longer suited the Chinese that French, English, or German industrial representatives had to declare in. Moscow who they were, thus revealing why Peking wished to see them.

The Chinese government thus tried to open an air route to and from Japan. This failed, owing to Japanese and American opposition. But when China came in conflict with India, when war broke out on the China-India border, an Asian ally fell almost automatically into the arms of the Chinese—an ally who not only concluded several pacts with Red China's leaders but was also willing to be of help in other ways: Pakistan.

As a result, Pakistani Airlines now has a weekly flight from Karachi to Shanghai via Canton, with the most modern jets and pilots who have received the best American training. That they are not allowed to fly to Peking, but only to Shanghai, indicates a developing awareness of prestige on the part of the Chinese. Because China has no jet transports of its own, and is therefore unable to fly the same route with its own equipment, it simply would not do to have such modern products of American monopolistic capitalism flying to its capital city.

Pakistan is a member of two Western defensive alliances (the Middle-East Pact and SEATO); but apparently the control over visitors that might be exercised by pro-western Pakistan does not seem to trouble the Chinese as much as Soviet control.

Besides, there is always the traditional door to China: the British crown colony of Hong Kong. Anyone can get a permit to visit Hong Kong at any British consulate, and he need not give many reasons. Communist China has always obtained the most important commodities it needs from the free world through Hong Kong; through this city it is able to settle its world-wide financial transactions. Even in the days of the Korean blockade, it was connected with the rest of the world through Hong Kong as through an umbilical cord. Such rights and concessions, grudgingly given by

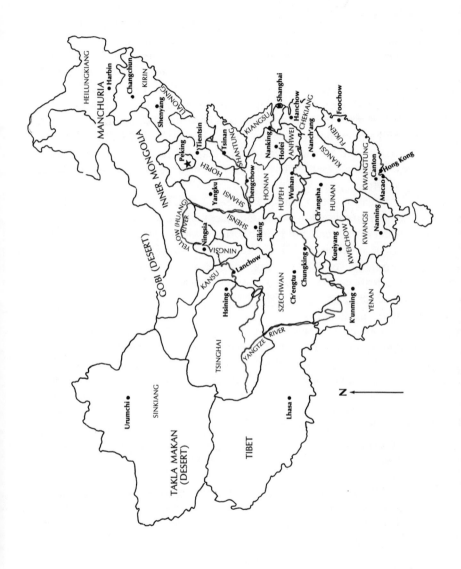

British colonial officials to their mighty Red neighbor, safeguarded Hong Kong from imminent "liberation" by the Red Army.

The number of Red Chinese establishments in free and anti-communist Hong Kong is surprisingly large. The biggest bank buildings in Hong Kong belong to the Bank of China—that is, the Red Chinese state bank. Red China even maintains a system of schools for the children of those Chinese who fled from the communist regime to Hong Kong. And quite a few big industrial installations owned by Red China are collecting hard currency for the communist motherland, not to mention certain non-communist Chinese industrialists and businessmen who are already paying a monthly tribute to China against the day of a possible "liberation," when it will be well to be in good standing.

On the other hand, Hong Kong obtains many millions of tons of fresh vegetables, meat, and rice, and millions of gallons of fresh water from the fertile neighboring Chinese provinces. A stoppage of these deliveries, which are paid for in hard Hong Kong dollar currency, would give Hong Kong serious supply problems. And so the British crown colony and its giant Red neighbor live and have lived for years in a sort of a symbiosis, a close relationship of mutual need and tolerance.

When I finally received my entry permit, after making many appearances at the Chinese embassy in Bern, Switzerland, the consular employee wanted to know how I intended to get to Peking. This would be important, he explained, because the point of entry would have to be noted on the permit. I posed a counter-question, asking which travel route the embassy would recommend to me.

The answer was cautious and yet direct: "The quickest way is by plane via Moscow to Peking, but the most comfortable way, of course, is by a Western airline to Hong Kong, crossing the border there."

I was reminded of the word "comfortable" when I sought out the Red Chinese China Travel Service upon my arrival in Hong Kong, only to be told there that mere possession of an entry permit did not give me the right to cross the border whenever I chose.

"Certain preparations are necessary," the smiling agent said in almost accent-free English. "The services of an interpreter must be procured for you, you'll need a reservation for the train from the border to Canton, and you'll also need a hotel-room reservation in Canton. And we'll have to decide now how you'll proceed from Canton to Peking."

It is significant that even today there is no direct air connection between Hong Kong and China. Travelers must board a local train at the Kowloon station in Hong Kong. It goes as far as the border, where they must change to another train in order to reach Canton. Once there, it is possible to take the Chinese interurban airline to Peking—but not on the same day; an overnight stay in Canton is unavoidable.

Just the same, I felt it would be more interesting to continue by train rather than plane. The railroad crosses China from south to north, passes through its most populous provinces, and touches a series of its most important cities.

Shepherding of the China-bound traveler by the Red Chinese begins in Kowloon. The porters here, employees of the communist railroad company, refuse to accept tips; instead, I was asked to pay a lump sum for porter services, and my luggage was tagged with a strip of colored cloth which alerted all subsequent Chinese porters to place their services at my disposal. The train's operating personnel had not yet put on their railroad caps with the Soviet star, yet they were fussing diligently over the Chinese travelers. Young men with American cigarettes, chewing gum, chocolate bars, and the latest issues of *Time* and *Life* passed back and forth constantly, making it quite clear that this would be my last opportunity to buy such things.

The closer we got to the border, the more passengers left the train; when, after a trip of about an hour, the locomotive came to a halt in the Lo Wu border station, emitting a long-drawn whistle blast, only a few passengers were left. All of these intended to cross the border.

Now I took a closer look at my traveling companions. There were eight West German captains of industry, a businessman from Belgium, a Netherlands diplomat with his daughter, and a few Chinese, who seemed to be quite well off—capitalist expatriates, on a visit to their homeland.

A peculiar atmosphere pervaded this little group. We all talked with one another, but each of us avoided saying who he was, where he came from, and what he was up to "on the other side." It seemed almost as if we were embarrassed to be caught taking such a trip. Only the Belgian talked straightforwardly: "I sell them special-compound oils which they cannot get anywhere else in the world. I'll remain in Peking just three days. Either they close the deal right away or I'm going home."

Much later, in Peking, I learned the German passengers' mission. They had come to sell China a large plant for the production of artificial fibers. The negotiations took longer than a month, but in the end the deal was made.

British border control, conducted by Hong Kong Chinese, runs as smoothly and routinely as at almost any West European frontier. Baggage is not opened and the passport examination is cursory. The way into China is free and easy.

Before us was a narrow railroad bridge framed by two high steel girders. Passenger trains do not go across this bridge. The traveler must cross on foot, carrying his own bags. In the middle of the bridge are more Hong Kong officials in British uniform: khaki shorts and blue police caps. A few paces behind them stand the first sentries of the Chinese People's Republic.

These are military sentries, clad in the sand-colored uniform of the People's Army; enlisted men and officers alike wear shapeless cotton jackets and trousers. But the shoulders of the officers bore the distinctive insignia with which I was already familiar: broad golden stripes with white stars, modeled after those of the Soviet Army.* The automatic pistols most of them carried were also Soviet models. Even to these sentries I had to show my Chinese entry permit. With a gesture, they motioned me onto the other half of the bridge.

At the end of the bridge, on a platform, I was met by my interpreter. Every foreign visitor is assigned an interpreter who knows the name of his "charge," where he comes from, and where he is to be guided. Later I discovered that these interpreters know a great

---

*These distinctive signs have been abolished, according to *The New York Times,* May 25, 1965.

deal more. They are informed about the traveler's occupation, his family life and circumstances, his political past, and his current affairs. The information disclosed during interviews and in the questionnaires, application forms, and *curriculum vitae*'s which must be submitted to any Chinese embassy in Europe as a prerequisite for an entry permit, is known to these interpreters and to almost all the other functionaries with whom it is necessary to deal in China.

So there was my interpreter. Because it was raining, he handed me an umbrella before shaking my hand. He then led me along the seemingly interminable railroad platform, straight through a cantonment of border guards, into a large, roomy border station. Here I first saw what was to become a commonplace in China: posters and slogans. I could not read the slogans, which were printed in Chinese characters. But the pictures spoke for themselves, At a glance, they showed happy, enthusiastic, determined Chinese peasants, laborers, and soldiers, struggling for greater productivity, better quality, more thrift, and, above all, the defense of the homeland.

As we moved on, other posters came into focus. These were directed against the "imperialists" and "colonialists." I asked for a translation of the slogans, which turned out to be the battle cries of international communism, although many had been somewhat broadened. For instance: "Proletarians of All Countries, Unite Against the Common Foe!"

The foe is imperialism, which is invariably depicted as either an American soldier or a monopolistic capitalist. The proletarians opposing this stereotype are at first sight only dark-skinned ones: Asians, Negroes, Arabs, Cubans, other Latin Americans. On the fourth poster, I finally discovered a white woman with blond hair in the phalanx of "proletarians of all nations." Later the Chinese were to assure me repeatedly that there was no desire to circumscribe "proletarian internationalism" along geographic, ethnic, or racial lines; the appeal went out to all nations, but, of course, primarily to the "oppressed."

We had come to the border station, which we entered. Never before had I seen such a well-equipped and imposing border station, and rarely such a large one. It soon dawned on me why this was so. China makes every effort to appear in the best possible light to all foreigners, and also to Chinese coming from abroad. Luxury, cleanliness, unexceptionable service, a friendly atmosphere, all contribute to this effect.

But the many rooms of this station served another purpose. Smoothly, almost unnoticeably, the travelers were separated from each other. The different groups were led into separate tea salons. The Chinese from abroad suddenly disappeared; the Netherlands diplomat and his daughter were no longer visible.

I, too, was guided into a tea salon, all by myself. Large, roomy easy chairs, all of them with slipcovers and lace antimacassars; next to the chairs, small end tables, also lace-covered; plants in flowerpots of the best Chinese porcelain; ash trays, teacups ready for filling, and fans to provide cool breezes.

Politely, the guide asked me to wait a moment. I whiled away the waiting period with what reading matter was available: eight booklets, with copies of each in German, English, French, Spanish, Russian, and Albanian. The content of all of them turned out to be the answers of the Chinese government to a letter written by the Communist Party of the Soviet Union.

The titles of the eight published answers are self-explanatory: "The Origin and Development of the Differences Between the Leadership of the C(ommunist) P(arty) (of the) S(oviet) U(nion) and Ourselves"; "On the Question of Stalin"; "Is Yugoslavia a Socialist Country?"; "Apologists of Neo-colonialism" (who turned out to be the Soviets); "Two Different Lines on the Question of War and Peace"; "Peaceful Co-existence—Two Diametrically Opposed Policies"; "The Leaders of the CPSU Are the Greatest Splitters of Our Times"; "The Proletarian Revolution and the Revisionism of Khrushchev." (Since then, answer number nine has appeared on the scene, under the title, "Khrushchev's Pseudo-Communism and Its Historical Lessons for the World," and is being diligently distributed, although Khrushchev has long since been ousted from office.)

Of secondary interest — likewise in the languages mentioned — were the pictorial magazines, *China in Pictures* and *China Reconstructs*. From then on, I was to find these brochures in every waiting room, hotel lobby, railroad coach, and airplane; in short, wherever a foreigner might conceivably venture in China. It is simply impossible to escape these ubiquitous reminders of the Chinese position in the ideological conflict with Moscow.

The interpreter returned, papers in hand. These were the applications I had to fill out before I could cross the border. There were two of them. On one, the usual personal data were to be set down. On the other, I was to declare how much foreign money I was bringing into China; the amount of money later exchanged in China had to be entered and certified on this form, which must be presented upon leaving the country. Furthermore, on this form were to be listed all objects that the Chinese consider valuable: cameras, watches, fountain pens, typewriters, any other technical gear, tape recorders, and also gold and silver ingots, jewelry, etc. Before one can leave the country, one's belongings must be checked against this list to make certain that nothing has been added or left behind.

There was another column headed: "How many exposed but not developed film rolls or film packs do you carry with you?" The same question is asked on the way out of the country, and those who don't know it soon discover that exposed but undeveloped film may not be taken out of China. In other words, all pictures taken in China must be developed before leaving the country, unless an official agency has been willing to make an exception.

Cooled by breezes from the fans, sipping bitter green tea, I sat ensconced in a comfortable easy chair, awaiting my turn to be called. The border officials spoke good English and were decidedly friendly. They threw only a superficial glance into my bag, saluted, and attested my declaration about currency and cameras. I noticed that even the baggage examination of the travelers was conducted individually, in separate cubicles.

This border examination lasted no longer than a minute. Already the interpreter was back. He obligingly guided me to a currency exchange and then into a different tea salon. This one was on the other side of the border control point. Again tea was poured. fans whirred to cool the air; again the same literature with which to pass the time.

Later, I was told that the train for Canton would not leave for several hours and was asked whether I preferred European or Chinese food. I was led in to lunch all by myself. In one corner sat the businessmen; my table had been set separately in another corner. The Chinese from abroad and the Netherlands diplomat did not appear here either.

Two hours later, China once again put her best foot forward for the travelers from abroad, this time in connection with the most important aspect of travel to a foreigner in any strange country — transportation. There stood the train, green with yellow side-stripes, sparklingly clean. At the door to each coach stood a female attendant in blue trousers, white blouse, and blue cap with the Soviet star.

Not only foreigners climbed aboard; many Chinese with loads and children also boarded. The loads were brought in Chinese style, hanging from each end of a bar carried across the shoulders, like balancing scales. The conductresses ran up, lifted the loads and carried them into the coaches, took the children from the arms of their mothers and then handed them up. All of this occurred as a matter of course; the passengers seemed to take this kind of customer service at railroad stations for granted.

Here on the platform all the passengers who had come from Hong Kong saw each other again. We had all been taken care of in separate tea salons, separate customs offices, and different restaurants in the border control building.

We were led through the train. The coaches are of two classes, a hard one and an upholstered one (and this is what they are called). Two benches each form a compartment; between them stands a table with the inevitable tea service for all passengers. Fans, which sweep in arcs, whir in all coaches; mosquito netting at the windows deters insects.

The foreigners were led neither into the hard nor the upholstered class. We walked to the very end of the train, the last coach of which had been reserved for us. With a friendly "Ni-hau" ("How do you do?"), the conductress greeted us at the entrance of a pullman without compartments. Heavy, large armchairs stood in two rows against the sides of the car, with a thick Chinese carpet between them. Next to each armchair stood a small table, again with a lace cover, flowerpot, tea service, and ash tray.

There were glass cases holding a collection of Chinese books and journals, several different board games, and foreign-language reading matter — and here again, of course, the eight answers to the CPSU. There were velvet-covered footstools to rest the weary feet of those stretched out on the wide easy chairs. For those who wished to engage a fellow passenger in a game of Chinese chess, checkers, or cards, folding tables could be set up in the middle aisle. At the rear of the car was a large glass-enclosed observation platform with a conference table and four armchairs.

At each window was a double set of curtains, open at the moment. I noticed the woven silk pictures hanging on the walls: "Lenin shaking the hand of Stalin"; "Mao Tse-tung bent over some work"; "The memorial to the heroes of the revolution in Peking"; and also a few old Chinese imperial palaces and nature scenes.

Hardly had we sat down when a female attendant appeared and offered to pour tea. Like almost all girls in China, she wore her hair in two braids, and she had on the summer uniform of the railroad personnel: blue cotton trousers and a white blouse with a red badge, on which her exact functions and service number were given in Chinese characters.

And then something began that I shall remember for a long time in connection with my travels through China: the loudspeaker. Mounted in all coaches, these operate by remote control and cannot be turned off. Announcement follows announcement, interspersed with marches, revolutionary songs, soldier choirs, but also arias from famous Peking operas, whose tone sequences sound discordant to our unaccustomed ears.

If one understood Chinese, one might find the announcements quite interesting. Passengers are told when the train departs, how long it will take to reach the next station, the length of the stop there, and whether there will be time to buy anything on the platform. Scenic spots on both sides of the track are called to one's attention. Announcements are made regarding the number of inhabitants in the next city, and its industry and commerce, including its achievements in production. By no means lacking are stories of the terrible hardships endured by the populace of that city before the communists took over, and how well off it is today. Names of outstanding communes situated nearby are called out, and "heroes of socialist labor" or the "war of liberation" are lauded. Again and again come admonitions to keep the coaches clean and neat, to make use of the spittoons (which are everywhere), and instructions on how to use the toilet.

Finally, passengers are invited, one coach at a time, to come to the dining car. The different menus are detailed, and so are the prices. And again, more announcements; this time (to be repeated often) a "socialist competition" is to take place among the conductors. The attendant of each coach competes against all the others in courtesy toward the travelers and in keeping the train neat.

My interpreter did not come along on this trip. He was a border interpreter, and his duties consisted of shepherding travelers through the passport and customs formalities. Foreign travelers in the pullman were left to their own devices for the five-hour trip. But there was a fresh contingent of interpreters on the platform awaiting our arrival in Canton, and this lot had cars.

We were driven to a newly built hotel, which I was able to identify on sight: it resembled, down to the smallest ornamentation, a newly built Soviet hotel in the city of Tashkent in Uzbekistan (Uzbek S.S.R.). The same Soviet architect must have been employed here; at least his blueprints had been used. The furnishings and layout of the hotel rooms were like the Soviet model. But when I asked, I was told emphatically that this hotel had been built exclusively by Chinese workers with Chinese material and according to Chinese plans: "out of our own strength" — how often I was to hear this assertive phrase!

That evening and the following morning, I was driven through the city of Canton on sight-seeing tours and was shown both old and new points of interest. Without fail, I had to visit the big, permanent industrial exhibition which had been established here — a few hours by rail from Hong Kong — to give those visitors from the West who were content with a mere side excursion into Red China an overall view of Chinese export products. The Catholic cathedral was pointed out to me; I learned that its doors stood open at all times and that the faithful were not hindered in attending regularly held religious services.

The next afternoon we returned to the railroad station. Most of my former fellow passangers had changed to a plane and had flown to Peking. This time I got a sleeping compartment. The journey, almost two thousand miles, would last two days and two nights, cutting right across China.

I had been granted a double privilege: the compartment, intended for four people, need not be shared, and the loudspeaker could be turned off from within the compartment. Just the same, I often turned it on and tried to discover what sort of things issued from it. (On this trip, also, there was no interpreter.)

Twice a day, Radio Peking puts a great bracket around all the people of China. At noon and again in the evening it addresses the entire nation, starting with the national anthem. Twice a day all Chinese people near and far, including those in the most remote regions of Tibet and Sinkiang, are spoken to directly, and the attention of the entire nation is focused on the important events of the day, both at home and abroad. In all trains, in all the people's communes, in all factories, in all the many places of work, these two important news broadcasts are listened to en masse. All the radio stations of this enormous country are linked at those times. Peking signs off with a vocal rendition of the "Internationale": "Arise ye prisoners of starvation!" Twelve hours later, it signs on again with the national anthem.

Trains are not only equipped with receivers and an internal loudspeaker system, they also have sending facilities. Each train can get in touch with any other train, or communicate with stations ahead or behind.

I soon noticed that ticket collectors came through the coach from time to time to draw the curtains across all the windows. Whether this was done just in my car, where I was the only foreigner, or also in the coaches for the Chinese passengers, I did not discover. As no one had asked me to keep the curtains closed, I at once ventured to look outside. I didn't see much that I considered worth hiding. Flooded fields, villages, and once some railroad ties which, curiously enough, had been burnt. Later I was to hear an official version of disastrous storms and the activities of the "Chiang Kai-shek bandits" on the Chinese mainland. Here and there, I saw peasants and other civilians at rifle practice. Every Chinese citizen belongs to the people's militia.

The train stopped in each of the larger stations for about ten to twenty minutes. During these stops, the train attendants would jump off, armed with mops, pails, and rags, to wash down the coaches from roof to rails with honest zeal. Most of the passengers also got off, to the accompaniment of rhythmic music issuing from the loudspeakers inside the train and others mounted on the platform. With the music came vocal instructions for gymnastics. Many of the passengers lined up along the platform and did the setting-up exercises as directed. Like every other place where the new Chinese state can reach a large number of people, the railroad has become a large drill ground.

On the long stretch of track between Canton and Peking, I observed another ritual conscientiously carried out by the railroad in its role of "socialistic training institution." Whenever the train entered a station, martial music blared over the platform. Dozens of railroad personnel stood at the edge of the platform at parade rest. Each was positioned precisely at a coach entrance, and they all waved red and green flags in salute. The same thing occurred when the train was about to pull out. There was the order to go aboard, to shut the doors, then the martial music and the salute by the personnel. A "train of socialism" got into motion. From then until the next stop, socialism was on the move over the loudspeakers in the coaches.

The platforms were painstakingly clean; whole columns of broom-wielding women worked to keep them so. Small vendors' carts were wheeled through the train for the passengers to buy ice cream, Chinese bread (a sort of puff pastry containing meat), chocolate bars, bonbons, cigarettes, wines, and spirits.

Apparently foreigners were not expected to mix with the natives, or to make their own purchases. When I approached one of these carts in a station, I found the attendant of my pullman at my elbow, giving me to understand that I should not buy a box of matches there. He guided me out of the crowd on the platform into a small park where, he indicated, I could stroll among the blooming jasmine shrubs and the fountains. Perhaps his sole concern was for my comfort. Two minutes before departure time, my attendant ceremoniously escorted me out of the park to the pullman, handing me a box of matches of markedly superior quality to those I had already bought at the cart—apparently he hadn't noticed my purchase. Later, I found these first-quality match boxes in all the hotels for foreigners in China.

Three times a day the dining-car chef called on me in my compartment. I could order from a variety of European or Chinese dishes, and I noticed that this variety was also available to all the other passengers. In this respect there was no preferential treatment of foreigners. On the other hand, I was asked politely to await the call from my attendant, who would then go with me to the dining car. Each time, the scene was the same: one-half of the dining car would be empty, and I would be put at a table in the middle of the car, but always so that my back was turned to the half of the car in which the tables were still occupied. I was left to stare at the empty section.

I admit that I interpreted this as a way of screening me from the rest of the travelers. I was, of course, determined to circumvent this measure. On the second day of the trip, I did not wait to be called and escorted. A few minutes later, I was almost sorry I had not waited. As I entered the dining car, all eyes turned toward me in surprised scrutiny; many diners stopped eating, feeling themselves observed. The conductors, attendants, and waiters were visibly embarrassed about the situation I had created.

This made me wonder whether the special treatment I received on this trip, and on several later occasions in trains and hotels, was truly designed to segregate me or whether it was simply intended as a courtesy. Perhaps both.

On the whole, I was grateful to the China Travel Service for advising me to go by train to Peking. Probably one of the most impressive experiences for a Westerner in the Far East is his first view of the Chinese landscape. Hour after hour, intensely green fields slid by the window of the pullman, each field surrounded by a small dam and a path, and with grazing water buffaloes. In the background, like a stage set, were mountains in the most bizarre formations, as blue and mist-shrouded as one sees them in the classical Chinese paintings.

The villages, which I saw for the first time at a distance, looked alien and somewhat forlorn in sharp contrast with the lovely landscape.

The first part of this journey carried me through southern China, where the principal crop is rice. Here it is the water-covered, terraced fields that above all give the landscape its Far Eastern character. Except when it rains too much or too little, nature here is kind to the people. Harvests can be gathered three times a year; while I saw on one field the ripe rice being threshed, I also saw the light-green rice seedlings being set out in an adjacent field.

And then I became aware for the first time that there were only small groups of workers in the fields. In the West this would surprise no one, but here I was traveling through a communist country where agriculture is collectivized; more, it has been concentrated into people's communes. I recalled the hundreds of Russian peasants whom I had seen, always in rank and file, shoulder to shoulder on the fields in the Soviet Union. Well, I thought, this may be due to the special requirements of rice cultivation. But a few days later, when I visited my first people's commune near Peking, I learned more about this planned distribution of the work force into small groups.

On the second day of this train ride, we left the terraced fields and mountains behind us. To the left and right of the right-of-way stretched a vast plain. The heat became oppressive, the air dry. Corn and wheat were growing in the fields. Wherever a cart or bicycle was moving, dust swirled high into the air.

We approached Wuhan, that industrial center on the Yangtze (Chang). The ground here was neither green nor gray but black as coal, and the sky was obscured by low-hanging smoke plumes from countless smokestacks.

This view from the window was the first indication I had that Chinese industry still lacks modern installations. I was to find this impression confirmed repeatedly in many of the industrial areas I visited.

Along the track, an unending procession of coal heaps passed my window. On each of these heaps, dozens, hundreds of people were busy shoveling coal and coal dust into small carrying baskets. Baskets balanced on poles across their shoulders, they raced down the slope, emptied each basket into a cart, and scurried back up the slope. The full carts were pulled by people, mostly women and girls, hitched to them by ropes. The sight of so many toiling, hurrying human beings must have given rise to the appellation "ants," used by former travelers in China to describe the great unresting masses of Chinese workers.

But such an impression of industrial backwardness may be deceiving. Nowhere else in China was I so impressed as when our train pulled into Wuhan.

Quite suddenly, the thousands of small suburban huts and houses fell away to make room for a broad silvery ribbon. This was the Yangtze, China's largest river and one of the greatest in the world. Even ten years ago the Yangtze was thought to be unconquerable; attempts to bridge the broad lower reaches of this mighty stream had never been successful. The river separates south from north China, and not infrequently in Chinese history it also constituted a natural boundary between different dominions.

I remembered reading travel accounts, some quite recent, that told how the trains from Canton would reach the terminus at Wuhan on the banks of the Yangtze, how the travelers had to be ferried across by boat to board the train for Peking on the other side. But our train did not stop; its speed merely decreased somewhat as it rolled thunderously onto a bridge, which one could not really identify as such at first. Because the rail line is so high above the waters of the Yangtze, one has the sensation of swooping in flight over the many junks plying between the two banks.

In the 1950's Russian and Chinese engineers succeeded in throwing this first bridge across the Yangtze. Even in comparison with similar structures in Europe and the United States it is one of the greatest construction feats of its kind, a truly brilliant technical achievement. It stood there in startling contrast to those thousands of coolies, whom just a moment ago I had seen running past my window with sweat-drenched, naked torsos, carrying their loads on poles.

Once more on the continuing stretch to Peking we pulled into another large industrial center: Chengchow. After that the trip went on for hours and hours without a stop. The landscape was a monotonous reach of arid plains as far as the eye could see.

We arrived in Peking after about sixty hours of train travel, punctual to the minute. As my foot touched the platform, I was as yet unaware that I was treading on one of the great symbols of China's "socialist reconstruction": the Peking railroad station, built by ten thousand workers in less than eight months in 1959, under the impetus of the "Great Leap Forward." It is designed to accommodate roughly 200,000 travelers daily.

There are nine other giant buildings in Peking, all of them erected in record time during the same period. Some of them I would get to see rather soon. But I had, first, another twenty-four hours to look at Peking at leisure, without a guide or time schedule.

2

In slalom style through Peking

At first I was not overwhelmed by Peking. Initially, I sensed neither the whisper of an imperial city thousands of years old, nor the exhilaration of a modern metropolis in the heart of a vast country.

When I walked out of the railroad station into the oppressive heat of a humid afternoon, I stood for a while in the really tremendous square in front of the station. Beyond it, by contrast, the low old houses seemed to cower. On the square itself, I could count no more than six cars, lined up to fetch prominent travelers at the behest of some official agency or organization. Five of the cars were Soviet products: a Zil, until a few years ago the parade vehicle of Soviet functionaries but now replaced in Moscow by larger, more modern cars; two cars of the intermediate class, the Volga; and two compact cars of the Muscovich type, plus one older model of the Czech Tatraplan.

Rickshas were available for those travelers for whom no cars were waiting. A couple of dozen pedicabs were drawn up at a sort of taxi stand, their drivers trying to shield themselves from the sun under old parasols.

These pedicabs have replaced the old-style rickshas that formerly were pulled by running coolies. Now the ricksha driver sits on a bicycle saddle, has a handlebar in front of him, and pumps the pedals. Over the two rear wheels of this tricycle, an upholstered bench is fitted into a body shell with room for two passengers. The old rickshas had room for only one.

Undoubtedly, introduction of the chain drive has somewhat mitigated the awkward feeling of being pulled by a running man. The ricksha driver, for his part, need no longer feel debased. This replacement of the running coolie by the ricksha driver is symbolic of the new China, where "man is no longer exploited by man."

Later on, I made use of rickshas on several occasions. Most of the older drivers still know a few English phrases, and the younger ones speak Russian. They were obviously pleased to be able to talk with a stranger in his own language, but even more pleased when they could show a foreigner that old, untouched Peking which nowadays not everyone who comes to the city is eager to explore, including even the Chinese. The ricksha drivers are forbidden, as are all service personnel, to accept tips. Gratuities, the Party says, are a symbol of debasement, of subjugation. But for the old-timer among the ricksha men, the thirst for tips is still in the blood. He will not mind if you leave the ricksha quickly at your destination without waiting for your change (whereas a waiter in a restaurant, for instance, will chase you across the street to give you your change).

But this was not the time for me to get into a ricksha. One of the waiting Volga sedans was for me, sent by the China Travel Service. Generally, it seems to be expected that foreigners want a chauffeur-driven car at their disposal all day. There is nothing more expensive in China today than a hired car. A private car is considered a luxury.

I got in. We started off. Now I became aware of just how many bicyclists were crowding the streets and squares. Four, six, or even eight abreast, they pedaled through the narrowest streets, turning intersections into circuses. Eventually, I found that, to a Chinese, the bicycle is his "car." His wealth, his material progress are measured by whether or not he owns a bicycle.

Now and then, a bus pushed through the bicycling throngs. The buses of Peking are painted red; all of them are products of the Czech Skoda plants. I have been told that there will be fewer and

Hand carts and "transports" bring most of the produce to the
many small markets in the cities. Supply and delivery are apparently
more prompt and efficient than in most other communist countries.

fewer of them because Czechoslovakia, too, has severely curtailed its deliveries to China. Above all, there is apparently a dearth of spare parts.

The Chinese try to make up for this virtual embargo by expanding their trolley-bus lines as rapidly as possible. It is remarkable how dense this network of electric motor coaches has grown already, both in Peking and in other Chinese cities. Furthermore, these light-blue trolleys are, all of them, made in China.

Mostly, Peking's inhabitants go about on foot. Tens of thousands, hundreds of thousands — no sidewalks are wide enough for them; they overflow into the streets.

We now turned into the broad central artery of Peking, which boasts ten traffic lanes in either direction. This huge avenue was constructed by the new government. Entire city blocks and sections were sacrificed so that it could traverse all of Peking and connect the most important buildings with the central city square in front of the Tien An Men, the imperial "Gate to Heavenly Peace."

On this square are also the Memorial to the Heroes of the Revolution, the new Great Hall of the People (seat of the National People's Congress), and the Museum for Chinese History and the Revolution. Incidentally, the residence of Party Chairman Mao Tse-tung stands at the main artery; two sentries of the People's Army, in their plain, sand-colored uniforms, are the only indication that a high communist functionary lives there. The gate before which they stand guard is a magnificent work of art from imperial times, one of those typically Chinese gates, with red wooden columns supporting a sweeping roof that rests on superbly carved beams. Behind this gate extends a large park with age-old trees, where once nobody but the emperor was allowed to walk.

While we were rolling along this broad avenue, I asked myself why it seemed so familiar, what it reminded me of. There is hardly anything to equal it in extent anywhere in the world; and yet, there was something about it that I had noticed elsewhere. Ah, I had it! Along the avenue stand tall lampposts crowned with large *luminaires*. Each of these light fixtures, of milk glass in the shape of a flame, rests on a highly decorated brass ring. They are exactly like those that line all the show case avenues in the Soviet cities and even in East Berlin and Warsaw.

This axial artery is an example of the grand-scale plans of the communist government. Not only is the avenue wide enough for twenty traffic lanes, it is also bordered on each side by six rows of trees, all of them still very young. And yet, with all of this, I did not get an impression of imposing modern dimensions; rather, I had the feeling that I was being driven across a large village square. This was probably because very few cars were in evidence, but instead many tricycles, bicycles, and carts.

At all intersections, traffic is regulated by policemen mounted on raised platforms in the center of the intersection, wearing blue trousers, white jackets, and tropical helmets and shaded by a parasol. Where there is no mechanical signal, they direct traffic very precisely with a white baton.

There are traffic signals at each intersection on the central artery. Their lights — green, yellow, red — are arranged in a horizontal rather than a vertical row. I had to hold my breath while we traversed the first few intersections, because neither the pedestrians nor the cyclists have to obey the red and green lights, which are intended exclusively for the drivers of cars. By the time we reached our third cross street, I had it figured out. As a car, bus, or truck comes along every five minutes, at best, the drivers honk their horns at the policemen long before reaching the intersection, whereupon the light will be held green for them, because cars are supposed to have precedence.

Nonetheless, quite understandably, my driver had his difficulties trying to get across these intersections. Moreover, it was almost impossible for him to steer a straight course, or to stay in one lane of this ten-lane thoroughfare. The reason is simple: any driver must navigate around dozens of pedestrians and cyclists—now a wide arc to one side, now a shorter one to the other side around the moving masses of people on foot and on wheels, who seem to pay no attention to any traffic rules. This prompted me to call such maneuvering "Chinese slalom," and also to shut my eyes tightly when one of the many cyclists suddenly veered in front of our radiator, or when a few children emerged from a throng of pedestrians and darted across the street, without looking either to the right or left, not more than a few yards ahead of us.

Soon, having become somewhat used to this, I was able to turn my attention to the people themselves. I had often heard and read that both men and women in the new China wear blue cotton suits. The catchword "blue ants" must have gone clear around the world. During my one-day stay in Canton I had been surprised to see only a few blue jackets and trousers. White and khaki were more usual there in the south of China, where the climate is tropical. But as I watched the inhabitants of Peking surging in great numbers up and down the avenue, I still saw no blue. People wore white or colored shirts, white or colored blouses.

However, both men and women wore trousers, and these were not well cut, more noticeably on the women; they seemed to have been made from a single ill-fitting pattern. Few of them were blue; most were white, khaki, gray, or brown.

Later I was told that the government has made efforts, in the last few years, to bring colored material onto the market. Like all dictatorships, this one is very sensitive to criticism. The communists are said to have been annoyed because the outside world regarded the sameness of dress among the Chinese as an external sign of mental conformity, and because of that term "blue ants." Appeals were published in the newspapers, urging girls and women particularly to dress more colorfully and to pay greater attention to their appearance.

The result of these appeals, and the corresponding availability of a variety of colorful fabrics on the market, was already apparent. Quite a few girls and women wore skirts instead of trousers. Somewhat later, I was able to see for myself that Sunday was a dress-up day when many women appeared in cotton and silk dresses in the traditional Chinese style, with the two long slits up the sides.

There was little variety in the way the hair was worn. Almost all girls wore braids—nowadays two, where one was the rule in the old days. Women wore their hair bobbed short and square or in page-boy style. Men's hair was cut short and, as a rule, parted.

There was something else I noticed on my first drive through

Peking. The walk of the girls and women had nothing feminine about it. Like the men, they strode through the streets with long steps. It was their footwear that made this possible. Their feet were thrust into flat plastic sandals, which looked rough-cut and were indistinguishable from those of the men. And yet, in Canton I had seen fashionably high-heeled western-style shoes in the shop windows. They were not only prohibitively expensive but most would-be buyers, said my Cantonese interpreter, "wouldn't dare to wear such shoes. The girls would be laughed at." The trend toward conformity, the desire not to be conspicuous, is still very strong.

Another thing that struck me was that not a single woman wore lipstick or showed the least sign of makeup. To want to appear more beautiful than one is runs counter to communist concepts, which castigate "fashion consciousness" and "the desire to please" as symptoms of bourgeois decadence.

Nevertheless, I did see one Chinese woman who had painted her lips red. That was in Canton. She also wore her hair in curls and had adorned herself with earrings. A crowd of children and adults were making fun of her, pointing fingers at this remarkable apparition which had, for reasons unknown to me, dared to venture into the streets in such a "get-up." This woman was defending herself vigorously, not just with words but also with a parasol, and trying to break out of the ring of detractors. My interpreter was unable to explain this scene, though he said that "there are still people whom this pleases, but, as you can see, the populace finds it a provocation."

But neither the pedestrians nor the cyclists nor the rickshas nor the lack of cars was entirely responsible for the strangeness of the Peking street scene. I kept turning to stare in fascination at certain vehicles I can only call "transport columns." These were of two types: a tricycle with a platform, usually piled high with a heavy load, laboriously pedaled along; and a two-wheeled cart, likewise heavily loaded, pulled by three, five, or eight men and women with ropes tied around their shoulders. These were loads that only horses would be expected to haul in Europe.

Hundreds of these "transport columns" could be seen by day and night on all streets in Peking, and in other cities too, as I saw later. "Co-operatives" (associations) supply the human motive power, although many factories, people's communes, markets, and industries have their own freight haulers and vehicles for transporting raw materials and finished products. One often sees transport columns of eight to fifteen tricycles or carts, all carrying the same product — the daily output of some small factory. It seemed odd to me to see perhaps eight men and women toiling through the streets with a cart holding a modern piece of equipment. The equipment was new in China, but the cart and means of locomotion have been unchanged for thousands of years.

However, this form of transport should not be underrated. On short hauls it serves its purpose very well, and it solves a transport problem that might stump other nations faced with a lack of cars and trucks. China has lots of people, and they help make up for sparse motorized transport. For example, later on in northeast China I watched as huge tubes, produced in an up-to-date factory by the most modern machinery, were fitted with a set of wheels at each end and then hauled to the freight yards by dozens of people.

Now and then, larger two-wheeled carts appeared on the Peking street scene, pulled by horses, donkeys, or mules. Most of them had come in from the country and were piled high with vegetables. A sack was hanging behind every animal—manure must not be wasted.

Because I had read so much about the dirtiness of the old China, not only the streets but also many of the people, I was struck particularly by the cleanliness of Peking. During the next few days, I would be wakened at five in the morning by the noise of many scratching whiskbrooms, and if I glanced out of my hotel-room window, I could see numerous columns of broom-wielding women, sweeping the street in unison.

Our car now turned off Peking's main street, and we drove past a series of public playgrounds, on which football and basketball games were being played before hundreds of wildly cheering spectators. I learned later that this is a popular form of recreation. We soon arrived at the Hsin Chiao Hotel, which is run but not owned by the state. This hotel had been financed by wealthy "patriotic overseas Chinese," and turned over to the Chinese government to run, for which the government pays 8 per cent interest a year. Many such arrangements still exist in China.

Incidentally, no foreigner may choose his hotel in Peking or anywhere else in China. A reservation is made for him by the China Travel Service. Furthermore, he has no say in the selection of a rental car or of the interpreter assigned to him. He can gauge the category in which he has been placed by the hotel at which he is booked, the quality and size of car supplied to him (at his own expense), and the proficiency of the interpreter detailed to him.

The largest and newest hotel in the capital, the Peking, is reserved for guests of the Chinese government. Others may not even eat there. They will be shown out, politely but firmly.

The Hsin Chiao Hotel, on the other hand, seems to be intended for foreigners who want as Western an atmosphere as possible in Peking, and who really cannot be counted as political friends of the communist government. Here can be found the industrialists from France, England, West Germany, Italy, Denmark, and Switzerland who have come to negotiate the sale of factory installations and machinery with Chinese government representatives. Now and then one sees guests from Albania and delegates of the Communist parties of Japan, Australia, and New Zealand.

Well, the China Travel Service had selected the Hsin Chiao as my hotel in Peking. In the lobby I was handed the customary notice-of-arrival form. In spite of its international flavor, there was not one word of English on the form; the column heads were in Chinese and Russian. So I needed my interpreter. Politely but without much warmth he had come up to introduce himself to me as Mr. Liu. From then on until the end of my travels in China, he was to be at my disposal whenever I needed him. He had been detailed to me for this purpose, at my request and naturally at my expense, by the China Travel Service. Mr. Liu spoke German well, almost without accent, although he had never been abroad.

"Not even in the German Democratic Republic [East Germany]?"

"No, I have never left China."

In the many weeks that he sat next to me for hours on end, in train compartments and on planes, he never said one single word about his family, his private life, or his personal opinions. Nor was he the least bit interested in how things were in Europe or in the country I came from. Whenever I ventured to make a comparison, he would turn his head away. He could not even be drawn into conversation about German literature, and he claimed never to have heard of Goethe, Schiller, or Heine.

"Then why did you study German?" I asked him one day.

"To be able to read the writings of Marx and Engels in the original language," was his answer.

The only textbooks he had studied were communist literature.

Only once — maybe — did Mr. Liu step out of character. That was when he proudly told me that he was a member of the Communist Party, and more than that, a cadre man, one who enjoys particular confidence, has to solve particular problems, and carries more responsibilities than ordinary Party members, let alone plain citizens. It was not necessary for him to tell me this. I had guessed it as soon as we met, just by looking at him. I had little doubt about the task set for Mr. Liu—to supply his immediate superiors with reports of my comings and goings, my inquiries and reactions. But I have to give him credit for being an exact and rapid translator, untiring even after eight or nine hours of heavy discussion during which he had to talk at least twice as much as I, since he had to translate not only my questions to the Chinese people but their answers as well.

Since my arrival at the hotel was expected, the registration formalities did not take much time. I was given a room on the fifth floor. Three elevators served the guests; these, too, had inscriptions in Chinese and Russian only, suggesting that the new China had initially been prepared for only one sort of foreign traffic, and that this hotel had served principally Russian guests, technicians, and experts.

The rooms, too, were furnished in Russian style — round construction, bulky tables, antiquated installations, many lace doilies and embroidered cushions, in the style of socialist realism. Similarly Russian was the arrangement of the hotel. Each floor had its own desk clerks, seated opposite the elevators and the staircase, so that they could see everyone who came or went. But they were also very service-conscious. No sooner had I entered my room than tea was brought to me; my shoes were taken away to be polished; fans

A view from the Museum of Chinese History in Peking, looking
across Tien An Men Square toward People's Hall, the seat of
parliament. The monument in the center of the square
commemorates the heroes of the revolution.

were turned on. Each floor had a refrigerator — a touch of the West—and cold beer, orangeade, and soda water were available. The clerks also sold cigarettes and matches.

Two or three small tables in every corridor displayed the already mentioned booklets: the Chinese answers to the Communist Party of the Soviet Union, printed in several languages. Above these tables were signs in the first English and French I had seen: "Help yourself" and "A votre disposition."

There were two restaurants in the hotel, one European and the other Chinese. Some of the printed menus were holdovers from the old days; they informed the guest that borscht, poljanka a la Warszawa, chicken a la Kiev, beef Stroganoff, and similar choice items were available. Borscht is unfortunately no longer obtainable; it seems there has been no demand for it of late. But poljanka a la Warszawa is very popular with guests, including those from the West. More up-to-date menus were printed in English, French, and German.

In the Chinese restaurant, tables groaned under the weight of an excellent selection of dishes. More than fifty were listed on the menu, and a meal consisted of at least five, and often ten, courses. The waiters were pleasant, very clean, and extremely quick and alert. This is certainly one of the outstanding differences noticed by a foreigner familiar with what passes for service in other "people's democracies." There are probably two reasons: one is the innate efficiency of the Chinese; the other, the fact that although there is "work for all," any number of jobs are less desirable than being a servant in a hotel for foreigners.

Yet, except for a few phrases of English or German, none of the hotel personnel understood a foreign language. This made it impossible to talk to any of them without an interpreter. Indeed I was unable to get any information at all except from the China Travel Service, which had offices in the hotel.

In addition, the foreigner can find whatever he needs in the way of everyday necessities right in the hotel; he scarcely needs to leave the building. The hotel's own post office and telegraph bureau are open weekdays and Sundays; likewise a men's and ladies' wear shop, a stationer's, a fruit and sweets shop, and, of course, one for souvenirs.

However, I was unable to find a telephone directory, city directory, map of China, or street guide, either in the hotel or anywhere else. Whichever official agency one has to deal with leaves its telephone number and address at the reception desk on the day of one's arrival. The only way to get the address or telephone number of a foreign embassy or legation in Peking is to bring it along.

But I was not cut off entirely from the outside world at that. The view from my hotel room window, from early in the morning until late at night, provided a direct link with Chinese life.

Directly opposite my window was the old city wall of Peking, about forty to sixty-five feet high, and the magnificent old city gate, the Tchong Wen Men. It bears no resemblance to the medieval gates of a European town, for it is crowned by a splendid old edifice, something like a Chinese temple, with a sweeping green-tiled roof. Each of the four cornices is adorned by fabled creatures of all sorts: unicorns, dragons, lion dogs, and others.

Thousands of swallows inhabit the multi-storied deserted building; huge swarms of them flew past my window, morning and evening, making an infernal racket. Below, in front of the gate, lies one of the city's most crowded squares. Several main arteries converge here, funneling traffic through the narrow gate. I could have spent hours just looking down on the hustle and bustle; the telephoto lens of my camera gave me a close-up view.

What humanity passed there! Thousands of cyclists, beginning about six o'clock in the morning, on the way to work; hand-drawn carts loaded with vegetables, carrying the produce of the people's communes for delivery in the city; two-wheeled carts, the axles of some rising almost seven feet above street level, the loads covered by reed mats; all sorts of rickshas. Then there were soldiers and policemen who marched past in single file to take up their posts in front of embassy buildings in the nearby diplomatic quarter. And in between, on and on, came the "transport columns," the tricycles piled high with cartons, boxes, barrels, tables, chairs. Sometimes I had to laugh heartily, when, for instance, ten of these transport-rickshas rolled past loaded with pyramids of spittoons. Or when a ricksha man came by, delicately maneuvering through traffic a light but precious load—a single television set with minuscule screen—and constantly looking back at it to make sure of its safety.

Now and then trucks crossed the square, solidly packed with men and women. They were being taken to some labor pool and would return in the evening. Whenever I saw them, I also heard them; they always sang, and their songs were Chinese lyrics set to Russian revolutionary and military tunes.

Then came donkey carts laden with enormous, green-blue cubes of ice. Peasants cut these in wintertime from frozen lakes, bury them deep in the ground, and deliver them to cold-storage houses, hotels, and restaurants in the city, where they serve the function performed by the modern freezers and air-conditioners of the West. In some of the hotels I stayed in later, chunks from such ice blocks were placed in large porcelain vases in the corridors to cool the air.

Frequently, in all this bustle, a troop of "Young Pioneers"—members of the communist youth organization—would march by, each wearing a red kerchief and swinging a triangular red pennant on a bamboo pole. Then a few old women might come hobbling painfully along, trying to cross the square. Their feet had been bound according to the old Chinese tradition, and their high Chinese slippers made it difficult to put one foot ahead of the other. This custom, incidentally, had been outlawed even before the communist takeover and is strictly illegal nowadays. The idea behind it had been to give women a graceful walk and an attractive sway—an idea that must have appealed chiefly to men.

Another thing that caught my attention was the large number of families setting out for strolls through the city, especially on Sundays: father, mother, two children in a perambulator, and another two, each holding the hand of a parent. During the week, grandfathers and grandmothers pushed these little bamboo carriages across the square.

Tea had been poured for me as soon as I entered my hotel room. As I was sipping it, the phone began to ring. At the other end of the line was a gentleman from the Chinese Foreign Office. My arrival in Peking was hailed, my presence in China was welcomed. The foreign office would be at my disposal. All efforts would be expended to accommodate my wishes. I was invited to meet with Madame Ma next morning at nine o'clock to discuss my further plans.

I spent that evening in the bar of the hotel. Don't imagine any resemblance to a bar as we know it in the West. It was a big, old-fashioned counter, and behind it a shelf on which stood a row of bottles of Chinese wines, spirits, and liquors, including those most in demand by foreigners—Chinese whiskey and Chinese cognac, which had replaced their noble Scottish and French counterparts. Imported intoxicants were not available even in this hotel for foreigners. However, some things were available here that one could no longer obtain in the Chinese provincial cities: ice cubes, chilled soda water, and orangeade.

The room was furnished with a few heavy, old-fashioned tables and much-used leather-upholstered chairs, bathed in the cheerless light shed by green-shaded lamps. In addition, there were three large billiard tables, usually occupied by well-dressed young Chinese.

The same peculiar atmosphere prevailed among the foreigners here that I was to encounter everywhere in China: they avoided the people at neighboring tables, shunned introductions, and seemed not to want to know about the others so as not to admit what they were there for. But always one sensed unspoken questions: Where are you from? Who are you? What are you doing here? And from the businessmen: Are you a competitor? Were you asked to come here? Are you getting preferential treatment, are your negotiations going better than mine, or are you as tired and exhausted as I am?

And, above all, question number one: Are you a communist?

English conversation drifted to me from one of the corners. Was the accent American? No, Australian. Tourists? Businessmen? Might be nice to talk with them. But after I heard one of them saying, "Comrades," I knew the score.

A married couple ordered drinks; evidently French, intellectuals. He looked as if he might be a writer. They would be interesting to know. "Bonsoir!" But a well-dressed Chinese gentleman got between us, nodded politely, and invited the couple to another table.

All this time, the man sitting next to me at the bar had been staring into his glass of Chinese cognac. Suddenly he beamed at me. "I should have met you six weeks ago," he said in French. "In that case, I might have stood it here much better. Well, that's life. Early tomorrow morning my plane leaves for Paris via Moscow, and I'll be home, you understand?" Somewhere in remote northeast China, I think in Changchun, I was to recall his words: "I'll be home, you understand?"

Next morning, I was driven in "my" car to the foreign office. It had been installed in an old palace, which stands dreaming in the middle of a park. Few would suspect that the narrow old alley leading up to the gate is the approach to the center of Chinese foreign policy. We drove past the customary two sentry guards, into the park, and over a long stretch of gravel driveway to the portals.

In the large foyer, a civil servant jumped up officiously, requested my interpreter and me to be seated in a tea salon, and soon came in with a steaming teapot and filled the cups. And very shortly, there was Madame Ma, a delicate young person whose large eyes regarded me through thick-lensed spectacles. She spoke in a murmur, in Chinese, although it became apparent that she knew English very well — I could see from the way she acted that she understood whatever I said before it had been translated. She had brought her own interpreter, who translated her conversation into English, and she asked me to speak in English. My interpreter offered to withdraw from the salon for the time being, but he was asked to remain.

Madame Ma began by asking me to tell her, freely and without reservation, exactly what I wished to do and see in China. I had more than fifty requests. To most of them she merely nodded her head without comment, while her interpreter wrote them down in Chinese characters. Now and then Madame Ma would look up to make a comment or to ask a question.

But nothing whatever could shake her composure, not even when I told her, "And then, I would rather like to go to Tibet, especially to Lhasa, but also to see something of the countryside."

Madame Ma's face showed no surprise; she remained polite

and ready to help. "In that case, something will have to be done about your visa," she volunteered in her monotone. "It will have to be extended to six or eight months."

My face must have reflected exactly what Madame Ma probably expected to see. "Oh, but why?"

To which Madame Ma replied, "You must surely know that there are no direct flights to Tibet. Lhasa doesn't have an airport. Nor are there any rail connections. The trip to Tibet would have to be undertaken by caravan. We have built a road there, but it's a very long one, many hundreds of miles, and it isn't a very good road. Floods and sandstorms often destroy the surface and cause the bridges to collapse. We estimate that a caravan would take three months, on an average, to reach Lhasa, but it's also possible that it might take longer. It depends on the weather and the condition of the road."

I was not willing to give up. "Aren't there any military flights to Tibet? Couldn't I hitch a ride on one of them?"

Smiling, Madame Ma shook her head; it was evident that she was not going to answer my questions. Instead, she asked, "You still wish to go to Tibet?"

Perhaps I should have replied "Yes." It would surely have been worth a try. Instead, I told myself that all the difficulties she described were mere pretexts, and that, in the end, I would not have been allowed to go to Tibet under any circumstances, since it had been closed off to all foreigners since the communist occupation. So why waste time? I went on to detail my other wishes.

I was able to say one thing at the end of my travels through China: of all my requests and wishes, which I augmented considerably three weeks later, only two remained unfulfilled. Number one: I wanted to discuss the status of women in present-day China with the female functionaries of the communist women's movement. Number two: I wanted to visit one of the great planning institutes that work out every step in the construction of modern factories, from the first cut of a spade down to the moment of starting production. My many other requests for conferences, visits, and travels were not only granted, they were arranged promptly and on a very

high level of efficiency, in sharp contrast with the slow and complicated bureaucratic methods encountered so frequently in communist
East Europe.

When I entered my hotel room upon my return from the foreign
office, I found a confirmation for my first appointment. An hour
later I was inside a coking plant on the edge of Peking, and soon
after that in Textile Factory Number Two, where I was to learn
about the work and living conditions of Chinese workers.

3

The proletarian gets the privileges

We went through one of the numerous gates in the ancient inner city wall, still almost intact. In "Chinese slalom" style we were off for the suburbs. Now no broad avenues, no new construction, no multi-storied buildings could be seen. Small houses stood huddled together, some of stone, some of wood, many surrounded by a wall, just as they used to be in the old days.

Here the street scene was even more colorful and varied than in the inner city. Children predominated. Hundreds, thousands of them thronged the broad strips of sand between the houses and the narrow asphalt streets, most likely because there was not yet room for them in the nurseries and kindergartens. The street was lined by wooden lampposts, which also supported the overhead wires of an electric supply line. Dense clumps of people stood waiting at the bus stops, while hordes of cyclists sped by.

Then the scene changed. Tenements came into view, or what we would call tenements. They are housing developments for laborers, built just a few years ago. Behind them I saw the first factories.

On the way, my interpreter briefed me on the condition of laborers in China. Rather, he told me what he knew about their condition before the "liberation" in 1949, when the communists came to power. He drew a horrible picture. No one had had fewer rights and less protection than a Chinese laborer. Foreign interests had exploited him, since native Chinese industries had been almost nonexistent. No one had cared whether the worker had a roof over his head, whether he would be able to share it with his family, whether his wages would be enough for the bare essentials. Most of these laborers had been the sons of landless peasants, had left their wives and children behind on the land, and had tried, by the tens, by the scores, to find a place to stay in overcrowded dormitories. Those who got sick had been tossed out into the streets. Medical care and clinics had been beyond their means. In a word, the Chinese proletariat had existed in dire want and misery. And now, in a few minutes, I would find out how laborers fared today.

For the rest of the trip, I reflected upon what we know in the West about the former and present-day life of the Chinese. The reports are still incomplete and too often tinged with propaganda. Naturally, the Chinese communist government declares that all Chinese, and especially the laborers, are better off today, that their material condition is good, and that they enjoy more freedom than ever before. Anti-communist observers, on the other hand, describe how communism has reached into the life of each one of the 700 million Chinese, how it deprives him of initiative, and how it has turned people into ants. No Chinese citizen, they say, can be sure he will not be conscripted into a work gang, separated from wife and children, and treated as a slave—perhaps one evening when he returns from work, perhaps early the next morning.

Outside China this view certainly sounds credible, and it has been confirmed by countless eyewitnesses. Nonetheless, it is an open question whether a regime of such magnitude can treat its population in such a fashion for long, with its economy—industry as well as agriculture—dependent upon unwilling slaves spurred to superhuman efforts.

I may perhaps anticipate here and report what I was able to learn for myself, both through personal observation and through many talks. Communism has now been in power for almost eighteen years, and the communists have tried various ways of handling the population in those years. Some of these have turned out to be dead ends.

Initially they tried to win popular support of the goals they set, repeating endlessly their appeals for the reconstruction of a great, new, powerful China. In that they succeeded to a much greater extent than the West wants to believe. However, in later years (about 1958-59) they managed to tire the willing populace beyond endurance, arousing opposition and resistance and producing a spent and exhausted people. That was the time of the "Great Leap Forward," when the government tried to create an industrial nation by fiat and set unattainable production quotas for agriculture.

Since then, the government and the Party have withdrawn many of their most ambitious plans. They have tried very cautiously to lead the population into more normal channels. Even these channels would not be tolerated by European workers and farmers, let alone by Americans. But in China, with a background of thousands of years of official and unofficial slavery, the population is only too willing and ready to believe in better times, in even the modest well-being promised to them. When the "Great Leap" ended, the people were not told that many of its exertions had failed. They were given celebrations, were assured that they had accomplished the most stupendous and incredible feats, and that they themselves had contributed to the general betterment. Strenuous efforts were made to share the so-called improvements with the people by increasing the food supply as well as consumer goods. Such improvements did indeed become reality a few years later, so that there is a renewed tendency to put faith in government slogans. That, at all events, was my impression, and it was arrived at independently, regardless of what official sources tried to make me believe.

Just the same, what the government accomplished for its population ought not to be overvalued. It has by no means established a modern social system everywhere, or instituted regular working hours, or provided a minimal welfare. Most of what is available tends to go to the industrial workers. However, out of the 700 million Chinese, only 10 per cent are employed in modern industrial plants. All the rest do just what they have done for centuries: they till the soil, and agriculture is still very backward.

In Peking that day we were to visit the "privileged," the industrial workers—and not just any industrial workers, but those who lived and worked near a large city; and not just any large city, but the capital. Our car turned into the large gateway of an industrial compound. We had arrived at a coking plant, about nine miles from Peking, where coke, illuminating gas, and chemicals are produced. We drove up in front of the central administration building. We were expected. Two polite young men in work clothes opened the car doors, shook hands with us, and bade us welcome.

We were ushered up a flight of stairs and into a big reception room.

This was just a few days after my arrival in China, but I was already aware that "reception-room conversation" was a routine procedure of Chinese etiquette. Every factory, every people's commune, every school, every hospital has such a reception room. They all have about the same furnishings: wide easy chairs with slipcovers and antimacassars over them, and small side-tables with teacups and cigarettes on each.

The people who confronted us also fell into the same categories: the head of the concern, usually accompanied by the Party secretary and the union steward. In addition, there was always a male or female secretary to attend to protocol. Every word uttered was written down, either to exert control or to gain experience for later interviews. Only on very rare occasions, when I sat opposite really high Party functionaries, was this protocol omitted.

However, there was no skimping on information anywhere, and if a plant was shown to me it was done thoroughly and competently. I was given the production figures (with a few exceptions, mainly in the steel industry), also the number of employees and their working hours. I was told what difficulties and obstacles had to be overcome. In fact, this last point was emphasized.

At the conclusion of almost all of these talks, I was given a stereotyped request to "engage in no-holds-barred criticism." Because: "We know that we are still backward, that we still commit many errors. There's much here that doesn't function properly. There may be much that we don't see. Tell us all!" I soon found out that foreign visitors must not take these requests too seriously. Criticism is ideologically prescribed in this communist system, but the visitor who practices it exposes himself to unending and fatiguing excuses and explanations.

Here, in this Peking coking plant, I found out about the working and living conditions of those privileged Chinese who are factory workers.

All over China, workers are classified in eight wage categories. The minimum wage amounts to between 34 and 36 yuan a month. (One yuan corresponds to about 40 cents in American money.) The largest wage, paid to highly skilled workers, is between 100 and 120 yuan a month. The directors, who are not classified as workers, receive wages somewhere between 120 and 170 yuan a month. The monthly earnings of the average Chinese worker or employee are about 60 to 80 yuan (equal to about $24 to $32).

The purchasing power of the yuan is hard to determine. Food, rent, utilities, and public transportation are much lower than in Europe. On the other hand, consumer products of all kinds are considerably more expensive, and technical instruments are exorbitantly high. So, for a simple existence, the wages are undoubtedly sufficient; for raising the standard of living appreciably, they are much too low.

In factories and offices, working hours are uniformly regulated: the workday consists of eight hours, the work week of six full days. Sunday is not always a holiday; to assure continuous production, factories must shift the day off, in a seemingly arbitrary manner, to the different weekdays. For that reason, all stores are open daily and on Sundays until late at night, to give shift workers the opportunity to shop.

I inquired about the right of workers to vacations. At first everyone looked blank, but then the director understood: "Yes, vacations. Every worker whose family doesn't live in the same city — that applies mainly to the unmarried workers — is entitled to twelve days off every year so that he can go to visit his parents. His travel time to and fro is not counted in, the travel costs are paid by the factory, and his wages continue during that time."

"And the other workers, whose families live here?"

"But they do have one day off a week. That is their vacation. Beyond that, there's no time off."

"Is it planned eventually to give workers a legally established right to a vacation?"

Director, Party secretary, and union steward looked at each other, exchanged a few words. Then one of them answered hesitantly, "Yes, perhaps, perhaps one day." Then this management team hastened to explain to me how many other advantages the Chinese worker had, especially in comparison with his former state of inequity.

The program for free medical care always came up in these discussions. This is an innovation in China; there has never been anything like it. Most factories nowadays have their own clinics, and some boast large hospitals.

"Here, workers and employees are treated free of charge. Their dependents pay only half price." This sentence also was repeated everywhere. Half of what? Of the actual costs, which depend on the type of illness, the length of time one is hospitalized, and the price of nursing care. In other words, dependents are only half-covered by this insurance.

With regard to the care of the aged, no fixed age for retirement is set by the government. In theory, men between the ages of fifty-five and sixty and women between fifty and fifty-five years of age can be pensioned off, depending on the state of health in each case — if they have been workers or employees!

This relatively low retirement age may well be ascribed to the incredibly huge manpower reserve, which exerts pressure on the Chinese labor market. Whereas in theory no one in China is permitted to remain without work, it is undoubtedly not easy for the state to provide adequate work for everyone. Pension payments amount to between 50 and 70 per cent of the wages earned and depend on the length of service in the plant.

"Is there such a thing as a pension for widows?" That question was also not understood at first; I had to explain extensively what I meant. This provoked signs of suppressed amusement when it was finally understood. "No! No pensions for widows exist here." And they explained that it would be almost unthinkable in China for a married woman not to have children. The children are required by the state to care for their parents, especially the widowed mother.

China's age-old social system continues in effect even now:

For the first time in China, women have been integrated into the industrial process and receive wages equivalent to men.

children are there to take care of the aged, and the more children, the better the care. The new government is making some attempt to replace this system by modern social insurance. But the effort has barely started. Those for whom the new insurance system is already providing — as was said before, this applies mainly to factory workers — need not make any contribution either to the health service or to the pension plans.

"In this way, their relatively low wages get equalized, and their standard of living is raised," the director declared.

But it is not the state that provides these social services. The clinics, the nurseries, the kindergartens, often even the primary schools, the pensions, and — what weighs most heavily in the balance — housing, all come out of the budgets of the factories, almost everywhere in China. True, the factories are state property (in China this is called people's property), and for that reason the costs are ultimately and consequently met by the state. But every one of these factories is, in this respect, a completely self-sufficient economic unit, to which belong, besides the plant itself, all housing and social installations. They are modern islands in the sea of Chinese life—a life that has few modern features for most of the population.

I asked questions about factory management everywhere I went but soon discovered that they were unnecessary. All business establishments are run according to the same scheme. "The director heads the factory, under the guidance of the Party collective, with full responsibility," was the stereotyped reply. This means that all important decisions are reached by the Party committee of the factory, under the chairmanship of the Party secretary. The director must carry out these decisions, and he alone is responsible for the results.

"Isn't it possible for differences of opinion to occur between the director and the Party committee?"

To this question, too, the answer was invariable. "No, that's impossible, because the Party committee listens to the masses [all the people connected with the factory], and the director also listens to the masses. As the masses have only one desire, this desire is expressed as much in the Party committee as in the actions of the director. How could there be differences?"

In theory, it is possible, as I learned eventually after intensive questioning of the management team, for a director to reject a decision of the Party committee, and to appeal directly to "the masses [factory workers]" to fight the decision. But only theoretically. In no factory I visited had such a thing ever occurred, or so I was told.

"And what happens when a director fails?" This, too, was nearly incomprehensible to my interlocutors. But, again in theory, there is an answer even to that. "The masses turn to the people's council of the province [provincial government], which investigates the dispute. The masses are heard, the Party committee is consulted, the director is instructed. The desire of the masses must prevail. The decision is handed down accordingly."

As the desire of the masses is unequivocally manipulated by the Party, the decision will undoubtedly be that of the Party. And that is probably the characteristic sign of present-day China: all concerns, all people's communes, all schools, all spheres of life are under the strictest control and are subject to the decision of the Party, more strongly so than in other communist states. Neither directors nor rectors enjoy even that iota of self-determination that is already being accorded to their respective counterparts in East Europe.

Trade unions in China, on the other hand, have the same functions as the unions in other communist states. "The union organizes the socialistic competition, in the first instance," I was told when I asked about it. This "socialistic competition" is as a matter of course guided by the directives of the Party. At the time of my visit, three such mandatory directives were in force: to produce more, of better quality, with greater economy. And the unions see to that by exercising strict controls. Lagging workers are called on the carpet and made to see their responsibilities; enthusiasm for work and increased production are generated by various means. Bonuses for outstanding achievements can add up to a supplement of 10 to 15 per cent of wages. Other inducements are medals and the display of exemplary workers' photos on the factory bulletin boards.

"However, we don't like the materialistic inducements," the union leader told me. "Though we still live under a socialistic system, in which everyone gets paid according to his achievement, we must strive for the communist ideal, in which everyone does the best of which he is capable without inducement."

The particularly orthodox Chinese communist ideologists must feel in their souls a keen distress that even now they cannot keep their economic system functioning without material incentives. As I was to see later, these play an even greater role in the people's communes than in the factories.

A union has other tasks, which resemble those performed by unions in the West in a rudimentary way. These are: to raise the educational level of the workers (evening courses); to arrange for art exhibits and amusements (amateur theatricals, visits of touring companies, movies); to distribute introductory coupons for health resorts and vacation spots; to administer the workmen's aid fund, which makes contributions and gives credit in case of dire need.

But in no instance may the union take the side of the worker against the interest of the employer, that is, the state. Strikes are unthinkable. They are treated as "counter-revolutionary activities" and punished severely.

When I asked whether workers at times found the work quotas too high, the brisk answer was, "The Party always evaluates the work load very realistically, so it is impossible for the quota to exceed the possible. It is true, though, that the utmost is demanded." (This was not always so, as I shall explain in the chapter on the "Great Leap Forward.")

"And how far does the ideological training of the workers extend?" I could never get a clear-cut answer to this question. "We don't know that. Workers congregate freely and willingly for discussions, and so determine for themselves when, where, and how often they wish to deal with ideological things." However, I noticed that in many plants Wednesday afternoons seemed to have been set aside for such "gatherings," and that very often on Saturday evenings discussions in a more intimate circle were in progress. This ideological training seems to have been somewhat curtailed since the time of the "Great Leap Forward," if for no other reason than economic necessity (infringement on working hours).

The next plant we visited was Textile Factory Number Two in Peking. It is situated near the center of the capital; its great entrance gate stands right at the edge of a main thoroughfare. Only when we came quite close to this gate did I realize how it differed from the entrance of the coking plant. That plant was far away from the inner city, and since only the workers and employees passed the gate, it completely lacked political posters, exhortations, and red banners. Here at Textile Factory Number Two, where people by the tens of thousands streamed past daily, the short stretch of roadway from the street to the gate was plastered with huge billboards and posters, reflecting the current Party slogans. Billboards also listed the production achievements of the factory, with exhortations to improve quality and to practice greater thrift.

Here, too, we were conducted first into the obligatory tea salon. Every member of the management team of this factory, which met us there, was a woman. The factory was run by a directress. The assistant directresses were at her side, and Party and union were represented by female secretaries and stewards. They all gave the impression of competence. They not only seemed to know their business, they also glowed with ambition.

I cannot rid myself of the feeling that communism probably elicits a stronger response from the women of China than from the men, perhaps because, for the first time in several thousand years of sociological development, it has actually granted women full equality of rights and has transferred to them responsibilities that, until eighteen years ago, were in the exclusive domain of men. And so they try doubly and triply hard to justify the trust placed in them.

The hour-long talk in the tea salon did not add much to what I had already learned at the coking plant about the status of the workers, their duties and rights. I did learn that a good many more women than men worked in the textile factory. This affected the nature of the problems with which the social welfare committee must concern itself. First among them are the pregnancies. Absences from work due to pregnancy are very high. The new state grants mothers-to-be fifty-six days off, beginning a few weeks before the birth, and mothers can take complete care of the infant in the first few weeks after birth. For the next few months the mother's workday is reduced from eight to seven hours, to give her "nursing pauses" during which she can seek out and breast-feed her baby in the factory's nursery. But otherwise, the female work force has no day off besides the variable Sunday. And if the female worker lives apart from her family, the same conditions apply for her as for the men.

We started on our inspection trip of the factory. As it turned out, this one was really worth seeing. We entered workshops in which spindles by the thousands were revolving, others in which three thousand looms produced cotton bands without pause. I was accompanied on this inspection tour by the directress, one of the assistant directresses, and the female Party secretary.

In China today only one general form of person-to-person address is current: "Comrade." I found it so in the factories. Female workers are addressed as "Comrade," the directress as "Comrade Directress." But despite these forms of address I had seldom seen in any capitalist enterprises I had visited in Europe and in the United States such strict discipline as here in Textile Factory Number Two of Peking. These female workers did not act servile, but they were very much aware of standing before their highest-placed superior. And yet, just a few minutes earlier I had been assured, "The directress has to listen to the wishes and demands of the masses. She may only execute what has been decided by the collective." And while going through the workshops, I gained the impression that in this plant nothing else was done but what had been decreed by the directress and the Party secretary.

When we had completed our inspection of the production facilities, the directress asked me, "Would you like to see our district for life maintenance?" This expression was new to me, but I wanted to see this district in any case. I soon found out that the "district for life maintenance" was simply the workers' housing quarter. It had been built by this factory, as by practically all others in China, to accommodate its work force and their dependents.

The "district for life maintenance," consisted of the housing development, open spaces covered with greenery, markets, stores, canteens, nurseries, kindergartens, schools, etc. All the buildings had been planned and financed by the factory and, with the exception of the secondary school, all the various furnishings were also maintained by the factory.

We walked slowly toward the four-storied apartment buildings, the walls of which were raw red brick. "Point to whichever building you wish to inspect, and select in each building whatever apartments you want to see," I was told emphatically. Apparently, previous foreign visitors had wondered aloud whether the buildings and apartments shown to them had been specially chosen.

I pointed to one of the buildings and in it selected at random three apartments to visit. The first one comprised three rooms, a minuscule kitchen, and a toilet. Total area, about 375 square feet. A family of eleven lived there. "Generally, according to regulations, a married couple having one or two children occupies a room that has an area of between 160 and 215 square feet," I was informed. This means, roughly, that 54 square feet per person is the rule in living quarters.

"For grandparents and in-laws, a second room is often made available, even though the family thus gains more living space than it is entitled to." The reasons for this apparent largesse did not occur to me until later. It seems evident that it is desirable to preserve peace in the family, as discord is reflected in lowered work output. And there is something else. The older generation has a lower level of "awareness"; that is, it is not so solidly grounded in the communist ideology as are the younger people who have, in most cases, been through communist schools. If grandparents and parents are put together into just one room, there is always the danger of ideological contamination. Much is made of this danger in the many Chinese movies, stage shows, and operas which I have seen. Obviously, it must present a problem. But more about that later.

Apartments are sparsely furnished by our standards. The stone or reinforced concrete floor is without cover or carpet. Two of the rooms in the first apartment I visited were furnished only with broad, low Chinese beds covered by bamboo mats. Several persons must sleep together on each of these beds. In the third room was a roughly constructed table, an equally rough easy chair, and an old armchair. There was also a sort of chest and a dresser. On the dresser was a radio set, apparently the most valuable piece of furniture, for it was decorated and veiled with several lace covers. A large Thermos bottle for hot water (in China, only hot water is drunk; even nowadays the Chinese simply cannot understand why Europeans and Americans pour ice-cold beverages into their stomachs), a picture of Mao Tse-tung, and several family photos completed the furnishings.

In this apartment the kitchen was equipped with a small gas stove. Nowhere else in China were there any gas or electric stoves in the living quarters I visited. Generally, kitchens are equipped only with the traditional, minute Chinese iron stove, even in the newer buildings. The stoves are heated with a mixture of a coal dust and peat. The glow is blown up into flame by a fan, and the dishes are placed one after the other on the small cooking surface over the glowing fire.

Even where running water was available there was rarely a sink, but almost always a basin of porcelain or plastic, and I saw neither shower nor bathtub. That this was not a coincidence seemed to me to be substantiated by what I saw on the blackboards in most of the schools. On these were admonitions about body care and hygiene. The children were shown how the face, hands, and feet must be washed, the teeth brushed, and the hair combed. Without exception, only wash basins and spittoons were depicted.

Incidentally, the spittoon is a standard fixture in China. One of them is sure to be in each room, and in all waiting rooms, railroad coaches, etc. The reason may have to do with climatic conditions and age-old habits, because the Chinese clear their throats often and spit a great deal. It must have taken a considerable educational effort for the government to get the populace to the point where they would spit only into the spittoon, in contrast with former practice.

If the apartment dweller owns a second pair of trousers or another dress, this item of apparel usually swings freely in the room, suspended by a wire from a nail in the ceiling. Chests for this purpose seem to be virtually unknown.

The tenants greeted me with utmost friendliness. They, and the other tenants whom I encountered on the stairs, clapped as soon as they caught sight of me. On the whole, a foreigner in China is received pleasantly and often with applause. In factory halls, hospital rooms, kindergartens, lecture halls — everywhere — activities are interrupted and vigorous hand-clapping begins as soon as a visitor enters. "We educate our people in the spirit of proletarian internationalism — the peoples of all nations are our brothers," explained my woman companion.

When I had shaken the hands of everyone (and this handshaking is also an innovation in China), the *pater familias* showed me around the apartment. He pointed proudly to the radio and confirmed my supposition that it was the most valued possession. Then he pointed to his wristwatch and to the wristwatch of his wife, and made clear to me with much enthusiasm that both he and his wife already owned bicycles. So this was, in Chinese eyes, a well-to-do family.

The interpreter was translating: "All of this was completely out of the question for workers before the Liberation [the year 1949, when the communist state was created]. Housing developments simply didn't exist at all. Workers lived in huge barracks or corrugated metal huts, crammed together like sardines. And in the summer, often under the open sky. All that we possess today we owe to the Party."

I heard explanations of this sort again and again during my sojourn in China.

I inquired about the rent. For a room of about 100 to 160 square feet, the rent being asked is 2 yuan (80 cents U.S. currency) a month; for a three-room apartment, the amount is a corresponding 6 yuan (including electricity and water). Meals eaten in the canteen cost between 9 and 12 yuan a month per person; it is somewhat cheaper to cook and eat at home. Children are often away at the kindergarten or in boarding school. As a rule, both parents work. For the kindergarten, the fee is

TOP: Pictures of worker "heroes" are frequently exhibited on bulletin boards. BOTTOM: Automobile Factory No. 1 produces a six-cylinder truck designed by Soviet engineers—but copied from American Dodge models.

between 7 and 10 yuan a month for each child; in the boarding school, in the elementary grades about 12 yuan and in secondary school about 18 yuan a month.

Parents take their children home from school on Saturday evenings, and the children remain at home until Monday morning — provided that Sunday is also the day off for the parents. This system is not the rule everywhere. If there is a grandmother, and there usually is one, children return to their homes after school, and they live at home. For one thing, it is much cheaper that way.

In the second apartment I visited, a young woman described her monthly budget for me in rough outline. She, too, was a textile worker. Her husband was a skilled artisan and she herself was a highly qualified worker. They earned considerably more than the average, a total of 160 yuan a month. They had two children, one away in boarding school, the other at home with grandmother. They spent about 100 yuan a month for rent, food, and school. "We are in a very fortunate situation," she told me. "We can put aside about 50 yuan a month for consumer goods. That is enough for simple clothing, but not for more expensive types. And we have already bought two easy chairs, a bicycle, two watches, and a radio."

Where only one of the parents works, or where the combined wages of the two are not this high, the budget for consumer goods shrinks accordingly, especially in families with several children. So, as the Chinese themselves repeat endlessly, "Our standard of living is still very low."

However, the greatest efforts are made to make sure that there are no record wage-earners, that the difference between the earnings of a simple laborer and the salaries of a director or high government official do not show too great a spread. Wages of 150 yuan a month are considered peak earnings, although there are some few high positions that pay 300, 350, or even 400 yuan a month. Into these categories fall university rectors, famous physicians, the highest bureaucrats, and extraordinarily meritorious opera singers and movie actors.

But even their salaries do not permit them to live much above the level of the masses. A motorcycle costs no less than 3,000 yuan ($1,200); cars are almost out of the question for private individuals, as they are neither freely available nor easily afforded. They cost between 25,000 and 30,000 yuan ($10,000 to $12,000). There are a very few exceptions; the "capitalists" who remain in China have private cars.

At the beginning of my visit I wondered whether such consumer goods as were offered to the nation were within its means, or even actually existed. I was not left in doubt about that for very long. I visited several department stores and shops in each city I came to, at the urging of my Chinese companions. These department stores are the pride of China. All guided tours include a trip through some department store. This is apparently an effort to counter unfavorable reports by foreign travelers and also, as I was told, certain "pronouncements of leading Soviet politicians" about economic conditions in China.

There can be no doubt that China's economy was a very poor one until recently. Under questioning, Chinese functionaries repeatedly admitted this to me. Yet today the department stores of China are well stocked. The necessities of daily life and some luxuries are available. The quality of the products, however, is invariably poor, in some cases very poor, and those items that would satisfy a more discriminating taste are almost beyond the means of the average consumer.

Rationing is still in force on cotton textiles. Also rationed are wheat products and candies, but otherwise there are no food shortages. Vegetables and meat are available in great quantities.

New department store buildings have risen in all the cities. All of these are multi-storied and are laid out like those in the West. On the street-level floor can be found all those consumer products that are in constant demand: foodstuffs, preserves, soap, washing powder, paper items, writing supplies, etc. Prices for these basic articles correspond exactly to those in the West. The prices for linen, suits, dresses, shoes, and even furniture and radios are about the same as they are in Europe, although the merchandise is of inferior quality.

Despite all this, there is a great disparity between the standard of living in China and Europe. This can be ascribed to the much lower income level in China. For instance, the price of a shirt (12 yuan) is about a fourth of a month's wages; a pair of shoes (24 yuan) is half a month's wages; a suit of bad quality (80 yuan) is more than an entire month's wages. And these comparisons apply only to wages earned by factory workers. The agricultural workers have a much lower disposable income.

This creates a condition in China that is unusual even for a "people's democracy." With the exception of refrigerators, washing machines, vacuum cleaners, and other high-priced appliances, everything is available at the department stores. Their shelves are fully stocked, but there are few customers. Even during the principal shopping hours, there is no crush in the aisles, and service is prompt.

Special departments exist in almost all Chinese department stores for "our friends from foreign countries." In these, articles of better quality and even imported products are for sale. I assume that high government and Party functionaries are permitted to make their purchases there.

The disparity between low income and relatively high prices explains the drabness noticeable in Chinese everyday life. The people are clothed neatly but poorly. Although all sorts of fabrics are offered in many colors and patterns, only a few are inexpensive, and these are the plain solid-colored fabrics in very little variety. The high prices, which few can afford to pay, thus make their contribution to a certain uniformity of appearance, not only of the populace but also of their utensils and the furnishing of their homes.

I was surprised to find, in all department stores, small sections devoted to cosmetics — and more than just soap and hair tonics. In some showcases I saw a few cheap lipsticks which seemed to be gathering dust. During all the time I spent in China, with the exception of the Cantonese woman I have already described, I did not see a single Chinese female wearing makeup. I came to the conclusion that these lipsticks were left over from the time when the wives of the Russian experts had requested such things. It is also possible that lipstick and powder are used in the numerous Chinese theaters where amateur performers appear.

Viewed objectively, it must be admitted that the standard of living in China is still one of the lowest in the world. However, I began to notice after some time that the phrase "Today our life is assured" came up every time I got into conversation with Chinese, no matter where I met them.

If it is true that the life of 700 million Chinese is assured nowadays; if not one of these 700 millions has to suffer from hunger even at times of natural catastrophes; if everyone has a roof over his head and a place to work, even though the pay is low — if all that is true, then indeed much has been done already for China.

What I had seen so far was life in the cities, the life of a privileged sector of the population. In China the urban worker is indeed privileged by reason of his income, which is relatively high for China, and the welfare provided for him by the state through the factories.

But for a true evaluation of conditions in China, the lives and destinies of its peasants must be examined. At least 500 million, and probably 600 million, Chinese are still engaged in agriculture. Here the communist government has introduced a totally new system, a system that includes guidance, economic control, and administration in a way that has not been tested in any other country of the world. This is the people's commune.

4

What happened to the people's commune?

Once again I was riding through the Chinese countryside, this time looking at it from a car. Whenever I wanted, the car would stop and we could get out to have a closer look at the fields, villages, and dams.

Nowhere else in the world but in Japan had I ever seen such carefully tended fields. The smallest speck of ground is utilized, the terraced fields climb up to the top of the steepest mountains. Many of the highest terraces are no larger than a few square yards. These fields are practically free of weeds. The shoots stand like soldiers in rank and file. Among them, here and there, small groups of peasants are endlessly busy cultivating. Now and then a water buffalo passes, pulling a plow.

Suddenly, I was amazed to see plows pulled not by animals, but by five or six girls. Exposed to the full force of the subtropical sun, they hauled the plows on long ropes. Old peasants steered them and guided the girls by calling out directions.

A little later we encountered the water wheels. They spread water from the canals onto the fields, as they have done for thousands of years. Young boys and girls operate these treadmills, holding onto a strong cross-beam while the water buckets fastened to the ends of the wheels revolve. As an accompaniment, they sing songs in rhythm with their running feet. A peculiar melancholy pervades these songs, but is frequently broken by exultant shouts, as if the monotonous running is made bearable by the prospect of a rich harvest, a better future.

As we neared these wheels, one runner after another would stop singing and slow down, and then the wheels would suddenly stand still. The surprised youngsters looked me over. Then one of the girls would begin to laugh, and soon all of them would be shaking with laughter. They would let go their hold on the cross-beam, applauding as they balanced precariously on the motion-less wheels. An expression of old Chinese hospitality? Or had they been told to extend this sort of friendly welcome to all foreign visitors? Perhaps both.

I covered enormous stretches of China by railroad and car, and in all those thousands of miles I did not see one single tractor. It may have been coincidence, but similarly, I could have counted on my fingers the trucks I saw. Manpower turns the wheels of China's agriculture, as it has for hundreds and thousands of years, with the help of a few water buffaloes, horses, and donkeys.

"To mechanize our agriculture will take at least another twenty-five years." I was told this by the head of the "October" people's commune (named after the month in which the communists came to power in 1949), in the vicinity of Nanking. This commune consists of a single village (a rarity, as most communes include several villages). A total of 10,544 people, 2,420 families, lived in the "October" commune. They had 13,399 acres of arable soil.

"We own 314 draft animals, mainly water buffaloes, but also 33 horses and mules. The commune was established in September, 1958. Since then, we have been able to buy three trucks. They have materially reduced our transport problem, but for the most part we must still rely on manpower."

I was soon to see another example of the use of manpower. On a country lane, dozens of carts laden with vegetables and fruit were being pulled along by three or four people each. This is how the commune delivers its produce to the state's distribution depot.

A drive through the people's commune, "Red Stars of Friendship with Korea," made an even stronger impression on me. This was near Peking; 55,000 people lived in the commune, which covered an area of 15,444 square miles. We drove through several settlements. The houses were of stamped loam with reed reinforcement. The children who crowded the lanes ran around stark naked, the women were bare to the waist, the men wore patched pants.

And yet this was a rich commune. If the chairman spoke the truth, it owned 64 tractors, 11 reapers, and 35 trucks, and had its own repair facilities. The fields yielded about 10 (short) tons of wheat an acre, and raised 5,300 cows, 30,000 pigs, 1,200 horses, and 150,000 ducks.

With pride, the chairman mentioned the "60 television and 3,000 radio sets and 4,000 bicycles" in the commune. In the 15 schools owned by the commune, 11,000 children attended the primary grades.

These impressive-sounding statistics seemed to contrast sharply with what I saw. Although I was conducted through the horse and cow stables, which were well kept, I had no way to verify the cited numbers. Nor could I detect any sign of television antennae on the roofs of the earthen huts. On the other hand, I was not able to inspect the entire commune in the time available.

Exactly what is a people's commune?

In theory, it is quite different from the kolkhoz (collective farm) found in eastern Europe. But I found more similarities than differences between the two. All the fields, formerly the property of individual peasants, have been thrown together. Private property has passed into collective property. That is, all real estate "belongs" jointly to all inhabitants of the commune, who are equally responsible for the tilling of this large acreage.

This is how the commune is organized: At its top stands the administrative committee, headed by a chairman assisted by a Communist Party secretary. The administrative committee is chosen by the so-called representative assembly (each group of peasants delegates a representative) but on the recommendation of the Party secretary.

This commune management organizes the available work force

(i.e., all able-bodied men and women from all the villages incorporated into the commune) into several production brigades. Each brigade in turn is divided into several production groups.

The production group is the smallest work unit that can be put into the field. Each group is composed of fifty to one hundred workmen, on an average.

In theory, the people's council (roughly corresponding to a county government) sets the goals for the individual communes and decides what they are to plant and which crops they are to give the state. The commune management team, in turn, assigns the tasks to the several production brigades on the basis of the council's production plan. The brigades parcel out these tasks among the various production groups.

These are the groups which actually carry out the tasks — the plowing, harrowing, cultivating, and harvesting. They are assigned to work in particular fields, set out the desired crop, and reach the corresponding harvest quotas. Whatever is reaped from the communal fields must be delivered to the state, which maintains a collection depot on the site of the commune. The delivered produce is paid for at the price set by the government.

Out of this payment, the individual workmen in the commune receive their wages. Obviously these wages cannot be uniform. Communes situated near large cities can bring in several vegetable harvests a year and dispose of them at favorable prices. Other communes, situated farther from cities, bring in grain harvests; and even here, differences can be substantial. In the southern part of the country, two and sometimes three rice crops a year are possible; in the north, there is only one wheat harvest. These yields determine how much is earned by the commune, which in turn determines the wages of its residents.

In the communes that I visited, there were marked differences in the wages of the workers. For example, the peasants of the relatively rich "Red Stars of Friendship with Korea" received 330 yuan (about $132) a man a year; those of the "October" commune, far less well mechanized but blessed by the southern climate, received 400 yuan (about $160) a man a year. In both communes, about 30 per cent of the wages were paid in produce or commodities.

About this, a commune chairman commented, "In the country, about five yuan a month are sufficient to meet a person's needs. Even ten years ago, peasants earned less than 180 yuan (about $72) a year. So we can point to an appreciable rise in the standard of living."

But there is no such thing as a uniform wage scale in the communes. "Our country is still in the socialist stage, and so everyone is paid according to his efforts." To evaluate these efforts, a complicated system of accounting has been instituted. At the end of each workday the achievements of the individual peasants are "discussed" and rated. Each group has a bookkeeper who credits the "work unit" performed by each peasant to his account. Every month, about 30 per cent of the wages due are paid out in cash. Once a year, the remaining 70 per cent is paid, usually soon after the harvest.

"The standard work unit is discussed daily?" I asked, quite surprised. "Doesn't that often lead to severe differences of opinion? Who decides objectively how much an individual peasant has accomplished?"

The chairman seemed not to find my question unusual. "That isn't so difficult. After all, everyone in the production group knows what everyone else has accomplished. Agreement is reached rather quickly."

Rumors had gone abroad that the communes were run on a quasi-military basis. According to these tales, all the able-bodied adults had to line up at dawn, to be divided into columns and marched off to the fields under the command of a group leader. They worked under strict supervision. At midday, units were marched back for the meal, which had to be eaten communally in canteens, as was also the evening meal. Meanwhile, the children were tended in nurseries, kindergartens, and boarding schools. Parents and children were able to get together only once a week; in some communes husbands and wives even lived apart.

This account did not fit any of the people's communes that I visited, and it was hard for me to imagine that such harsh measures could be introduced and maintained in the villages of China. However, the head of one commune admitted to me that when the people's communes were first introduced in 1958, the communal eating in canteens had been planned "to spare women the household chores and thus to free them for more valuable and productive work in the fields."

Further, it had been announced that the introduction of the communes would mark the true age of communism, in which there would be no need for money. And so the serving of free meals in canteens was said to have begun: children were fed in the kindergartens and schools, the peasants supplied with commodities and consumer products—all free of charge.

No mention is made of this nowadays. Meals taken in a canteen must be paid for, and, as this is undoubtedly more expensive than eating at home, the canteens are frequented by barely 20 per cent of the commune membership. Nurseries, kindergartens, and schools also charge for their services. These are very inexpensive if children just attend the classes; they are relatively expensive if the children are boarded. Consequently, most children, and in some communes all of them, remain under the care of their parents. This is feasible because every family seems to have a grandmother. Frequently, too, the mother does not go to work but performs the household chores and tends the offspring. In families where this is not the case, children are simply taken along to the fields.

In the communes there is no real compulsion to work. However, wages are so low that each family tries to put as many hands as possible into the fields, in order to earn as much as possible and to increase its living standard somewhat.

This living standard is still appreciably different from that of workers in the cities. First of all, there is the matter of housing. Living quarters, even if small, are provided for the workers by the factories. The peasant has to build his house himself and pay for the construction materials himself. In cases of severe need, the commune will help out with a contribution or by granting credit. But in the communes I visited I saw hardly any new houses. The rural population lives, now as formerly, in old peasant dwellings.

The worker is automatically covered by health insurance. Not so the peasant. Although many communes have a hospital, medical care and hospitalization must be paid for. For that reason, some communes have resorted to self-help, initiating their own insurance system within the framework of the commune. I was surprised to learn that this was on a voluntary basis. "Anyone who wants to have medical insurance pays three yuan a person a year, and that entitles him to treatment," explained the chairman of the "October" commune.

What I saw in the Chinese people's communes was essentially a normal village life, with one considerable difference: the arable soil no longer belonged to the individual peasants but had become "collective property."

Harsh words were used by the commune chairmen I talked with when they compared their communes with the kolkhozes that are prevalent in the Soviet Union. They considered the kolkhoz system, "as it is handled nowadays in the Soviet Union," an instrument that "encourages the spontaneous private-capitalist impulses of the peasants." They believed the kolkhoz peasant gave little attention to the collective property but cultivated as best he could the private plot allotted him — "The size of private plots gets ever larger in the Soviet Union" — to sell his produce at high prices on the open market and to accumulate private capital with the proceeds.

That is why the people's commune, they said, is not only a much more advanced type of socialistic collectivism, but also a strong bulwark against "every kind of revisionism" and "backsliding into a private capitalistic society."

My flights over China made me doubt these theories. The view of the Chinese landscape from the windows of the plane impressed me even more than my earlier observations on the railroad trip from Canton to Peking. In the Soviet Union, as in the United States, I had been accustomed to a bird's-eye view of fields stretching almost to the horizon. That is typical of a form of agriculture in which large surfaces are cultivated by highly mechanized methods.

The people's communes of China should actually have served the same purpose. They were meant to halt the splitting up of arable soil into small private fields; combining the fields made possible their cultivation on a large scale and a greatly increased yield.

It was also planned to supply the individual communes with tractors, trucks, and sowing, reaping, and threshing machines, so that mechanized cultivation of large areas would be feasible in the near future.

At the same time the communes had a definite ideological purpose; if a person were not allowed to own a private plot, he would be prevented from amassing capital.

So I expected to see huge fields in my flights over China. Nothing of the kind! Most of the fields looked even smaller than ours in Europe. From the air, it appears that cultivation of the soil proceeds within narrow confines.

Thereafter, one of my first questions when visiting the communes concerned the methods of cultivation. And that is where I got a big surprise. The fields do not belong to the people's commune, nor to the production brigades. They belong to the production groups, the smallest work units of the commune.

As each production group consists of roughly fifty to one hundred field hands, it can take care of about ten small fields. When I asked who had owned the fields before the people's communes were established, I was told, "Mainly those peasants who now constitute a production group."

Since the production group has to work the fields as a unit, since it is not allowed to split up into subgroups for work on separate fields, the fields have not actually reverted to their original private owners. Not actually—but almost.

I had a second surprise. The plows, sickles (the scythe is unknown in China), all agricultural implements, and even the draft animals belong neither to the commune nor to the brigade but to the individual production groups. Thus the means of production are also in the hands of the smallest labor unit.

In addition, peasants have again been ceded small plots to till as their own. "On the average, 5 to 7 per cent of the commune fields are cultivated privately by the peasants," was the answer I generally got when I inquired.

These small private plots are immediately distinguishable from the communal grounds. On them, the corn is twice as high. The secret is revealed in the appeals by the communes and newspapers: "Members of the commune should feel obligated to donate a portion of the human dung to the communal fields." Apparently, this happens only in rare cases, and the "private" fertilizer is used primarily on the small private fields.

Artificial fertilizer is largely unknown in China. The economist Yung told me, in Peking, that roughly five million tons of artificial fertilizer were being produced in or imported into China at the time. He declared, "To reach Japan's production, it would be necessary to produce or import between 100 and 110 million tons of artificial fertilizer a year." China is not able to do so at this time.

What the peasants grow on their private grounds they may either use or sell to their neighbors. The stirrings of "capitalistic" sentiments through such transactions are prevented by forbidding the peasants to take their vegetables, fruit, and meat to the large markets in the cities. Out in the open countryside, they may exchange their produce for other products in small markets; in some cases they may sell freely. But they are constantly encouraged to deliver even this surplus to the governmental purchasing agencies at the official price rates.

Chinese officials are trying to counteract a rumor now spreading abroad: that the people's communes have "degenerated" until they no longer resemble the original concepts; that they have sunk to a level even lower than that of the Soviet kolkhozes.

The chairmen of the communes I visited were emphatic in explaining the advantages of the commune. First, they had to admit that almost all means of production are in the hands of the production groups; more, that the production groups actually constitute separate economic units. It is they who receive the money for the delivered produce, they who pay the wages. They administer their ten or so fields independently. Here is how it works out: 72 per cent of the money taken in is distributed to the members as earnings; somewhat more than 17 per cent is expended on production costs, that is, the replacement of implements or the rental of tractors and horse carts; a little more than 5 per cent has to be put aside by the group as reserve, which the Chinese term "accumulation" but which really represents a build-up of capital; roughtly 5 per cent is paid by the production group to the state in taxes (the commune itself has to pay between 12 and 15 per cent in taxes).

All this raises a question about the function of the production brigade. What are its tasks, if the group acts completely independently anyhow?

The chairman tried hard to make me understand that the brigade, which is larger and therefore much more significant in the communist concept, has to fulfill very important tasks. But all that remained for the brigade, really, was to indoctrinate the production groups with the communist ideology and to pass on to them the planting plans set up by the commune administration.

In a few cases the brigade leadership assembles the groups under its control into a single unit, to construct large projects such as canals and dams. However, I saw only such water projects as had been carried out by the production groups for their own fields, or erected by the commune administration itself.

This brings us to the function of the commune administration. It buys, as soon as it is able to, the heavy technical equipment — tractors, sowing and reaping machines, trucks, horse carts, etc. This equipment is cared for in its own machine and tractor depot, to which a well-equipped repair facility is often added. The individual production groups can borrow any of this equipment, together with the technical personnel to run it, to cultivate their fields. "But the groups have to pay for that, both a rental fee and the wages of the tractor driver."

The commune thus earns money from the rental of machinery. It also makes money in other ways. It maintains the nurseries, kindergartens, elementary and secondary schools; it runs the infirmary and convalescent home; and where one exists it administers the culture center, which shows plays and movies for an admission fee.

The commune administration has another special task: establishing small industries within the commune. Each people's commune is urged to start as many such small industries as possible. Originally, when the communes were being set up, it was hoped that they would soon include small industrial centers, and that China would become quickly industrialized in this fashion.

The dreams have faded. "We erect industries on the basis of concrete realities," I was told in explanation. In most cases, this means that the commune administration controls brickworks, small cement factories, and, in rare instances, minuscule artificial fertilizer plants and repair shops.

The "October" people's commune had made a little more progress. "Come, let us end the theoretical talk. Why not see for yourself what we have done by way of industrializing this commune?" the chairman urged me after I had questioned him for about three hours.

It was a hot, sweltering day, but we set out on foot for an inspection tour. First we went into the village. It consisted mainly of the old peasant houses that had stood there for generations. The chairman pointed to one new settlement of row houses, which had been built to accommodate the influx of truck drivers and mechanics for the new pumping station. Each family had one bedroom and a kitchen. Along the street, the chairman kept pointing out shops which he said were newly built. "Formerly, traveling salesmen came with supplies for one privately owned central store, to which all the peasants were in debt. Today we have a long row of shops which belong partly to the state and partly to the unions. They supply the peasants with all kinds of consumer goods. The individual peasant cannot make purchases in installments, but his production group can make installment purchases possible. It can even buy bicycles, which it passes on to its members and for which it deducts part of their wages."

Next the chairman showed me the pride of the village and, as the commune in this case consisted of this one village, the pride of the commune: a newly built secondary school. I had to inspect every classroom, the small school library, the lecture hall, and a collection of teaching aids. The experimental equipment and demonstration models had almost all been made by the peasants themselves. The stuffed birds had been caught by them, and so had the other animals. Several small models of physics apparatus had been cobbled together by the most primitive means, but they all worked and apparently fulfilled their purpose.

And then we walked along a narrow lane, which brought us quickly to the periphery of the settlement. The chairman gave me a meaningful look. "Now I'll show you our factories." We turned a corner around the last farmhouse. In front of us was a large yard, and from the stacked wheels, iron hoops, and horseshoes, I gathered that we were approaching a large blacksmith's shop.

"A smithy?" I asked.

"Yes," he conceded hesitantly. "But it's really more than that, it's a factory. A factory for the production of agricultural implements, and all that is needed in the way of tools and utensils by the people's commune."

This "factory" consisted of three large sheds, two fireplaces, three anvils, two workbenches, and a few planing tables. Possibly fifteen to twenty workers could work there. They would make wheels for the wagons and traces for the horse carts, forge plowshares, sickles, hoes, and other tools. Some of the raw materials would come from the city, the wood from forests belonging to the commune.

But this was obviously not why the chairman was so proud. He grasped me by the arm and led me to a shed in which stood a peculiar little machine. "You know that the Party has appealed to us to create technical innovations," he said. "May I present to you this comrade?" and he called over an elderly worker who was busy nearby. "This comrade has invented a machine that has enabled us to increase production by 500 per cent."

I examined the machine with great interest. It consisted of an old-style electric motor, a transmission belt arrangement, two long metal tracks, and a plane fastened to one of the tracks. I asked to see how the machine worked. The comrade worker jumped to it with alacrity, pride, and joy. He reached for a half-finished wooden water pail, fitted and fastened it onto the lower track of the machine, lowered the plane on its upper track onto the pail, and threw a switch. The belts began to hum, the plane moved rapidly to and fro, smoothing the outside surface of the pail. In a second operation, the plane smoothed the inner wall of the pail.

No doubt there are better and more efficient machines than this one, performing the same operations more quickly and accurately. But here, in the 1960's, the machine-driven plane had been newly invented by a Chinese peasant.

"And now to the glass factory," said the chairman. The glass factory turned out to be mostly a large roof, supported on a few pillars, under which a melting furnace had been erected. On a brick platform were three form presses, into which the molten raw material was poured. The molds were handled by workers with long iron bars.

"Do you have the raw materials for glass-making in this commune?"

"No," said the chairman, "we drive once a week to Nanking to fetch a load of broken glass."

He pointed to a small heap of glass fragments and splinters of all kinds, mostly broken bottles. "These pieces are melted here and made into medicine bottles. We deliver them every week to the city, where they end up at pharmaceutical houses and hospitals."

At that moment, workers pulled two such bottles out of the molds with tongs and stood them on a sheet-metal tray, which a young girl carried to the furnace. "In this oven the bottles are tempered, made heat-resistant," I was told. That was the glass factory of the commune.

In addition, the commune owned a brick-making plant, a small cement works, and a workshop where the traditional Chinese fans were made of bamboo and paper. The bamboo grew in groves behind the village, the paper came from the city. The commune had a few amateur artists who made themselves useful in the shop with their pens, brushes, colors, and inks. They painted miniature scenes of Chinese village life on the fans, which were delivered to the state purchasing agency in the city, to be sold cheaply.

It is no wonder that the foreign visitor departs without being very impressed by the so-called rural industrialization. Nevertheless, these tiny workshops and factories, like the invention of primitive machinery, should not be underestimated. They play their part in raising the living standard of the Chinese peasants, slowly but perceptibly. Further, they acquaint the peasant for the first time with technology — however primitive — and open up the possibility of educating his sons to become artisans, whose sons in turn will eventually be skilled workers. Thus a certain reserve of trained workers is being created in these communes.

As to the primitive machines, I got to see several later on: for example, simple wooden rollers which facilitated the sowing of grain seed or the setting out of rice seedlings in the swampy ground of the fields. On the streets, I admired a kind of street-sweeping machine. It consisted of a box on two wheels, pulled by a donkey. A differential of wooden gears transferred the rotation of the axle to a kind of paddle wheel, which projected far out from the rear of the box and had a broom attached to each paddle. As this contraption was pulled along the street at a good clip, the broomed wheel turned and the brushes deposited the street dirt against the curb, where it would be quickly collected and put into cans by the female street cleaners.

But building small factories and encouraging technical innovations are not the only tasks of the commune administration.

One great advantage of the commune derives from the fact that it is not merely responsible for agricultural production, but that it simultaneously acts as the basic administrative unit of the government. The commune chairman is, in effect, both the highest administrative official and the highest government representative of his district.

In the same way, the commune is also responsible for all administrative tasks. Among them are: (1) agricultural production; (2) livestock raising; (3) industry; (4) culture and education; (5) welfare and health; (6) planning and finances; (7) people's militia (each adult citizen of China is in continuous military training, has to practice target shooting, and must join a guerrilla group in time of emergency); (8) justice and public safety; (9) purchasing; and (10) sales.

Several people's communes together make up a district; several districts are a province, and the provinces combined form the entire Chinese nation. It was plainly not a bad idea to let the production units serve also as administrative and political units.

But how does the Chinese peasant feel about giving up his private property, and its absorption into collective property? Has he acquiesced in this system or does he only endure it? Is he prepared to turn against it as soon as he sees a possibility of doing so?

Without a doubt, the initial demands on the people's communes were excessive. The quotas set at the time of the "Great Leap Forward" (1959 until about 1961) for the people's communes can only be described as irrational. Within very short periods, requests for production increases of 30, 50, then even 100, 150, and 300 per cent were made. I shall go into this in the chapter on the "Great Leap." But today, all this has been moderated. The people's communes are no longer asked to do the impossible.

When I asked whether the state's expansion plans were always realistic or whether the production groups would have to protest against excessive quotas, I was told that the plans were geared to the "concrete conditions," and that the district and provincial functionaries who set these quotas were required to work in the people's communes several weeks a year. All of them were formerly peasants, and by actually taking part in farming they could determine for themselves what could or couldn't be got out of the soil.

Some national policies have been steered into totally new channels since 1961. In contrast to the Marxist principle which puts heavy industry first, the slogan in China today is, "Agriculture is the foundation of the state, industry has the leading role." It cannot be stated more clearly without verbally deviating too far from Marxism: nowadays agriculture in China has absolute preference.

The "concrete conditions" have forced the Chinese national leadership into a change of policy so decisive that I was prompted to ask whether a population in the hundreds of millions could have assented without protest to such a sudden shift in policy, one that has drastically changed their lives.

Wherever circumstances made it possible, I tried to get an honest answer from the people with whom I talked in China. Most of the time all I got was official propaganda phrases: everything was done for the benefit of the nation; the masses understood exactly the measures adopted by the government; everyone tried diligently to give his best; although life was harsh, the people were content.

One evening I met an elderly Chinese who had spent many

years in the United States and Europe, and who not only knew the history of his country and the habits and ways of thinking of its people, but understood how to explain them to a foreigner.

"Look here, for nearly four thousand years agriculture has been China's pivotal question. That's understandable, because 90 per cent and more of our people have always been peasants and are to this day. Whoever ruled China had to consider two things: agriculture had to see to it that the state remained wealthy and strong, and the state had to see to it that the peasants (which means the Chinese nation) were content. Sounds simple, doesn't it? I can tell you that it has always been as difficult as squaring the circle. In a word, impossible."

This was to be a long explanation, for the speaker reached far back into Chinese history. First, the peasants had to work at maintaining the strength and well-being of the state. This they often did unwillingly; the emperor and the dukes forced them to it. The methods they used changed in the course of Chinese history, but they remained the same over long stretches of time. On big projects such as the Great Wall, the imperial palaces, the temples, the administration buildings, etc., the peasants were pressed into forced labor for the state. In tranquil times, when the emperor and the dukes were powerful, this forced labor was regulated. Each ablebodied man had to serve the state for thirty to seventy days a year. Peasants were enlisted for state service if they were not urgently needed on the fields or in the villages. Under some emperors, this corvée service amounted to slave labor; under the better regimes it was a sort of labor service, in which the peasants were relatively well treated and provisioned.

In addition, a village, or several villages together, had to till a large piece of ground for the emperor, the dukes, or the state. On this piece of ground, which was called the duke's field, the peasants had to supply the labor as well as seeds and fertilizer. They were expected to reap a rich harvest from this field, even though they did not own it. As with the Incas in South America (who are supposed to have been of Asiatic origin), the harvest of this central field was delivered up to the state and was at the disposal of the dukes and the emperor. Sales from this harvest reserve brought money into the sovereign treasury for the construction of roads, dams, and canals.

"So you can see that the Chinese people were conditioned for thousands of years to perform corvée service for the authorities, that this forced labor was often arranged rather arbitrarily, and that the peasants were reconciled to their fate," my informant explained.

I took this explanation to mean that interference in the lives of the peasants of China had always been the order of the day, so that the measures decreed by the present-day government might not seem as strange to the Chinese as to a visitor from the West.

He continued. "Moreover, there is a considerable difference between the agriculture practiced in China and that of Europe or America. Your farmers plow, sow, weed, reap, and then leave it to heaven to provide a bountiful harvest. They can afford to do so, because in Europe and America the rainfall during the summer months is fairly even. That is, rain comes down at regular intervals; there is seldom too much or too little. It is quite otherwise in China. As you know, rice is our staple food, and rice must be kept constantly under water. But the heavens here are either too prodigal or too miserly, and hardly ever reward us with just the right amount of water. So we had to start practicing water conservation and irrigation thousands of years ago. Have you already seen this from the air?"

Yes, I had. Several of my flights in China had been over rice fields, during clear weather, hour after hour. And so I knew what he was talking about.

As he spoke, I recalled vividly a most striking sight during a flight from Peking to Nanking. For a good hour we flew along the Yellow River. In Europe a river tends to meander through a valley, bordered on both sides by hills or mountains. The Yellow River flows through a plain. Not a sign of hills and mountains, near or far. But— it took me some time to grasp what I was seeing — people had built mountains to the right and left of this stream, not over a mere stretch of ten or twenty miles, but for hundreds of miles.

A chain of hills without a break ran along each riverbank. I should call them dams, because that is what they were; but seen from above they gave the impression of even, unending hills. Work on these dams has gone forward without stopping for hundreds, even thousands of years. Each generation had not only kept them in repair but strengthened them and increased their height. Every year the floodwaters of the Yellow River carry away millions of tons of alluvial mud, which, deposited on its bed, increases the water level considerably. To tame this river, to prevent catastrophic flooding of the fertile plains on both sides, the dams must match the riverbed for growth. This means that the base of the dams must be widened each time the height is increased.

The Great Wall in the north of China is considered the greatest human construction feat in the world. Compared to the two dams along the Yellow River, it looks like a small city wall.

That was the sight I remembered when I was asked what I had seen from the air. But there was more. The dams along the Yellow River are perhaps the most impressive in China, but they are a mere fraction of all the nation's dams, which had to be built along many other rivers thousands of years ago. All these dams together have certainly used only a small part of the labor that was and is required to build the hundreds of thousands of canals; to dig and maintain the ditches leading from the rivers to the fields. Many of these begin as broad, even navigable waterways and continue in smaller streams to the individual villages, which must then be connected to the separate rice fields by hundreds of runnels. Seen from the air, this resembles a gigantic spider web of water courses.

To build and maintain them and to prevent yearly silting over has always been the great task of the Chinese governments. The village communities could do no more than keep the runnels on their own fields intact and flowing. To construct the main canals must have required the combined efforts of huge numbers of people; so, too, the building and maintenance of the dams along the rivers. Without the engineers (who existed in China even in antiquity) and without the organization provided by state officials, it would never have been possible to keep the irrigation and conservation systems of China functioning.

"That was another product of corvée labor," my Chinese informant went on. "It too served the state, although its planning and execution really ought to be regarded primarily as an accomplishment of the state for the benefit of the peasants. If you wish, we could call that an early form of true collective labor. Our peasants have not always regarded even these labors as a necessary intervention by the state on their behalf. Nowadays, the responsibility for building canals and dams, and drilling cisterns for times of drought, lies with the communes. When the people's communes were established, it was thought that the entire able-bodied population of the commune could be put to work as a unit for this sort of task. But, as of old, there was resistance. The new government believes that now it has found the right way. It has created in the communes so-called investment brigades, to which all construction work is referred. Only when this work force is insufficient can the rest of the commune population be drawn upon. In effect, what took place was the retraining of a part of the peasantry, mostly its younger members, into construction workers. This is at least an attempt to solve an age-old Chinese problem.

"And don't forget that the most severe emperors of China, those who herded the peasants together by the millions for these labors, were and are considered the best in Chinese history. It was they who improved the condition of the people, who assured their food supply, who guarded them against floods and droughts. Those emperors who neglected to repair and expand the system of canals and dams were popular at the beginning of their reigns because they waived a part of their corvée rights. But then, when the dams broke, when the canals silted over and the floods came, or the countryside changed into a desert in a time of drought, then it was the peasants who cried for revolt. Through dire need they instigated civil war, deposed the emperor, and not infrequently even chased dynasties off the throne. Chinese history is full of such peasant insurrections, and only the major ones were recorded at that. We have a saying: 'The first three generations of a dynasty are always good.' Three generations of rulers remembered that they had come to power through the revolts of the peasants, and that they would have to serve the peasants. In the fourth generation they usually began holding a lavish court and forgot the source of their power."

I was to think of these remarks later, when reading the lead articles in the Chinese communist newspapers. The communist leadership seemed to be afraid that coming generations might forget that communism had come to power through a revolt of the peasants, and that it might wither in the third generation. This same thought seems to play no small part in the split between China and the Soviet Union.

But my host of the evening had not yet exhausted his subject. He wanted to remind me of a third weighty argument. "Surely you are aware that the Chinese reveres nothing so much as his ancestors. To him, the ancestors are not dead. They still abide within the family circle. Formerly, the altars in the homes of the peasants were dedicated to the veneration of the ancestors; the graves of these ancestors outside, in the fields, were the sites of their prayers. Now you'll ask me what this has to do with agriculture. More than you may believe, because this ancestor cult creates a problem for everyone. Ancestors can have a happy life after death only if as many descendants as possible honor them. For thousands of years this has encouraged the Chinese to bear as many children as possible. Many children meant much veneration and many prayers at the grave of the father. This was the only way he could hope for a better life beyond the grave. Besides, with a large family he could hope that at least one or two of them would be lucky and successful. Perhaps they would even become well-to-do and care for their parents in their old age. In other words, as you rightly suggest, a form of social insurance.

"But the many children have been the ruin of Chinese agriculture. As everywhere, in China the children inherited the father's land. That is, the estate had to be split among the sons, and because there were many children and often many sons, the land of the father was divided into smaller and smaller plots, often in the second generation. In the third or fourth generation, at the latest, these plots were no longer big enough to support a family, much less a large family. You have this problem in Europe also, but never in such a serious form. The development of technology, the emergence of many large cities, and finally the industrialization of Europe draw the surplus population away from the countryside. Not so in China. Even in this century — yes, even now — our industry is unable to absorb the surplus rural population. What has been the consequence? At intervals of three generations, the peasants have

Chinese farmers use bullocks and crude wooden equipment to harrow the rice paddies. (UPI Photo)

been unable to feed themselves. In times of flood or drought, the crops were totally inadequate.

"In another way, too, the ancestor cult helped to impoverish the peasantry. Our customs decreed that the father receive a costly and elaborate funeral. Families had to sacrifice everything they had and plunge into debt to finance such funerals. The splitting up of the land and the financing of these expensive funerals have repeatedly forced our peasants to mortgage their small holdings, then finally to sell them and to hire themselves out as field hands. Starting in antiquity and continuing into the twentieth century, this led to the formation of a class of wealthy landowners, consisting of those few peasants who were clever enough to exploit the needs of their fellow citizens. Usury flourished in the countryside, money lenders became a scourge, and the peasants themselves became more and more dissatisfied; unable to endure being day laborers, they rebelled again and again to repossess their fields and homes. Wise emperors adopted preventive measures. Two thousand years ago they introduced in China what the rest of the world thinks of as a modern innovation — land reform. Chinese history is full of references to extensive land reforms. Emperors and dukes would decree a redistribution of the soil, seizing from the great landowners, often without any compensation, the real estate acquired through money-lending operations and giving it back to the peasants. Our history evaluates such emperors as good emperors."

This is where my informant's talk ended that evening. From what he had told me, I was able to draw my own conclusions, which were amplified later by the functionaries I met. They explained that Mao Tse-tung and his Communist Party had started their triumphal march through China by promising the peasants a new redistribution of land. Each was to get a piece of ground as nearly uniform in size as possible; the great landowners, the usurers, the village despots were to be chased off. This land reform was actually one of the first measures effected by the communist government. With only the support of the peasants, it was able to bring the revolution to a successful conclusion, to seize power and achieve victory. And at first it gave the peasants what it had promised them: their own acreage. Even anti-communist observers believed at that time that the Chinese communists were no communists in the Soviet sense; they were land reformers, and they were precisely what the country urgently needed.

These opinions changed when Mao Tse-tung ordered that kolkhozes be established, just a few years after the land reforms. Not that they were called that in China. They were called "production units" and were divided into "lower" and "higher" kinds.

At first the peasants had been urged merely to pool their tools and agricultural machines, to bring in the harvest and to sell it in common. When this led immediately to disputes and confusion over property rights, the production units of the lower type were converted into those of the higher type. The latter closely resembled the Soviet kolkhozes. All fields were thrown together and became collective property. Individual ownership was nullified, and the means of production, especially the draft animals and plows, likewise became the property of the kolkholz.

Now it is asserted that even establishing the higher type of production unit did not deter the Chinese peasants from trying to keep their own plots of ground and their own water buffaloes — in short, from showing "spontaneous capitalistic sentiments." This led to the decision to establish the people's communes. The Soviet Union did not have much luck with its kolkhoz economy; Soviet agriculture slid into a constant state of crisis with the kolkhozes. Nowadays, the Soviets are accused in China of not being able to master the basic problem of their country, agriculture, because they were not courageous enough to progress further along the "road of socialism" and convert the kolkhozes into the more rigorously socialistic system of communes. Only the people's communes, I was told, insure against the Chinese peasantry's regression into capitalistic sentiments, against that striving for private property which could lead to the destruction of the communist structure. In addition, people's communes were the only solution to the ancient Chinese problem of divided land, a debt-ridden peasant class, and a general shortage of foodstuffs.

However, I doubt that the people's communes have made the

Chinese peasants happy. On the contrary. What has already happened to these communes, what I myself saw and have reported earlier in this chapter only strengthened my doubts. And even the government has begun to pay closer heed to the "concrete conditions."

5

The center of the earth

"Chinese communism is incomprehensible to anyone who does not search for its roots in China's past. When Lenin initiated the October Revolution, he revolted not only against the czar but also against the history of his country, against the nature of the Russian people, or at least against that of the Russian peasant. The Soviet state initially broke with history and to some degree with the culture of old Russia. But Mao Tse-tung and those around him mobilized Chinese nationalism when they called for revolution. They even appealed to Chinese traditions, and they were able to lead the country back to a Chinese way of life in certain spheres. When you have considered all that — unfortunately few visitors from the West have as yet taken the trouble to do so — you'll comprehend much more readily what has occurred here during the last forty years, what significance it has, and what kind of China it is that confronts the world today."

This advice came from another educated Chinese, well versed in his country's history. One thing had already become clear to me in the first week of my stay in Peking: no one can understand present-day China without a knowledge of its most recent political past; no one can interpret this recent past without paying attention to China's history and the forces that motivated it.

During my first weekend in Peking, I visited a most singular and impressive building dating from the time of the empire. In the official *Guide Through Peking* this building is listed as the "Temple of Heaven." Here the emperor gave thanks to God and the gods for rich harvests and held dialogues with the celestial powers.

When we had crossed a beautiful park to reach the "Temple of Heaven," I discovered that it consisted of not one but two temples, connected by a broad street surfaced with large, square stone slabs. But, magnificent as those two temples are, with their blue-glazed ceramic tile roofs, they did not make nearly as strong an impression on me as the round plateau nearby. The plateau is reached by passing through two marble gates and consists of three immense round terraces piled up like pyramids, decreasing in diameter toward the top. Each is encircled by a marble wall, richly carved with old Chinese signs and symbols.

On reaching the topmost terrace, one is struck by a curious geometric arrangement. The ground is covered with large stone slabs, arranged in bands around the center point. Each band is made of nine slabs, diminishing in size toward the center. (The number nine has always played an important role in Chinese mysticism.) In the exact center lies a round stone.

"This is the center of the earth," said my guide, pointing to the stone. Feeling somewhat peculiar, I did what many visitors have undoubtedly done, though it would have been an outrage even a hundred years ago. I stepped onto that round stone.

I was standing on the center of the earth. At least, many generations of Chinese have believed this, and the Chinese emperors had this center point calculated and verified by their best astronomers and astrologists and geographers. Here, and nowhere else, was the center of the earth. The emperor alone was permitted to stand here. Had any of his subjects dared to do so, they would not have remained alive very long.

The round stone on which I stood reveals more about the history of China, the attitudes of its rulers, and the mentality of its populace than many of the other things I subsequently heard and saw in China. It was neither accident nor conscious presumption that led the Chinese to place the mid-point of the earth in their realm, thus elevating their country to the central position on earth.

"In this world, there have been only two truly great cultures and civilizations, the Occidental and the Chinese," the Chinese professor told me. "Everything else, magnificent as it might be in its own way—the realms of the Aztecs and the Incas, the cultures of the Middle East and of India—all pale beside the achievements of these two spheres of culture and civilization. Above all, these are the only two cultures that have survived in the stormy history of humanity until this very day, and that are still effective."

I tried to recall what Western schools teach about China. China is a large country; it is a very old country, having possessed a very well-developed culture. Its mores had been refined, philosophers of the highest rank were its teachers, and scientists delved into and discovered the secrets of nature and made epochal inventions, in many instances long before the Europeans did. China was ruled by mighty imperial dynasties — "the emperor of China" is a proverbial saying in Europe. With an area of more than three and one-half million square miles, China is as large as the continental United States plus Alaska and Hawaii. Something like that, perhaps a little more, is what we learn in school.

But it is really only when one sees the cultural sites of China that one begins slowly to understand the significance of this country, its history and its philosophy. Walking through the imperial palaces, visiting the legendary graves of the Ming emperors near Peking, or standing on the Great Wall, which is 2,500 miles long and was built 220 years before the birth of Christ, the visitor begins to comprehend China.

Some of the objects on exhibit in the old imperial palace of Peking date back two thousand years before the birth of Christ. Among them are a few thousand tortoise shells and animal bones incised with complex Chinese characters. Ancient scribes made use of these durable materials in place of paper, then unknown.

Nearby stand magnificent large bronze vessels, richly decorated; long passages engraved on their inner surfaces proclaim these to be gifts presented to victorious commanders and benevolent dukes 3,500 years ago.

It is estimated that Chinese culture had its beginning about four thousand years ago, that is, two thousand years before the birth of Christ. In that remote period, thoughts were first recorded in written characters, Chinese political organization began to develop, legal decrees were issued that established order in the country. By 1500 B.C. the Chinese had a highly developed political organization. It gave the country a comprehensive administration: property and labor were regulated, commerce was channeled, art and science were cultivated, and philosophy was exalted.

"However, Chinese culture developed mainly in isolation, unlike the European," the Chinese historian said. "China had no contact with other highly cultivated peoples. That is, there were no Egyptians, no Assyrians, no Hebrews, no Persians who might have fructified our culture. As long as 3,500 years ago, the Chinese had already put large sections of the country in order and were trying to live in harmony with the gods and the universe. Europe, if I may say so in all modesty, was still shrouded in the fogs of pre-history."

I suggested that individual Chinese tribes, under advantageous climatic conditions, had developed their culture at about the same time as other peoples living under similarly favorable geographical circumstances. "Yes," replied the professor, "but Chinese culture has remained intact and continues to this day. It has suffered no interruptions. In Europe one culture is replaced by another; peoples spring up and disappear. Remember, China has been one country and has remained one country, except for periods of dismemberment, in contrast with what has happened in Europe. Further, this realm has been settled principally by one ethnic group, the Han; the non-Chinese minorities have played hardly any role in Chinese history. Moreover, this nation belongs to one single race, the Chinese, which is different from other races. Let me try to explain how strongly this has influenced our thinking, our opinions about the world. We Chinese call our country the 'Middle Kingdom' (Chung Kuo) to this day, have done so for 3,500 years, and don't recognize any other name for it. Today, on the postage stamps of the People's Republic, you'll see the same written characters, 'Middle Kingdom.' This, too, is no accident. Because, again in contrast with Europe, the Chinese for centuries knew no other world than China, for thousands of years no other highly developed culture than their own. Even our greatest thinkers assumed that nothing outside of

China was worth knowing, nothing was worth striving for, nothing was worthy of emulation, except what we had known for a long time. The realm of the Han was the center of civilization, the center of the earth."

On modern maps of the world we can see that China borders on other large nations inhabited by large numbers of peoples. To the north is the Soviet Union. But even a century ago this northern region was sparsely populated, and the Chinese came upon nothing but nomadic tribes in the inhospitable reaches of Mongolia and Siberia. True, they were often warlike men who fell upon China in its moments of weakness, and at times even usurped its sovereign throne — as for instance the Huns, Genghis Khan, and the Manchus. But in the eyes of the Chinese they were barbarians who had hardly any culture of their own worthy of the name.

In the west, China bordered on Tibet, on the Himalayas. There the mountains were too high and the terrain too inhospitable to make explorations in that direction worthwhile. Although there is historical evidence of caravan routes at a very early time from China to Afghanistan and Persia, and also of some contacts between Chinese and Indians, the fact remains that the tales of traders could not convince the Chinese court and the sages of the existence of nations and peoples that could compare with the greatness of China and with its cultural development.

In the south and southeast, where Korea, Viet Nam, Laos, Cambodia, and Burma are located today, the Chinese met nothing but insignificant peoples, barbarians in their eyes, who were soon persuaded or forced to accept Chinese culture and Chinese domination.

The same was true of the insular realm to the east of China, Japan. The tribes inhabiting these islands had not yet developed much of a culture or civilization when the first Chinese seafarers and, later, armies brought them news about the Son of Heaven and of the Middle Kingdom, taught them the Chinese written characters and Chinese customs, and in this way laid the foundation for a future Japanese culture.

"Weren't there really sufficient grounds to believe that nothing in the world outside China counted for anything, or even that the world consisted of China?" the professor continued. "When we suffered a military defeat, when barbarians usurped the sovereign throne, they could survive only by adopting our culture, by submitting to our customs, by surrounding themselves with Chinese advisers, philosophers, and administrators. Barbarian chieftains sent embassies from afar to the Chinese throne to plead for a highly cultivated Chinese princess whom they could marry, for Chinese scribes and organizers so that they too could share in the achievements of Chinese culture. And if they occasionally had something worthwhile to offer, we were flexible enough to adopt their ideas, to enlarge upon and to transform them, and often within one generation to make them an integral part of the Chinese cultural heritage."

6

Grass must bend

In the first century A.D. the already highly developed Buddhist faith crossed the Himalayas from Tibet into China. Astonishingly, until then this great Chinese culture had not managed to put together a distinctive religion of its own. Although today Lao-tzu and Confucius (K'ung Fu-tzu) are regarded as the founders of an in-digenous Chinese belief, they did not create a religion.

All Lao-tzu tried to do was to explain and systematize the other-worldly powers. He traced them back to a kind of innate spirit, the Tao. The Tao comprised the entire universe; it existed even before there was God. He never made it clear whether there was one god or many. The heavens, about which Lao-tzu spoke, had space for many gods and goddesses, for spirits and demons. But to interpret them, to determine a close connection between them and human beings, seemed too presumptuous and impractical even to Lao-tzu. He urged human beings to strive for inner and outer harmony, to grasp that the entire universe, including the world and humanity, the good and evil spirits, constituted a single entity, and only those who were aware of themselves as an integral part of this great unity could achieve peace and wisdom.

The Tao was everything—the universe, the unity, the harmony, the way which human beings sought, the innate spirit, the original oneness of the cosmos. The *Tao Te Ching* (Scripture of the Way and Its Power) is the name given to a collection of sayings attributed to Lao-tzu, in which his philosophy as well as that of his teachers and their teachers have been preserved for posterity. "Before heaven and earth came into being, something nebulous already existed: in silence, for itself alone, unchanging in itself, always circling, deserving to be the mother of all things . . . ," explains this scripture. And further, "Let all things have their natural course, and do not interfere, for whatever opposes the Tao will soon perish. Though the heavens do not engage in battle, they are ever victorious."

Lao-tzu also inveighed energetically against warfare: "Soldiers are the weapons of evil. Even in victory there is no beauty. Whosoever finds it beautiful has joy in slaughter."

And for governments, Taoism prescribes: "Peace and freedom are assured only when governments refrain from interfering in the lives and concerns of their citizens."

Taoism also teaches moral precepts that come close to those of the Christian Occident: "You must return good for evil. Love is victorious in the attack and invincible in the defense. Heaven arms with love those whom it wishes to save from destruction."

But the core of this teaching proved to be dangerous for the Chinese. Man is exhorted not to disturb nature, not to take a hand in natural occurrences. "For whosoever disturbs the rhythm of the Tao confounds the cosmic order." It is because man wants to act, because he strives to follow his own aims, that there is so much evil in the world. Therefore do not act, merely give yourself up to the search for harmony with nature. Inaction is the right action. Let things happen, accept them without resistance.

The consequences of this attitude were often disastrous. Partly because they truly believed in it, but partly because it presented such a convenient excuse, the Chinese followed this principle of action through inaction during long stretches of their history, bore their fate with fatalistic lethargy, and ceased to develop further what their high level of civilization had already brought them in knowledge, experience, and inventions.

I found proof of this in my walk through the Museum of Chinese History in the square before the Tien An Men gate in Peking. There I stood in front of a Chinese water clock, designed to be driven by a mill-wheel. Because the velocity of the current in the stream that drove the wheel would surely change from time to time, the clock was provided with a complicated, cleverly devised system of gears that regulated the flow. This power was transmitted to a cylinder, about six feet tall, from which protruded twelve large wooden leaves. The ancient Chinese had divided the day into twelve units, each equal to two of our hours. Every two hours, one of these leaves would tumble over, indicating the elapsed time.

Not far from the clock stood the world's first seismograph, a gigantic bronze vessel with a rod in its center, which had been placed so that the least tremor would cause it to fall. In whatever direction the rod dropped, it fell on wooden tines which caught the fall and transmitted its power over a complicated mechanism to set a series of balls in motion. The balls left the vessel through artfully decorated channels, to tumble into ready-placed dishes. In this way, Chinese scientists were able to ascertain that an earthquake had occurred and could determine the direction in which the epicenter lay and the intensity of the tremor.

In the same museum I saw several models of a so-called compass-car. These were two-wheeled carts in whose center a kind of mast was set up. On the tip of the mast a figure indicated the direction with an outstretched hand. This figure needed merely to be turned so it faced a certain quadrant of the sky, such as the direction of a certain town or village which one wanted to reach by cart. A system of gears, coupled to the axle of the cart, made sure that the desired direction would be constantly shown by the hand on the mast. Despite detours around mountains, or circuitous paths through woods and fields, the driver could always resume the proper course and finally reach his goal. Such compass-cars were in use in China three thousand years ago.

It was also the Chinese who, long before the Europeans, invented the magnetic compass. This enabled them to undertake long ocean voyages without having to depend on the stars for guidance. With the magnetic compass, Chinese overseas junks made harbor in Arabia and the east coast of Africa at a time when these regions were practically unknown to Europeans. But they returned bearing news only of barbaric peoples, great deserts, an inferior culture.

The Chinese discovered gunpowder long before the Europeans. And long before the Europeans they produced paper and used it to record documents, letters, and books. Long before the Europeans, they had movable type and were masters of the art of book production. Chinese mathematicians figured out the complicated number pi (π), hundreds of years before the Europeans. This would have made it possible for them to make technical computations, which could have spurred a rapid development of mechanics and technology.

"But our junks remained junks into the twentieth century despite the compass. The galleys of the Romans, on the other hand, were developed further in Europe to the point where, finally, they appeared on China's coasts in the form of battleships," the professor observed.

Not least among the forces that kept the Chinese from seeking further progress was Taoism. Its principle of action through inaction led the people to feel that their culture and civilization could go no higher.

Likewise Confucius, the greatest Chinese philosopher and political scientist, gave China neither a religion nor a spiritual incentive for further development. He lived from 551 to 479 B.C. In contrast with Lao-tzu, he did not even try to delve into supernatural matters. As the inexplicable (Tao) could not be explained, it would be senseless to waste time on it. Confucius was of the opinion that the more man kept himself apart from God and the supernatural powers, the better off he would be. Man ought rather to order his life and to bring about order in the state.

Thus Confucius concentrated on giving China a civic and moral order. The core of his concepts he epitomized in the maxim: "Act always as you would have others act toward you." That is, human beings ought to be capable of maintaining a moral balance within themselves; only then will they achieve social, and with it political, peace.

True to this basic tenet, Confucius taught that man's morality ought to have its origin within the smallest group, the family, which is the basic unit of the state. Consequently, morals and order must begin in the family.

Confucius formulated this order, based on the "Li"—morality, ethics, the law—and making use of old Chinese traditions, which in his time had been in effect for about a thousand years.

Confucius saw an essential unity in everything, expressed in reciprocal relationships. His moral law for the family is explicit. Children must revere and obey the father. The father must love the children. The younger brother must show humility and respect for the elder brother. The elder brother must be gentle toward the younger brother. The wife must obey the husband. The husband must let righteousness prevail in dealing with his wife. Youngsters must show absolute deference toward their elders. The elders in turn must practice tolerance toward the youngsters. Subjects must be unconditionally loyal and faithful to their sovereign, and the sovereign must treat his subjects benevolently.

Above all, the ancestors must be respected and revered. They continue to live within the family, and, as the eldest, are granted an almost godlike status.

This is how Confucius regulated relationships within the family, within the clan, in the village community, and in the state: The eldest must rule, the younger must obey. But the emperor is the supreme power, the father of the nation, the Son of Heaven, the elect of the supernatural powers — and he alone can always reconcile his people with the heavenly powers.

Beyond this, Confucius gave the Chinese people a great number of precepts, not a few of which became the bases for laws. Here are some of these: "Direct your will to the right path. Hold fast to doing right. Better than to know truth is to love truth. Better than to love truth is to find joy in it." But also: "When the country is on the proper path, one may be daring in one's words and daring in one's deeds. When the country is not on the proper path, one ought to be daring in one's deeds but cautious in one's words." And "When order prevails in a country, then poverty and humility are a disgrace; when disorder prevails in a country, then wealth and renown are a disgrace."

Confucius himself wrote little, but his numerous disciples preserved the sayings of the master, and in them the content of his teaching, for posterity. Many of them founded their own Confucian schools, and some of their students, and theirs in turn, developed further the intellectual inheritance of Confucius.

What Confucius gave the Chinese was a grandiose moral philosophy, a code for the social structure of China, and a foundation for the laws of the state. But he always accepted the established order. He himself spoke of the commoner and the nobleman, of the uncivilized and the civilized, of the unintelligent and the intelligent, of peasants and dukes.

On the other hand, he developed an incredibly progressive system of state administration. Neither the sons of noblemen nor the feudal lords should administer the state. The best minds, Confucius thought, came from all walks of life. He laid the basis for a system of examinations through which future Chinese civil servants should be selected. The examinations were held in all of China from the second century B.C. until the beginning of our century. China's civil servants were selected in this way from among the entire population, since anyone could take these examinations. If the son of a peasant found a good teacher in his village, or moved into the next village or next town to serve his apprenticeship; if he learned the Chinese classics and their wisdom and was able to follow their thoughts and thus to understand the world, he could pass the examinations and be elevated to the rank of an official. We know these officials of the old China under the name "mandarin."

This enlightened and democratic system of state administration accounts for the fact that China's unity and its political stability remained unshaken for so long. Revolts and revolutions ended the reigns of many Chinese emperors, but not the empire itself or the governmental order.

That stability was the towering achievement of Confucius. When the communists today declare, "We must root Confucius out of every nook and cranny of our hearts and minds," this only shows how much they fear that the Chinese people may not forget the class theories of Confucius and may want to reestablish them.

But according to the teaching of Confucius, man is the measure of all things. Confucius did not offer the people a divinely ordained power, a means of salvation, or a revelation. This lack made itself felt, as mentioned earlier, two thousand years ago, when

Buddhism penetrated to China and swept through the country. The Chinese people seemed eager to fill those gaps left open by Taoism with the teachings of the Buddhist religion.

True, there were some who had already become too enlightened for Buddhism, thanks to Lao-tzu and especially Confucius. On the other hand, the mass of the Chinese people had been too long without religion and had abandoned itself entirely to superstition. Ghosts and demons, gods of all sorts were thought to direct the destinies of man. Even in India and southeast Asia, the teachings of Buddhism had not been able to retain their original purity and clarity. When Buddhism reached China, the Chinese already knew many heavens and gods and were only too willing to add a few dozen of their own. These were further surrounded by entire princely courts of inferior gods, demons, spirits, fairies, and other supernatural beings.

Until 1949, when the communists came to power, and to some degree even now, the Chinese believed in all these gods, spirits, and demons, and conducted their daily lives according to their whims and foibles. But where did this lead?

The moral precepts and principles formulated by Confucius provided for no effective supernatural power to call human beings to account for their deeds. As long as there were strong emperors who knew how to enforce the principles of Confucianism in the land, the social structure and political organization remained intact, supported by lofty moral purpose. But when the government was weak, rot soon sapped the moral fiber; responsibility toward one's neighbors soon disappeared from the conscience of large segments of the population. The admonition of Confucius that morality should be firmly established above all in the family—and order would then prevail in the whole country—proved detrimental during these periods. In years of want, the Chinese drew back wholly within their families, gave help only to their nearest relatives in most instances, had little sympathy for the needs of others and often no concern for the common welfare or the state.

The consequences were easy to see. Communal property was not preserved, park lands were trampled down, trees felled, streets dirtied without consideration; the stairwells of large tenements became junk piles. Beggars were chased from the door, the homeless were refused asylum, the sick were shown little sympathy. Formerly, travelers in China were impressed by the strict morality within the family, by the unconditional obedience toward the elders. They brought back reports about the strict discipline and high morality. I suspect that this patriarchal type of family conduct displeased younger members of the family; it may actually have promoted the growth of strong resentment in them, not only against their elders but against the entire social structure of China as well. In any case, the biographies of almost all the present communist leaders of China show that they became revolutionaries in their youth while still under familial control; they hated their fathers and considered the entire state and social structure to be obsolete and ripe for destruction. This is certainly true of Mao Tse-tung.

In old China it was a considerable obligation to be helpful, respectful, and socially responsible toward one's relatives and clan. The clan consisted of no less than 262 degrees of relationship, each of which carried a distinct Chinese designation. Often the clan also took upon itself the supreme duties of the state.

There was another important factor: according to Confucianism the Chinese woman was virtually without rights. As a girl, she was unconditionally obedient to her parents; as a wife, she owed this obedience to her husband. It was customary to send girls while still children into the homes of their future in-laws, where they would work as slaves. Older girls were betrothed without seeing the bridegroom face to face before the marriage ceremony took place, with rare exceptions. One clan negotiated with another for the marriage. Barely ripened into womanhood, the girl most often became the slave of the husband. It was a woman's duty to bring as many offspring into the world as possible, and to work harder than a man.

If the man was well-to-do he could also afford concubines, whom he brought into the home. These, too, bore him children. They all belonged to the clan, but their rights were not easily maintained. When the husband died, the main wife often exacted revenge from the concubines and their offspring.

With enlightened Chinese, above all with those who had

learned the ways of Western civilization, this system was moderated with time. But they were not many in relation to the mass of common people.

When communism promised equality and freedom to the Chinese women, it must have exerted a powerful attraction on many women — and also on many young men. They, too, had formerly had no voice in selecting a mate, but had to take the wife chosen for them by the clan.

"Communism will not have a long life in China. It clashes with the national character of the Chinese. It is impossible that such a highly cultured people will support such a system for any appreciable length of time." How many hundreds of times such predictions were voiced by politicians and sociologists, by old China hands and sinologists! For years they awaited the supposedly imminent collapse of communist rule in China. To reinforce their theories, famous descriptions of Chinese family life were cited; the power exerted by Confucianism, which had endured for more than 2,500 years, was invoked. So were the inborn egoism of the Chinese, their love for property and the soil, their natural bent for trading, their ability to seize and use advantages.

In my opinion, all these factors make for an eventual transformation of Chinese communism, as has happened in the Soviet Union. But today it can hardly be doubted that the communists, by destroying the Confucian family system and the Confucian social order of China, based on a series of outdated precepts, have freed the Chinese from medieval chains. In so doing they have evoked an especially strong response in the young people.

But, paradoxically, Confucianism is not least among the influences that render the Chinese pliant to the communist regime. Confucius said, "The essence of a sovereign is the wind, the essence of the inferior is the grass. The grass, when the wind sighs across it, must bend." Or, in another place: "Outwardly, to serve the superior and the duke; inwardly, the father and the elder brother."

If, with this, Confucius appealed to something in the national character of the Chinese, or if this teaching became the common property of the Chinese people, we can well understand how the Chinese were able to withstand all onslaughts from outside for so many millennia. "The grass must bend"—what can that mean other than the counsel Confucius bequeathed his people, to show no resistance to those placed above them?

Would not the grass also bend under the wind of communism, under the alien and European teachings of Marxism-Leninism, only to spring up straight in a calm and windless moment?

Yet the influence of Chinese philosophy and religion on the Chinese mind and its acceptance of authority is not enough to account for the victorious march of communism and its ability to maintain itself in power in this huge country. To account for that, one must leave the sphere of purely theoretical considerations and search for further causes in the more recent history of China.

7

The "white peril"

Accompanied by my interpreter, I made a sightseeing tour through Canton. One of the oldest structures of this city is the so-called "Five-Story Building." It is situated on a hill and dominates the city. In former times it was the symbol of imperial dominion over this large seaport in the south of China. Marble tablets affixed to one side of this building are said to list all existing Chinese written characters, preserving them for future generations. My interpreter was unable to read many of these, because of the modernized language program that has been conducted in recent years.

We walked past these tablets toward the entrance and came to a platform on which, to my surprise, stood a row of cannon. These, and the tablets with the written characters, are kept in spit-and-polish condition because the communist regime apparently considers them important as an eternal reminder. Next to the cannon are plaques inscribed with names and dates. One name occurs several times: "Friedrich Krupp." These cannon were brought here in the nineteenth century, when the European powers began to subjugate China.

During a similar conducted tour through Shanghai, I was taken to the roof of Shanghai's tallest building. This high-rise structure stems from the days when the center of the city did not belong to the Chinese but to Europeans and Americans. "Do you see the park down there on the bank of the Hwang Pu River?" my companion asked. "At the entrance of this park stood a marker that read, 'Dogs and Chinese forbidden.' "

When we were walking through the streets of Shanghai, my companion pointed out certain rows of houses. "This used to be the border between the French and the Anglo-American sectors of Shanghai. Over there is where the international settlement began." The functionaries who accompanied me on such tours seemed never to tire of describing the humiliations that China had suffered at the hands of the "European-American imperialists" who had invaded and occupied their country. Europeans and Americans were not subject to Chinese jurisdiction. Had they murdered or cheated the Chinese, they would not even have been handed over to a Chinese court. The Chinese police were not permitted to enter the foreign concessions. The entire trade structure—and most of the China trade flowed through Shanghai—was monopolized by the foreigners, who grew rich on China's raw materials and Chinese labor, while the country itself sank deeper and deeper into poverty. Customs control was entirely in the hands of Europeans, and all customs duties accrued only to European countries, above all England, France, and Germany. In these tales the words "shame" and "disgrace" recurred frequently.

This is a chapter in the lexicon of European crimes which the Chinese enjoy retelling today. The Japanese do not fare much better. Their imperialism went hand in hand with that of Europe and America. Broad areas of China were conquered by the Japanese, who governed with an iron fist.

The traces of colonial rule in China—by European, American, Japanese, and other nations—are manifold. Penetration of China by the colonial powers contributed greatly to the development of communism in that country a century later.

It all began with the large-scale discovery of China by Europe, just as Europe and America had discovered Japan at an earlier date. The industrial powers were intent on disposing of their products in the Far East and obtaining raw materials in return.

Japan was forced to open its ports and submit to Western civilization. It offered hardly any resistance. On the contrary, Japan

fairly jumped at Western civilization, embraced it, and itself became a highly industrialized state in the Western sense. Shortly
afterward Japan was itself a colonial power, whose hand reached
out to Asia, to Korea, to Manchuria, to China.

It was entirely different with China. The Japanese were constantly aware that theirs was an island nation, and that most of
their culture and civilization derived from China, that great and
mighty people existing not far away. China, on the other hand,
was the "center of the earth." It was, for a long time, unaware
of greater or mightier peoples, near or far. It had a very strong
indigenous culture and civilization, which had been accepted willingly by the peoples at its borders.

At the end of the eighteenth century, when the English first
tried to establish firm connections with China and to send an ambassador to the Heavenly Throne, the emperor of China, Ch'ien
Lung, replied to the British:

> Despite your reverence for our heavenly dynasty, and despite
> your yearnings after our culture, the installation of an ambas-
> sador has no purpose. Even if your envoy were capable of
> absorbing the merest rudiments of our culture, he could not
> transplant its ways and mode of existence into your homeland.
> I, who rule the world, have one aim only: to govern excellently
> and to carry out the duties of the state that comprises the world.
> The strange and valuable objects [among them the first techni-
> cal treasures of Europe] mean nothing to me. The products of
> your country have no value whatever for me.

This is why the English ambassador was sent packing, and
many another European mission after him. Chinese emperors
thought of their country, the Middle Kingdom, even in the nineteenth century, as the most advanced, most civilized, and mightiest
state on earth. Chinese morality, postulated by Confucius for all
eternity, was far superior to all other moral doctrines. The Chinese
way of life was unsurpassable. The technology being offered by the
Europeans to the Chinese emperors elicited only a smile: What is
that for? For whose happiness?

The Chinese had invented gunpowder, which they used mainly

to set off fireworks. Long before the Europeans they had invented the rocket and shot it into the sky to amuse spectators. Iron and other metals had been known to them for thousands of years, although the extraction of these had been placed under imperial monopoly. Only a limited amount of the metals was mined, just enough to produce important religious vessels, temple statues, weapons, and coins.

Thus the Chinese made one invention after another but did not take them seriously or develop them further, because of the prevailing lofty sentiment that Chinese civilization was already perfect and not in need of any newfangled gadgets.

As for the Europeans, that white race whose envoys now landed more and more often in China's ports, and who even got as far as Peking, were they not mere barbarians, ignorant of the wisdom of the Chinese classics, to whom the moral precepts of Confucius were alien, who did not know how to comport themselves, showed no respect toward their elders, and barely managed to perform the prescribed kowtow before the Son of Heaven?

The emperor and his councilors had no idea with whom they were dealing. They had no conception of the might and power arrayed behind these barbarians, nor did they know what political and economic concepts were already being realized in the European metropolitan centers of the nineteenth century. They were to find out soon enough.

In 1839, after China had placed an embargo on the import of opium, England demanded the opening of the Chinese ports. British ships and marines equipped with the latest weapons broke the veto of the Chinese emperor—the Opium War. Several Chinese ports were occupied once the initially strong Chinese resistance was broken. China was forced to cede Hong Kong and Kowloon to England.

With that, the signal had been given. A race began among the European powers, and finally Japan, to put China into a position of colonial dependency, to secure for themselves the most valuable positions in China, and to incorporate them.

England and France again went to war with China in 1856, forced the opening of additional ports, and exacted the condition that European legations having extraterritorial rights would be established in Peking. The Yangtze River was declared an international waterway.

The Russians marched in 1858 and 1860 and occupied the Amur province and the eastern part of Siberia, which until then had belonged to China.

French troops landed in Indo-China and occupied Annam.

England wrenched Burma from under Chinese hegemony.

The Japanese landed on the Ryukyu Islands.

In 1894 Japan went to war against China, won, and obtained Formosa and the Pescadores Islands. Japan forced the Chinese to declare the independence of Korea, and established Japanese hegemony over it.

In 1898 the Germans finally appeared on the scene. The Bay of Chiaochou, with the important harbor of Tsingtao, was occupied by German troops.

Russia marched once again. The Liaotung peninsula, with its large Port Arthur, fell into Russian hands. Manchuria and Outer Mongolia became Russian spheres of interest.

England occupied the harbor of Weihaiwei; France, the Kwangchow Wan peninsula.

Within China there were insurrections against the government and the emperor. The people sensed the weakness of the imperial house and resented the disgrace inflicted on China by foreign powers.

Hung Hsiu-ch'uan, a Chinese educated by European missionaries, organized the Taiping Rebellion (1850–1865). The European powers at first supported this rebellion because it promised to weaken China. But when the Taipings besieged Peking, England and France placed troops at the disposal of the central government. The Japanese, too, were busily engaged in lending support now to one side, now to the other, as Chinese armies and parties met in conflict.

The Taipings were defeated, but the civil war, which lasted for thirteen years, brought China to the brink of disaster. This is why the Europeans and the Japanese had fairly smooth going in China in the following years.

In 1900 one of the many powerful Chinese secret societies called anew for rebellion, this time not against the imperial house but against the "real enemies of China," the Europeans. The insurrection broke out in Peking. The European diplomatic quarter was stormed. The German ambassador, Clemens von Ketteler, was murdered. The European colony barricaded itself, to fight for its life.

This incident brought about a unique solidarity of all interested states. Germany, England, France, Russia, the United States, Austria-Hungary, Italy, and Japan sent out a punitive expedition. In England the Peking rebels acquired the name "Boxer," and the conflict has gone down in history as the Boxer Rebellion. The supreme command of the punitive expedition was entrusted to the German general field marshal Count Waldersee. Two months after the start of the rebellion, he entered Peking at the head of the international units and liberated the diplomatic quarter, which had withstood the Boxers for fifty-five days.

Count Waldersee forced the imperial house to arrest and punish the culprits. Beyond that, China had to pay huge war reparations. China did not recover from these debts until 1949.

*   *   *

One Sunday in Peking I visited the so-called summer palace. It is not really a palace. The name applies to a splendid park, large enough to take in almost the entire population of Peking. In this park stand several pagodas, palace-like structures, teahouses, shrines, and guest houses. The imperial widow of China, Tz'u Hsi, had this park built. She insisted that her architects make it a smaller but faithful replica of China's most beautiful region, the "paradise of Hanchow." Here they created a small-scale but accurate version of the large lake of Hanchow. To afford a promenade for the dowager empress in inclement weather, a covered walk, many miles long, was erected on the shores of the lake, and each of the hundreds of cross-beams supporting the roof was a choice piece of art.

My companion told me the history of this park. "At that time (1894), Japan was making preparations for the invasion of China. The state council was of the opinion that China ought to defend herself with a strong fleet. The money to build this fleet was allocated. But the imperial widow thought it over. She came to the conclusion that the money would be ill-spent on a fleet. Who could conquer China! So she decided to use the money for the construction of the summer palace, for the creation of this great park."

In the final analysis, the Chinese emperors were proved right. China has never been conquered. Neither the Europeans nor the Japanese were able to subjugate the country in its entirety. But what was the consequence of this European-Japanese onslaught?

Unlike the emperors, many Chinese began to doubt the superiority of their culture, and even of their country's governmental and social institutions. They understood that they were confronted by a civilization stronger than their own. Their concept of the world, their belief in the traditional wisdom and law collapsed, and with it their faith in the emperor and the political leadership. The young Chinese began to ask why their country, for thousands of years the center of the earth, was not able to stop the Western invasion. Before too long, they thought they recognized the cause. China had not paid enough attention to the natural sciences and to technology. It was the superior technical knowledge of the West that had forced China to its knees.

A generation of young, open-minded Chinese plunged into a study of the Western sciences. With the sciences Western political thought came to China.

At the beginning of the twentieth century, China had a small but extremely intelligent and determined group of students who were prepared to make use of European knowledge for the defense of China against Europe. They demanded the overthrow of the imperial dynasty and the introduction of Western democracy and Western technology. Their goal was to make China strong, on a par with Europe, and so to rid it of foreign influences.

In this group of revolutionaries who were ready to overthrow the dynasty and to transform China into a Western liberal democracy one man stood out: the physician Dr. Sun Yat-sen. He had attended American schools. He understood how to gather around him open-minded friends and energetic supporters from among the overseas Chinese. He visited the United States, England, France, and Germany; he studied the Western system. He was one of the few who knew that China could not be freed of its backwardness and made over into a Western democracy overnight.

His program was aimed at freeing China from foreign influence, re-establishing its sovereignty, gaining equal rights among the nations, and introducing necessary reforms, especially land reform. After the fall of the dynasty, a military government was to guarantee the unity of the country. This government should be succeeded by a "guided democracy," which was to educate the Chinese people for true democracy. Only after this second period of government would Sun Yat-sen introduce democracy after the Western model.

Just as the Germans discovered Lenin in World War I and brought him to Russia to tear down the hostile regime of the czar, so the Japanese discovered Sun Yat-sen, provided him with sufficient means, and brought him to China in the hope that he would topple the imperial dynasty and thus further weaken China.

In 1911 all was ready. Revolution broke out under the leadership of Sun Yat-sen. Its target was the overthrow of the Manchu Dynasty. Many political groups knew the cause of China's decline and even agreed that China must regain her power. But they did not know how to achieve this goal.

The friends of Sun Yat-sen founded the National People's Party, the Kuomintang. They refused to listen to Sun Yat-sen, who warned them that China was not yet mature enough for the introduction of a Western-style democracy. They wanted to achieve an advanced political system without any transition. A provisional national assembly in Nanking elected Sun Yat-sen president of the government of China (that is, of the rebellious southern provinces).

It was then that the threatened dynasty, under the widow of the emperor, turned to the tried and proved General Yuan Shih-k'ai, obviously in the hope that the general could secure better treatment of the deposed imperial family. However, the general had political ambitions of his own. He threatened civil war and demanded that Sun Yat-sen renounce the presidency and leave the country. Sun Yat-sen, who himself had not believed in a direct transition from imperial to democratic rule, and who also knew the military strength of his opponent, resigned his office to spare China a new blood bath. That was the end of the Manchu Dynasty, the end of imperial rule in China, but it was not yet the beginning of a new democratic China.

Shortly afterward, Yuan Shih-k'ai had himself proclaimed the first constitutional president of China. In 1915 he tried to have himself crowned emperor of China and to found a new dynasty, but failed.

Yuan Shih-k'ai died in the next year, 1916. The democratic forces of China gathered new hope. In Europe, the First World War was raging. Its effects could be felt in faraway China. Japan declared war on Germany. Japanese troops attacked and conquered the German-Chinese enclave of Tsingtao. Then from the United States came promise of salvation: President Wilson proclaimed the right of all nations to self-determination. That would mean that China, too, could free herself from all foreign influences, that the foreign troops would depart and Chinese sovereignty would be re-established.

But China was torn apart internally. Warlords governed in the provinces. The government in Peking was not only weak, it openly collaborated with the Japanese. In vain were the rulers in Peking urged to enter the war, to align themselves with the Allies. Not until the last year of the war did they bring themselves to this decision, in the hope of being granted a place and a voice in the great peace conference to come.

This peace conference was convened in Versailles. There, the Chinese representatives demanded the return of the former German possessions in China from the hands of the Japanese, demanded the withdrawal of the English and of the French from the Chinese ports. The United States backed these Chinese demands — sufficient reason for the Chinese students and intellectuals to believe in a good and just conclusion of the Versailles Conference. But neither Japan nor the West European powers were ready to accede to the Chinese demands. They ignored the promise of President Wilson regarding the right of nations to self-determination and apportioned the world according to the contributions made by the individual nations to the Allied victory. The United States was outvoted at Versailles, whereupon it quit the peace conference.

On the fourth of May, 1919, the decision of Versailles became known in China, and the hopes of thousands of politicians and intellectuals were ruined. Disillusionment with the West was marked, to such an extent that the popular belief in democratic principles was reversed.

In front of the Tien An Men in Peking, the Gate to Heavenly Peace, the largest political demonstration in China's history took place. First the students marched before the Tien An Men. They were followed by the intellectuals and the politicians, and finally by a large number of Peking's citizens. It was a demonstration against their own government, which was accused of collaborating with Japan, and of showing weakness vis-à-vis the might of the West; and it was an outbreak of hate against Europe.

With good reason, the present-day Chinese rulers refer to May 4, 1919, as the day on which the foundation for the communist victory over China was laid. Quite a few of today's leading politicians were present as students among the demonstrators in front of the Tien An Men. Until that time most of them had believed in democratic and liberal ideals and had wanted to introduce the parliamentary system into China. There, before the Tien An Men, they determined to search for a new and indigenous form of government.

Sun Yat-sen evinced a very similar reaction. His slim hope of support from the Western powers had soon turned to disappointment. Like many Chinese students and intellectuals, he began to listen to a voice that expressed what the Chinese had hoped to hear from the Western democracies. This voice, speaking from Moscow, was the voice of Lenin. Vehemently it condemned imperialism and colonialism and proclaimed the equal rights of all peoples. The new Soviet government declared itself ready, even at this early stage, to support the national democratic movements in the colonial and semi-colonial territories of the world.

Openly the communists announced that they did this in the hope of subverting these movements to communism at the right time. The founding of the Chinese Communist Party (CPC) followed promptly, in 1920. The CPC, incidentally, was founded simultaneously in several countries. Chou En-lai, at that time a student in Paris, organized the CPC in France; Chu Teh, later a general and fellow campaigner of Mao Tse-tung, founded the CPC among Chinese students in Germany. The weakest of the founding committees was the one in China itself. Eight anarchists, social democrats, and so-called Marxists in Shanghai decided to found a Communist Party of China. And one of them was called Mao Tse-tung.

In the same year, Sun Yat-sen succeeded in getting a foothold in Canton. Moscow was alert, sent its advisers, urged Sun Yat-sen to organize rigorously and to discipline the Kuomintang. It remained a national-democratic party but was organized on the model of the Communist Party of the Soviet Union (CPSU). Shortly afterward, it concluded a treaty of mutual defense and offense with the Chinese communists, on the advice of Moscow.

A school for Party cadres was established, also a military academy. The communists joined the Kuomintang as individuals while retaining their membership in the CPC. Mao Tse-tung, then twenty-six years old, became a member of the executive committee of the central committee of the Kuomintang, and was simultaneously a member of the executive committee of the Politburo of the CPC. Chou En-lai, having returned home from France, was an instructor at the military academy for Kuomintang troops, which was commanded by a certain General Chiang Kai-shek.

It was the aim of the so-called blue-and-red coalition to rid the country of the warlords, to unite it, and to form a central government. At this point Sun Yat-sen died, in 1925. The destiny of China took its course.

8

The blue-and-red coalition

Nanking. This city has always played a great role in China's history, and recently a particularly important one. In 1911 the first national assembly of China met here and proclaimed Sun Yat-sen the first president of the republican government, before the imperial dynasty had even been overthrown. Here liberal and democratic revolutionaries defied the military dictatorship of General Yuan Shih-k'ai. Later, Nanking became the capital of China under General Chiang Kai-shek.

Our car rolled along a well-kept, paved street through park-like scenery, through subtropical forests, along lakes densely covered with lotus blossoms, past small, open tea pavilions, and onto hills from whose summit one could see, along the horizon, China's largest river, the Yangtze. On one of these hills had been built the monument to Sun Yat-sen.

We got out of the car and stood in front of a large Chinese gate, the roof of which was covered with blue-glazed tiles. It was a gate like those in front of the burial grounds of the Chinese emperors, and served as a passageway to the first outer temple at the foot of the hill. In the outer temple was a large marble plate carved with gold letters: "Here the Kuomintang buried Sun Yat-sen." And above gleamed the white star of the Kuomintang.

Behind the outer temple, some three hundred steps almost ninety feet wide led us over large terraces to the summit of the hill. Chinese architects have achieved a brilliant feat here. From the bottom of the hill one sees only endless steps running up into the sky. But from the top, none of the steps can be seen. The large terraces hide them and create the impression of a flat marble carpet extending from the outer temple to the top.

Up here we saw the memorial proper, consisting of an antechamber and the burial room. In the antechamber was a white marble statue of Sun Yat-sen. A low, narrow corridor led into the burial chamber. The grave itself was closed by a marble slab, and on this slab was another marble sculpture of Sun Yat-sen. The body of the great politician has been buried hundreds of feet under ground to safeguard it against depredation, in keeping with an ancient tradition.

But probably no one has ever intended to plunder the grave of Sun Yat-sen. It was General Chiang Kai-shek who arranged for Sun Yat-sen's burial here, thus according him imperial honors. Yet on the anniversary of his death, year after year, the highest communist leaders assemble to render homage to him under the inimical star of the Kuomintang.

No one has tried to replace the many Kuomintang symbols on this monument with those of the hammer and sickle. Even today the Chinese communist leaders profess emphatically their adherence to the pact which they concluded with the Kuomintang at the beginning of the twenties. Now as then, they regard Sun Yat-sen as the precursor of the communist revolution and co-founder of the new China, although Sun Yat-sen was certainly not a communist, having advocated the step-by-step transformation of China into a democratic state. In the Peking Museum of the Revolution, and elsewhere, I saw six pictures, in this sequence: Marx, Engels, Lenin, Stalin, Sun Yat-sen, Mao Tse-tung. It is as if European Marxism, on its way through Petrograd, Moscow, and Georgia, and finally through Canton and Nanking to Peking, developed by degrees into a Chinese idea.

In this chain the Kuomintang is a vital link, not yet broken. Even today the revolutionary committee of the Kuomintang exists in Peking, while Sun Yat-sen's widow has earned great honors and exerts considerable influence as the Kuomintang's representative in Communist China. Incidentally, her sister is the wife of Chiang

Kai-shek; and Chiang Kai-shek also considers himself a Chinese revolutionary, legitimate successor to Sun Yat-sen.

But the coalition between the Kuomintang and the communists did not long survive the death of Sun Yat-sen in 1925. General Chiang Kai-shek, the commander of the military academy and Sun Yat-sen's brother-in-law, was called upon to assume leadership of the Kuomintang. At the same time he was commander-in-chief of the communist units within the Kuomintang army.

Even at that time, the communists began to have grave doubts about Chiang. He did not appear to be a reliable confederate, though he had received his military education in Moscow and had numerous friends and allies in the Soviet capital.

But it was precisely this circumstance that caused Stalin to put his trust in Chiang Kai-shek. The Soviet dictator did not believe a communist revolution possible in China, an opinion first voiced by Lenin. In colonial and semi-colonial territories, the proletariat was thought to be too weak to revolt. The bourgeoisie in these territories, economically much stronger and often allied to the army and the police, should first trigger a national and democratic revolution and lay the basis for industrialization, thereby strengthening the proletariat. Not until much later would a strengthened proletariat be ready to embark on the communist revolution. And so, in the opinion of Moscow, Chiang Kai-shek was to be supported; he had to be trusted to keep the alliance with the communists. Even if he had tried to suppress the communists, they would have supported him.

We do not know whether Chiang Kai-shek knew about this concept. One thing is certain: when his troops began to march in 1926, when they began to storm China's large cities in 1927, when Chiang Kai-shek's victory over the numerous warlords of China was no longer in doubt, he decided not to share the victory with the communists. Probably rightly, he feared that after the victory he would not be able to assert himself against them but would have to hand over the victory to them.

What occurred in China in 1927 was a tragedy for both sides. Chiang's troops surrounded and besieged the cities. Not a few of the troops were under communist command. In the cities, the communists understood how to organize the workers. Strikes were called under communist leadership. As a result, there were armed clashes between the workers and the local military commanders. Chiang Kai-shek's troops would have had little trouble at that point in taking over the cities. But the command was not given.

The communist units of the Kuomintang troops came to the brink of mutiny but were held in check by their commanders. Moscow had placed absolute trust in Chiang Kai-shek; his orders were to be followed. So the troops surrounding the cities had to stand by and see the fighting groups of city workers defeated. Strangely enough, suddenly the local military commanders seemed to have gained precise knowledge about where the centers of the communist underground were located. They raided them and stood the communist leaders against the wall. But still Chiang's army did not attack.

And then came a command from above. The communist sections of the Kuomintang troops were to be disarmed. They would have been strong enough to put up a last bloody battle, or they could have withdrawn from the Kuomintang army and sought refuge in the remote provinces. But Moscow, under Stalin, confirmed the command of Chiang Kai-shek.

"Treason!" The word spread like wildfire through the communist cells. "Treason, treason!" they cabled to Moscow. But there Stalin was arguing with Trotsky. Even before the turnabout of Chiang Kai-shek, Trotsky had demanded the dissolution of the alliance between the communists and the Kuomintang. He had advocated the creation of a separate Red army in China. He distrusted Chiang Kai-shek. But Stalin opposed Trotsky. He wanted the coalition with the Kuomintang maintained under any circumstances, even at the price of disarming the communist units and seeing the communist organization broken and scattered. Even the word "treason" did not change his intentions, which would have proved Trotsky right and himself wrong. His envoys ordered the Chinese communists to lay down their arms, to deliver them to the Kuomintang, so as not to provoke Chiang Kai-shek.

Chiang Kai-shek regarded this as a further sign of communist weakness. On his own initiative, then, he broke the alliance with the Chinese Communist Party and ordered the communist officers and political commissars shot.

During that time, a Communist Party functionary named Mao Tse-tung operated in Hunan Province. There a great peasant revolt had broken out. The order from Moscow was to keep this peasant revolt down, true to the Leninist principle that the revolution may not be set off by peasants but by the city proletariat, as happened in Russia.

But Mao Tse-tung, who was now ordered to hold the peasants back, was himself the son of a peasant. He knew their poverty, he knew how they were being oppressed by village tyrants and usurers. He recognized an opportunity for communism to exploit these feelings of the peasants. Instead of calming them, he wrote glowing accounts to the Central Committee (CC) of the Communist Party about the progress of the peasant revolution. And he promptly fell into disgrace.

Mao founded an all-Chinese peasant association, placing it under communist leadership. In 1927, his association is said to have numbered more than ten million members.

When Chiang Kai-shek turned against the communists, Mao acted quickly. His army of Red peasants disengaged itself from the troops of the Kuomintang and withdrew to a mountain plateau in Kwangsi Province.

The Red troops, poorly armed, were constantly harassed by the armies of Chiang Kai-shek and by local military commanders. But Mao had come to a decision. He was not satisfied to be the leader of a small horde of insurgents. On the barren plateau, in 1927, he proclaimed the establishment of the "Soviet Republic of China." He placed it under the control of the Central Committee; he was the leader.

But even Mao did not know how long a few thousand peasants, poorly equipped with weapons, could hold out against superior forces. The troops made frequent sorties, occupied villages in the plains, and persuaded the peasants to sell them food. Mao developed —without communication with the Central Committee, which had gone underground in Shanghai—his own military and political tactics. He himself worked out the rules for effective guerrilla warfare.

He compressed his rules into a few catchwords, set them to music, and taught his peasant-soldiers to sing: "The foe advances, we yield to him. The foe stands still, we wear him out. The foe tires, we beat him. The foe retreats, we follow him."

These tactics permitted him always to withdraw before an attack by the enemy, to avoid decisive defeats, to weaken the foe at auspicious moments much more effectively than either his numbers or equipment permitted. Mao had no inkling at that time that these tactical instructions, written down in mountain caves, would be used fifteen years later as guidelines for the Russians and above all the Yugoslav partisans in their battles with German troops.

But Mao the politician was no less active. The chances that his republic would be annihilated within weeks were strong. Yet he began to lay the foundations for the conquest of China through communism. He originated the now famous "Three Tenets and Eight Disciplines." They, too, were easy to grasp; they, too, were set to music; they, too, were sung by his soldiers, so that everyone could hear them, and must hear them.

The Three Tenets:
1. Obey orders in all your actions.
2. Don't take a single needle or piece of thread from the masses.
3. Turn in everything captured.

The Eight Disciplines:
1. Speak politely.
2. Pay fairly for what you buy.
3. Return everything you borrow.
4. Pay for anything you damage.
5. Don't hit or swear at people.
6. Don't damage crops.
7. Don't take liberties with women.
8. Don't ill-treat captives.*

Today it can be asserted for good reasons that these

---

*These Tenets and Disciplines were altered several times. In 1928, for instance, the first two of the then six Disciplines went like this:
1. Put back the doors you have taken down for bed-boards.
2. Put back the straw you have used for bedding.

"Three Tenets and Eight Disciplines" made it possible for Mao and his Red Army to survive from 1927 until 1949 in the most inhospitable regions of China. When they came to a village, the peasants had nothing to fear from the Red Army. Mao Tse-tung's soldiers went without pay for months, but each cup of rice they received from the peasants was paid for. On the other hand, it is true that the Reds took the money from the big landowners and money lenders and did not issue them credit notes for it.

Emissaries of the Central Committee of the Chinese Communist Party arrived in Mao's Soviet Republic with orders: "The class struggle is to be intensified and the 'kulaks' [rich peasants] in the liberated villages are to be liquidated without mercy." Mao turned a deaf ear. He did not even liquidate the big landowners. Not because he was so tender-hearted—on the contrary, he had no mercy for traitors. No, his instincts told him one thing: once the Red Army acquired a reputation for using summary executions among the civilian population, the middle and small peasants would begin to dread it; they would be lost to him as allies.

And so the Red Army made a show of friendship wherever it went. It was a friend of the poor peasants, even made common cause with the middle peasants, who were already kulaks in Soviet terms, and also left most of the big landowners alone—for the time being. The Central Committee of the CPC raged. Moscow demanded the dissolution of this "pseudo Soviet Republic." But Mao was successful. The youths of the villages swarmed to enlist in the Red Army. Some of Chiang Kai-shek's troops transferred their allegiance. Word had gone around that Red Army officers did not beat the soldiers (a common practice until then in China). Prisoners of war were fed by the Red Army, even if its own soldiers had to go without food, and were sent home with good wishes. Whoever wished to join the Red Army was welcomed as a friend.

Officers and men of the Red Army received the same pay or no pay, wore the same uniform or the same sort of rags.

These unusual military practices were well known. Often enough they were noted and reported by anti-communists. Today we can only assume that a man like Mao Tse-tung introduced and carried out these rules for cold-blooded considerations. And his tactics bore fruit.

In the Peking Museum of the Revolution there is a model of the terrain held by the Soviet Republic of Mao Tse-tung. It covered only a few dozen square miles. Next to the model are figurines in the uniforms and equipment of that time. The cloth is the thinnest cotton, nearly transparent, and was woven by the soldiers themselves. Around their necks they wore a cotton sack filled with gruel or rice; with this ration they had to maintain themselves for two to three weeks, as there were hardly any central provisioning points. Their guns were mostly homemade. Instead of land mines, they used sharpened bamboo spikes, which they buried in the ground.

The façade of a peasant house of that time is also exhibited in this museum. The slogans of the Red Army can be seen on the door posts: "Liberation of the peasants! Land reform! Chase off the big landowners!" I had an odd feeling when the directress of this museum invited me to step through the old wooden door of that house, for behind it was a luxuriously furnished tea salon for prominent visitors to the museum.

This museum is crowded daily by thousands of "Young Pioneers," children between the ages of seven and thirteen. Well disciplined, they sit on the ground in large groups in front of the exhibits and listen to the historical development of the Soviet Republic of China, to the wondrous, heroic deeds of Chairman Mao Tse-tung.

In the foyer of the museum, there are, as I have mentioned, four small and two large pictures. The small ones: Marx, Engels, Lenin, and Stalin; the large ones: Sun Yat-sen and Mao Tse-tung.

What, then, was Mao Tse-tung during those years in the mountain fastness of Kwangsi? A communist?

In his opinion, without a doubt. In the opinion of the Central Committee of the illegal CPC and particularly in the opinion of Stalin, he was an opportunist, if not a rebel.

In 1930 Mao's Soviet Republic was sharply criticized in the illegal central organ of the CPC: "It will not do for the military forces of the peasantry to overshadow those of the workers. This is a deviation which expresses a lack of faith in the power of the working classes." The dissolution of Mao's Soviet Republic was demanded. "The revolution can never emerge from bases in the countryside. It must have its source in the cities."

Mao did not bother with all this. Better than the other CP leaders, he knew that a revolution of the working classes in China would be impossible for many decades, if not centuries. Of the 700 million Chinese, at best two million were workers. But the peasants were ripe for the revolution. They knew nothing about communism, but they had been oppressed too long; they had become too impoverished. They called for land reform and wanted to get rid of their burden of debts. So Mao Tse-tung devised a strategy for the revolution in the villages, formulated laws for land reform, and nourished the rebellion of the peasants.

Chiang Kai-shek knew better than Moscow how dangerous this Soviet Republic of Mao Tse-tung was. Between 1927 and 1934, seven long years, he attacked Mao repeatedly, unleashing five "campaigns of destruction" against the Red Army, with half a million soldiers powering these campaigns. The Red Army suffered severe losses but still held on; Mao's guerrilla tactics proved effective.

Then disaster struck Mao and his Soviet Republic. The Central Committee of the CPC was unable to maintain itself underground in Shanghai. By devious routes, its members pushed on to Mao's plateau. The Soviet advisers, among them purportedly a German general, whose cover name was given only as "Otto," accompanied the tired marchers.

Chiang Kai-shek, then about to undertake his fifth campaign of destruction, had entrusted the command for the operation to another German officer, General von Seeckt.

The planning for the defense against this attack was seized from Mao and entrusted to the representatives of the Comintern. German military strategy was then confronted by German military strategy. Chiang Kai-shek attacked on a solid front, but for the first time the Red Army did not yield. It had formed a main line of defense. And it was beaten, trapped by Chiang.

Nevertheless, Mao did not yield his authority. He commanded: "All troops will concentrate their strength on one sector of the trap, at night. We will break through the trap, and the Soviet Republic will then start to march."

On that night, neither Mao nor his Red Army knew where this march might lead them. They did not know how long it would take and where it would end. It was the beginning of the Long March, an October night in the year 1934.

Today it is impossible to visit a Chinese museum, factory, school, or cultural center without being confronted by pictures, models, and souvenirs of the Long March. The Long March has become the heroic epic of the Chinese communist revolution. It has left its imprint not only on the minds of the communist leaders but on the entire Party—in fact, on a large part of the Chinese people today.

9

The Long March

Since the success of the Long March the Chinese Communist Party has considered itself invincible, able to overcome forces much stronger than itself. Out of the ideology of the Long March comes the concept of the anti-communist enemy as a "paper tiger," such a paper tiger as is set on fire at Chinese public celebrations to show its impotence.

Out of the Long March comes the notion that an enemy may seize all China and still be defeated. And from the experiences of the communist leaders during the Long March comes their contempt for death even in the face of the atom bomb, a contempt incomprehensible to the Western mind.

We must know the story of the Long March if we are to evaluate accurately the thinking of Mao Tse-tung and his lieutenants. No other logic can be brought to bear on their thought patterns.

China today is employing the ideology of the Long March as her strongest weapon, not only against the West, but also against the Communist Party of the Soviet Union. "What we did then you too can do. You need not depend on outside help if you have enough confidence in yourself and if you are willing to endure deprivation and suffering. Then no one can take your victory from you." This is what the Chinese advisers and emissaries advocate to revolutionary groups in Asia, Africa, and Latin America, rather than the foreign economic aid extended by the United States and the Soviet Union.

The Long March began in Kwangsi Province on a night at the end of October, 1934. The troops of Chiang Kai-shek, under the command of the German General von Seeckt, surrounded the Soviet Republic of Mao Tse-tung and then prepared for the decisive blow. On that night the Red Army broke through the ring of Chiang's troops and swept like lightning through the valley.

There were 130,000 men in the ranks of Mao Tse-tung and Field Marshal Chu Teh. They started out, these 130,000 men with their wives and children, their primitive spinning wheels and looms, their blacksmith tools and sewing machines, their plows and sickles. They had no plan but to evade the troops of Chiang Kai-shek, to stay out of the hands of the enemy.

But Chiang did not give up. His troops pursued the marching Soviet Republic, headed it off, bombarded it from the air, and day after day raked it with machine-gun fire. Pushed back by superior numbers, it retreated to marsh and hill country, to impassible gorges, and almost to the border of Tibet.

Statistics on the Long March are available. To read them is to wonder how human beings could bear such hardships. Mao's Soviet Republic marched for 368 days, averaging 24 miles a day. In approximately a year it covered about 6,800 miles on foot. It crossed thirty large rivers, twenty high mountain chains, including the 16,000-foot-high Great Snow Mountains. Dozens of ravines were traversed with no help but hand ropes.

And at every mountain pass, every ravine, every riverbank stood Chiang Kai-shek's soldiers with artillery, grenades, and machine guns to halt the army in its tracks.

At the end of the Long March barely 30,000 of the 130,000 reached north China. But even this figure is inaccurate, because new troops joined the Republic all along the way, peasants and their families. The losses, therefore, must have been much higher than 100,000.

Mao Tse-tung himself, whose first wife had been shot in 1930 by Chiang Kai-shek's police, was accompanied by his second wife and their five children. His wife was seriously wounded by a bomb splinter from one of Chiang's planes and was carried by stretcher for the greater part of the march. The three youngest children, near death from starvation, had to be left behind with a peasant family. They were never found again—too many children had been handed over to kind-hearted peasants to save them from certain death by hunger and cold.

Countless stories about the Long March have been written, of which the best known are by Mao's former orderlies. They tell of incredible hardships, days and nights when death by drowning in the swamps seemed inevitable, constant strafing by Chiang's planes, and icy weeks in the Great Snow Mountains when almost half the troops died of cold and exposure at an altitude of sixteen thousand feet. They tell of astonishing but historically verified battles for bridgeheads, ravines, and streams in the face of powerful resistance by the enemy.

Scarcely a soldier had a whole pair of shoes. Their feet were wrapped in straw and bark. Only a few had coats. The leaders, who had horses or mules, were able to ride only for short stretches. They too traveled on foot for the greater part of the seven-thousand-mile journey.

But they "liberated" every village they came to. The advance units were accompanied by political commissars who induced the peasants to establish self-government. In every village they founded a small Soviet, organized a communist administration, and within twenty-four hours redistributed the holdings of the large landowners among the peasants and field hands. They requisitioned nothing from the poor but paid for everything they took. The main body of the Red Army passed through towns and rural communities with the song of the Three Tenets and Eight Disciplines on its lips. Although it knew it could never stand still for long—ten days was a long rest—it acted as if Soviet power in the area would last forever.

Behind all this was a cleverly calculated political scheme. As the Red Army advanced, it was followed by Chiang's soldiers, who immediately reversed everything it had done. The poor peasants, tenant farmers, and field hands were forced to return the land, so recently given them, to its former owners. Their self-administered government was dissolved. Naturally they hated Chiang Kai-shek and his government. For a long time to come they would dream of the days when the Red Army had been among them. If it returned, it could count on their support. This plan, laid by Mao, proved its worth fifteen years later.

On the Long March, in damp caves and under the open sky, during downpours and icy winter nights, Mao Tse-tung wrote countless political pamphlets, worked out the policies of a Soviet China yet to come, analyzed the classes of Chinese society, extended the theories of Marx and Lenin and revised them for Chinese needs. Interspersed with these activities he somehow found time to compose verses in the style of the Chinese classics. Most of these were paeans to the beauty and harmony of the landscape through which he was passing.

But that was not the only task Mao undertook. After covering twenty-five to thirty miles on foot in a day, the soldiers would fall down dead tired and go to sleep at once. It was then that the Central Committee of the Party would meet for endless discussions about the interpretation and implementation of communist theory, practice criticism and self-criticism, and call individual leaders to task for wrong opinions. Mao Tse-tung almost always came under vehement attack. More than once he faced expulsion from the Central Committee and even from the Party. The representatives of the Comintern wanted to get rid of Mao. His opinions, his politics, his traits as a leader went counter to the orders from Moscow. His viewpoint was opposed to Stalin's.

And so, after an exhausting day on the battle front, Mao had to fight at night to defend his claim to leadership. It is reported that these sessions lasted until the trumpeters woke the sleeping troops at daybreak.

Months passed before Mao had a majority in the Central Committee, establishing himself as leader. Not until 1935 did he become secretary of the Central Secretariat and thus the strongest man in the Party.

To his army he preached tirelessly: do not "liquidate" but ally yourselves with the well-to-do farmers, and win the artisans and workers over to the Soviet state. He went still further and courted the middle classes, even the capitalists among them. Mao realized that the well-to-do Chinese hated the foreign invaders, hated the English and French and most of all the Japanese imperialists. They were dissatisfied with Chiang Kai-shek because the Nationalist government had managed only with extreme difficulty to revoke the privileges of the foreign powers and to re-establish China's sovereignty piecemeal. Chiang sought the friendship and support of the West. His regime was internationally recognized, and he was reluctant to proceed without international sanction, preferring to obtain China's rights through negotiation.

This was too slow for many Chinese. In their eyes, Chiang was too conciliatory toward the Western powers and much too tolerant toward the Japanese.

The Japanese had taken advantage of unsettled conditions in China to invade and occupy Manchuria (Manchukuo) in 1932. They met almost no resistance, for Chiang was too weak to provoke a war against the aggressor nation. He wanted first to protect the rear, to restore order in his own country. That brought grist to the mills of the communists. They stamped him as a traitor to his people, invoking the popular anti-Japanese sentiment. And they found many sympathizers among the middle classes, even among the Chinese industrialists and capitalists. Using as his slogan, "Down with imperialism, down with colonialism, death to the Japanese!" Mao Tse-tung set about building a national solidarity front. Centuries of humiliation and shame endured by the Chinese helped his cause.

Thus, during the days and nights of the Long March, Mao developed his strategies and determined his policies, not only for the immediate future but for years to come. All this time not one of his men knew whether Mao would live to see the next day or whether the Republic would survive until the end of the march.

Although a strong framework of legend has already been built around the Long March, we may accept the reports that it was Mao whose faith in the future and determination strengthened the leaders and gave them courage to go on.

By that time they had abandoned all hope that the Red Army would be able to conquer and occupy an entire province and maintain itself there. Only in the inhospitable north, almost inaccessible to enemy forces, far from any strategically valuable city, railroad, or highway, could they find refuge. And so, the Soviet Republic marched northward.

At the end of 1935 the exhausted remnants of the Red Army reached Wuch-i and took shelter in the Yenan caves. Here they managed to establish a strong base. Chiang-Kai-shek seemed to have lost interest in liquidating their straggling forces. The strategic advance of Japan and the menace this implied for China absorbed his whole attention. Word that Mao had managed to find a refuge in the north trickled down to other fragments of the Red Army, scattered through south and central China, and to such bases as they still held in those areas. Many of them succeeded in getting through to him. Mao filled the ranks with fresh reinforcements and used the years that followed to train his troops and prepare them for a greater strategic role.

The people's communes that came into being in China in 1958 had their inception in the Yenan caves. Mao not only created a training school for political leaders, he also urged all the members of the Soviet Republic, including its soldiers, to live in a single great commune. The day was strictly organized. In the morning, gymnastics were followed by military drill. Then everyone had to work in the fields. The only privilege Mao asked for himself was to be allowed to plant a tobacco field. A heavy smoker, he was thus able to supply his own needs. But he too lugged human excrement onto the fields and worked beside the soldiers.

Primary attention, however, was directed to training the army for guerrilla warfare. This form of warfare gave the communists their lone hope of some day prevailing against superior enemy forces.

The success of the Long March and the reports of Mao's successes in Yenan finally convinced even Moscow that Mao Tse-tung was the strongest leader in the Chinese communist movement. He was confirmed by the Comintern as First Secretary of the Central Committee and the Party's leader. There was really nothing else for the Comintern to do. In the Central Committee and in his Party he had scarcely an enemy left.

Even those who had opposed him during the Long March now

acknowledged him as leader, although with some reservations. The difference between the Chinese communists and the Soviet leadership is nowhere more marked. None of Mao's former opponents were liquidated. Most of them remained on the Central Committee in high positions. The Long March, the shared suffering, perhaps the awareness that they had no backing in the entire world bound them together. The bond that formed during the Long March and the Yenan days remains until this day. Most of the present government heads of China went through the Long March with Mao and lived through the Yenan experience with him. Their differences were great then, and even greater after the victory and in the difficult days of the "Great Leap" and the break with the Soviet Union, but only two of them made an issue of their disagreements. Nor did they try to liquidate each other.

If Mao was usually able to range a majority behind his ideas, it stands to reason that he often did so only after some stormy battles. Many of his colleagues must have been arrayed against him. But after the votes were in, they apparently carried out his policies without demur and relied on his continued trust. To them the continuing struggle for power in Moscow, from Lenin's death to the present, seemed a sign of immaturity.

Naturally, the recognition of Mao as chairman of China's Communist Party by the Communist International in Moscow was little more than a gesture. The Russians had given up all hope of an imminent communist conquest of China. Moscow continued to recognize the Chiang regime as the legitimate government of China. It not only concluded trade agreements with Chiang but offered pacts of friendship and mutual aid. That was Stalin's policy.

Moreover, the Soviet Union stabilized its relations with Japan, and Stalin accepted the Japanese occupation of Chinese territory. He even confirmed his acceptance by making several pacts with Japan.

Thus Mao and his followers were virtually alone in the Yenan caves. But history came to his rescue in 1937. Japan renewed its aggressions against China, invaded the country over a broad front, marched against the capital of Nanking, and took it. Chiang Kai-shek's troops were defeated. Japanese troops quickly spread over the fertile plains of China and occupied most of the large cities, forcing Chiang to flee to Chungking.

That was the signal for Mao Tse-tung. In line with the strategy developed on the Long March, he declared an end to the fratricidal war with Chiang Kai-shek and commanded his troops not to attack the "blue units" of Chiang unless they started hostilities. Often enough this happened, and there were skirmishes between Red and Blue. Each time, Mao insisted that Chiang and his generals were shedding Chinese blood while the Japanese were penetrating further into China. He declared that the Red Army was determined only to fight the Japanese. Above all he called for the ancient land of China once more to defend itself against the invading barbarians. Whenever Red troops encountered Chiang's divisions, they urged them to unite against the Japanese. Often, Chiang's troops turned their backs on the Japanese and engaged the Red Army, but sometimes the soldiers refused to obey their leaders and deserted to the Red troops.

Now communist propaganda was set in motion: "The real patriots are in the communist camp." All who wanted to defeat Japan were invited to join the Red troops. Mao was clever enough not to merge the defecting Chiang soldiers with the Red Army; he kept them under their own officers, declared them "completely independent," but made it clear to them that they would have to proceed with a common strategy under his guidance. In this "anti-Japanese war" Mao thus laid another foundation for his "great coalition," in which, at first, the Nationalist forces were to find a place.

While Hitler attacked the Soviet Union and Japan bombed Pearl Harbor in the 1940's, further negotiations took place between Chiang Kai-shek and Mao Tse-tung. Under pressure from both the Soviet Union and the United States, an attempt was made to unite the Kuomintang and the communists in a common front. The alliance worked sporadically.

Ten days before the end of World War II, Moscow declared war on Japan. Soviet armies penetrated into Manchuria, meeting no resistance, and occupied northwest China and North Korea. Now the question arose: to whom would they cede this territory, the Red Army of Mao Tse-tung, or Chiang Kai-shek? Even then Moscow seemed not to believe in the possibility of a communist victory in China.

At that time, incidentally, with Soviet approval, U.S. navy and air force units airlifted hundreds of thousands of Chiang Kai-shek's soldiers into Manchuria, to keep them from falling into the hands of the Red Army after the withdrawal of Soviet forces. This is significant, for the exact opposite was happening in Europe, where the Allies were clearing a vast area to be handed over to Soviet troops.

At once there were renewed clashes between the Red Army and Chiang Kai-shek's troops, and the country stood on the brink of a great civil war. The United States and the Soviet Union again tried to act as mediators. The United States in particular urged the formation of a great coalition, in which the communists would hold second place under Chiang's leadership. Neither Chiang nor Mao would agree. The cease-fires urged by the Americans were constantly violated.

In 1948 the Red guerrilla armies had made their way to the banks of the Yangtze. Chiang Kai-shek had dominion only over the south and the large cities. And yet he clung to the belief that he could defeat the communists in open battle. Mao was not quite convinced that his armies would be victorious. He was afraid his guerrillas would never be able to conquer the big cities.

Chiang opened the battle. Mao had to accept his challenge. What happened was unexpected even to the communists. Chiang's huge armies, equipped with the best American materiel, showed no will to fight. Many fled. Others defected to the communist side, bringing along millions of dollars' worth of American arms.

"In those days we used to say that Chiang Kai-shek was our chief of supply," a former officer of the Red Army told me in Peking.

In a gigantic offensive, Mao's soldiers began crossing the Yangtze. There were few boats and no bridges; but as on the Long March, Mao's army acted with ingenuity. Hundreds of thousands of soldiers swam across in full uniform, with their rifles on their backs. They used a gadget that teaches Chinese children to swim: three bamboo stalks tied together like a triangle and held in the hands to buoy up the body while the feet are used as rudders.

The Nationalist General Staff is said to have refused to believe that any large number of communist soldiers would be able to cross the river. The Yangtze had always been regarded as an unconquerable natural barrier. The surprise and confusion were therefore great when suddenly thousands of Red Army men rose up from the waters of the river.

Furthermore, the civilian population was heartily sick of war, particularly civil war, after twenty years of peril. The soldiers Chiang had conscripted were no longer willing to fight, and his own battle-hardened troops were dissatisfied with the government and with their officers.

Chiang had no strong ally in the administration of his country. Influential positions had been distributed among members of his family and his wife's many relatives. Scandals and rumors of corruption were daily occurrences. Although Chiang had introduced new penal and civil codes modeled after those of the West, they existed mainly on paper. The old Confucian spirit ruled both the army and the civil administration, and was to a large extent perverted. The unconditional obedience toward elders and superiors ruled out democratic thinking, and led to suppression and to tyranny. This was exactly opposite to the principles constantly urged upon the people by the communists.

Thus the communist armies met with little resistance when they attacked Chiang Kai-shek's front. In the next few months, more than four million of Chiang's soldiers laid down their arms or deserted to Mao's "Army of Liberation." With the trucks and armored vehicles of American make which they had captured, the Red Army pushed on to the south. At the beginning of 1949 Chiang Kai-shek prepared to flee to Formosa.

From the terrace of the imperial gate in the center of Peking, the Tien An Men, Mao Tse-tung proclaimed the establishment of the "People's Republic of China" in October, 1949.

Again the belief of Mao formulated on the Long March seemed to be verified: "The enemy is a paper tiger." The best equipment, the aid of American advisers, even the help of the American air force in the struggle against communism had not prevented the "triumphant victory of the people."

From then on, Mao and the communists were regarded in China as invincible. They themselves believed it. They were also considered infallible. But they knew why they had triumphed. They were invincible because they had adopted the most intelligent tactics and had proceeded with extreme caution. They had never underestimated the opposition, and they had gone into battle only when they were superior. They had tried to win the majority of the people as friends. That was their secret—a secret they were soon to forget.

10

Seizure of power and calculated terror

The flag of the People's Republic has waved from the "Gate of Heavenly Peace" in the center of Peking since 1949. In one corner of the red flag are one large and four smaller yellow stars. They are not, or rather were not, without meaning. The large star stands for the central government, one powerful united Chinese nation. The four small stars represent the forces that are supposed to have brought the government into existence: peasants, workers, the petty bourgeoisie classes, and the national bourgeoisie. This is how it is explained in Peking today, and in the new Chinese history texts.

Officially, a number of "democratic parties" exist in China today, in addition to the Communist Party. Their representatives sit in the People's Congresses and on committees. Naturally, they have had no real voice for a long time. Many chose to affiliate with the Communist Party in order to regain some authority. Now as then, however, the thesis is put forth in Peking that the government represents a united front of "the most varied democratic elements of the population."

At the time of the 1949 coup this corresponded roughly to the facts. Again and again, Mao Tse-tung himself urged union with the petty bourgeoisie and the national bourgeoisie. This had practical results. When the "Red Army of Liberation" set out on its victory march through the country, the soldiers at first were moderate in their treatment of well-to-do peasants and farmers, artisans and storekeepers, traders and, in many cases, even "capitalists."

For the most part the new regime recognized only two enemies: the big landowners in the rural areas and the "capitalist bureaucrats" in the cities. For a long time the landowners were kept in the dark about their inevitable fate. So long as the communist victory still hung in the balance, landowners were asked to lower the rent of the poor farmers, to let them have land whenever possible, and to siphon the capital off the land and use it to start small industries.

The big landowners, recognizing these warnings for what they were, lowered the rent on the farms that had been worked by poor peasants, sold a large part of their holdings to the peasants at nominal prices, and retired to the cities. With the ready cash thus acquired they bought shops or started small industries. Those who did this were granted indulgence later; they not only saved their own skins but were integrated into the social structure by the communists. Although they lost part of their property, at least they were not stigmatized as enemies of the people.

Those who did not follow Mao Tse-tung's advice as issued in communist pamphlets, those who continued to charge high rents or were reluctant to give up their property, could count on standing trial after the communist victory.

It is certain that some landowners who had made themselves unpopular in the community or incurred the displeasure of the local Party secretary were liquidated without trial. But this was not the intention of the communist regime. Court proceedings cost nothing and they served the purpose of the new government to perfection.

"As a rule, this is the way it was," eyewitnesses who lived through the early days agree. "Political commissars appeared in the villages and called the peasants and field hands together. First, they reminded them how brutally they had been treated. Most of the peasants hadn't even realized that. Brought up in the spirit of Confucianism, dedicated to Taoism, taught gentleness of spirit by Buddhism, most Chinese were not only fatalists but resigned to their fate. It never occurred to them that things could be otherwise. There were times when the commissars and Party secretaries had a hard time convincing the peasants that they had been exploited. But after a while they accepted the communist explanations. Then they were invited to bring complaints against the landowners, village tyrants, and money lenders. They hesitated at first but were encouraged by the communists and the examples of a few brave men; the complaints soon came in thick and fast. Yes, yes, the peasants really had been exploited. If they needed money to bury the head of the family, they could get it only by paying usury up to 50, 70, or even 100 per cent. In consequence, their fields were often confiscated and they had to rent them back again and pay enormous interest on the mortgages, as a rule 50 per cent of their income. Not infrequently a landowner or village tyrant had his own gang of toughs or 'police force.'

"Some of these complaints were justified. Others were exaggerated. There were cases where the landowner was not really such a bad fellow, but the commissars were determined to bring a judgment against him anyhow. This was how it all ended: The accused was brought before the political commissars and forced by fair means or foul to confess his guilt—and much more. In the hope that such a self-accusation might save their lives, especially if it went beyond the original charges, the accused went too far. Then the commissars would call out to the assembled people, 'What should be done with them?' Usually only one or two answered, 'Kill them!' It depended on local conditions and the instructions given the commissars, and their own desire for a successful conclusion to the matter. If the death sentence was pronounced, the victims were executed without delay."

So run the reports on those days, reports I have collected in China and abroad. Quite a number of foreigners witnessed these trials, among them some Americans. Most of them turned away in horror and spoke of "the bloodiest regime of all time." Others described them as "not entirely unjust, in some cases."

Since that time it has become evident, as the communists themselves have stated in speeches and articles, that the events of those days were the result of a carefully planned reign of terror. Most of the large landowners had a tight hold on the peasants, who owed them money and whose position was virtually that of serfs. For years and years they had stood in awe of the village leaders. Then the communuists came along, seized the landowners' properties, and distributed them among the peasants and the dispossessed. If the landowners had been allowed to live they might have tried to regain their property. And they might have succeeded, since the social structure of the community kept the peasants under their rule. Some peasants would have been afraid to take possession of land that had once belonged to landowners they both respected and feared.

To keep this from happening, it was necessary to destroy or exile the landowners. So the communists decreed. One method was to transform the large estates into small industries and retire the landlords to the cities. Another was to execute the owners.

Some observers who were aware of this plan were inclined to be lenient in their judgment of the communists. There were those who called the Chinese "land reformers," who protested against any parallel between their methods and those of the Soviet regime in Russia.

For one fact was obvious to everyone who knew China: land reform was more than overdue. It had been urged by progressives in China since the nineteenth century and had been one of Sun Yat-sen's main goals.

After the liquidations, the communists distributed the land they had confiscated. Each Chinese peasant—and there were more than 500 million of them—was to be given approximately the same amount of land. It was this land distribution which won the favor of the Chinese peasants and, as related, a good press in the West, including the United States. At first the truth of the terror was not completely known, and some did not even want to know it.

The communists employed even harsher methods against the "capitalist bureaucrats." Who was included in this category? Above all, well-to-do industrialists, large merchants, wholesalers, and bankers who had worked with the Japanese or remained loyal to Chiang Kai-shek and had grown rich through corruption. Also counted among the "capitalist bureaucrats" were all high government officials, police officers, and members of Chiang's secret police. The communists acted without mercy against all these.

Public trials were held in the open squares of towns and cities.

The people were ordered to attend both trials and executions. According to the reports of eyewitnesses, tremendous pressure was put on the people to turn out for these executions. The intention was plainly to instill fear in the people, to assure their subjugation to the new regime. I am not so sure that it was always necessary to exert pressure. People in China, as elsewhere, had always enjoyed executions. But there was another reason. Most of the Chinese were sick and tired of civil war, insecurity, and inflation. They wanted an end to terror. This feeling was not restricted to the country people, who had borne the brunt of the war years; city people, too, longed for an end to the corrupt conditions of Chiang Kai-shek's rule and the barbarities of the Japanese military dictatorship.

Eyewitness accounts of those days show a sharp disparity. Some describe the untold suffering brought about by the "Red terror," which began immediately after the Liberation. Others insist that the "Red terror" was planned carefully, restricted to selected groups, and at first left the mass of the population unharmed.

In Shanghai, "old capitalists" were brought to meet me. They belonged to the so-called national bourgeoisie. That is, they had not collaborated with Chiang, they had had no connections with the "foreign imperialists," but had been simply Chinese nationalists who wished the liberation of China from its semi-colonial status and advocated a central Chinese government. They had not believed that Chiang Kai-shek could realize this goal.

The members of this group, whether bankers or entrepreneurs, were treated at first, in 1949, with consideration by the communists. They were asked to continue as heads of their companies, even to enlarge them and pour more capital into them.

Here, too, the reason was clear. A China lacking in economic resources and production facilities could ill afford to risk business and production reverses through the mass liquidation of experienced entrepreneurs.

The intellectuals, too, were courted. Prominent authors and poets, university professors and doctors who declared their allegiance to the new rulers could count on being honored and granted positions as "people's representatives." A large segment of the intelligentsia has survived not only the communist takeover but also the much more rigorous measures of the later government, and today enjoys high office and honors.

So the question remains unanswered. "How bloody was the inauguration of the new regime?" Opinions differ. From all available communist sources—and the communist newspapers were not squeamish about reporting the executions—we get a round figure of one million liquidated. Foreign appraisals based mainly on the reports of exiles mention nearly ten million executions. The truth will probably never be known.

Communist tactics from the start were based on a false premise, and this false premise is encountered in today's China. On several occasions I met people who told me that they had owned businesses or factories in the old days, that they ceded these to the state "of their own free will," six or seven years after the communists came to power. Some of them explained that they still served as managers or directors of their former plants and were financially well off.

But I was also told that there had been days when the people of Shanghai walked in the middle of the street. The sidewalks were not safe because of suicidal capitalists jumping out of windows. They jumped "of their own free will," after their books were found to betray "counter-revolutionary activities" that would have led to their prosecution and death.

Another page in the history of those days is filled with the persecution of religion carried on by the communists, the expulsion of missionaries and religious orders. The situation is still confused. I saw quite a few priests, monks, and nuns of various orders. Churches and temples are open most of the time. More of that later. I merely mention it at this point because it seems to substantiate the second interpretation of the conduct of the communists during and after the takeover. The terror they unleashed had been planned. It was strong enough to discourage any action against the regime and to keep the masses docile. But it had not been an all-out horror that engulfed all classes equally. In this it was typically Chinese, carefully planned and put into operation in full awareness of the Chinese character. It had not swept the country like a sudden storm, as had, for example, Russia's October Revolution. The screws had been tightened much more slowly.

Mao Tse-tung (right) with Chang Kuo-tao, president of the communists' "frontier government," in a photograph taken in 1938. (UPI Photo)

So the entrepreneurs were left alone from 1949 to 1956. Only then, and "of their own free will," did they have to give their holdings over to the state to administer. The campaign against religion started earlier, but it too was a calculated attack against certain groups, especially the three million Chinese Catholics.

The great mass of peasants were able to enjoy their newly acquired fields from 1949 to 1953, then were prevailed upon to form, first, "agricultural production cooperatives of the lower type," which were no more than joint cultivation projects. This move was soon followed by the founding of "agricultural production cooperatives of the higher type," which were really a form of collective farm or kolkhoz.

In 1959 the communist newspapers began to publish articles on the "desire of the peasants" to convert these collective farms into people's communes. The government consented "hesitantly," after a four-month period of consideration. In a few weeks 750,000 collective farms were transformed into seventy thousand people's communes.

To become a member of the commune was, like everything else in China, "voluntary." In each commune I visited peasants were pointed out who had not joined up "for a long time." "The advantages to be gained by joining finally persuaded them to take that step," I was told, "and their fields have been incorporated into the commune."

In this way the communist regime in China felt its way slowly and cautiously toward solidifying its position, transforming China from a "new democracy" to a "socialist state under the dictatorship of the proletariat."

It was ten years before the new regime felt sufficiently sure of its powers to throw caution to the winds, to abandon the "exact appraisal of concrete conditions," and to call on the 700 million Chinese to "pull the country out of its backward condition" in an exertion without parallel.

That was in 1958.

Even today political observers, after the most intensive study of all available sources, cannot agree on the factors that led the government to put caution aside and start the Chinese people on an adventure unprecedented in the history of the human race.

One thing is certain. Mao Tse-tung had been feverishly seeking a way to lead China out of its backward state, first during the Long March, then in the caves of Yenan, and later during the War of Liberation. At first there were no means to accomplish this goal. There was little capital, much less than the Russians commanded when the czarist regime was overthrown. China lacked even the limited industrial capacity Russia possessed at the time of the Soviet takeover in 1917. There was insufficient raw material to keep industry alive. The Japanese had opened up mines in Manchuria, but there was virtually no crude oil; for a century China had been forced to import foreign petroleum products ("oil for the lamps of China"). Electrification of the country, which Lenin declared to be the foundation of the dictatorship of the protetariat, was unthinkable for a long time to come.

Where was China to get the power to lift itself by its bootstraps, as it were, out of its backwardness?

A basic design soon emerged from Mao's year-to-year deliberations, his writings and speeches. China possessed something that other nations lacked—a tremendous reserve of manpower. Hundreds of millions of Chinese were agricultural workers. If some of these were taken from the fields and put to work gathering raw materials, building production facilities, and making tools, then this immense work force ought to make up for any lack of capital and machinery and eventually bring an end to backwardness.

This must have been a reason, perhaps *the* reason, why the communists, who had advocated birth control after their accession to power, began encouraging people to have more children. Hands instead of machines!

For example:

China had always been plagued by flies and mosquitoes. Even in our era of DDT and other insecticides the Chinese had not solved the problem. Foreign exchange to buy insecticides in sufficient quantities was lacking, and in any case primitive transportation facilities would have made it extremely difficult to distribute imported chemicals. Nor was it possible for China, at this stage, to manufacture its own insecticides.

Mao Tse-tung called on his people to eradicate flies and mosquitoes by themselves. Every day, every Chinese was to kill as many of these insects as he could. The Party cadres concentrated all their efforts for months on reaching the goal set by Mao. In a few months, a nation as large as all Europe was practically rid of the pests. In every hotel room I occupied, one of the most important furnishings was a fly swatter. They were always available on trains. One fly appeared in a dining car; dozens of Chinese were as agitated as if the car had caught fire. Two conductors armed with swatters and cheered on by the passengers went after the insect, and a sigh of relief went through the car when it was finally dispatched.

A similar campaign was waged against sparrows. Some unknown statistician had calculated that these birds ate thousands of tons of food, especially rice grains, in the course of a year. If the birds were liquidated, would not a large reserve of food be made available to the people?

The sparrows were hunted down much as the flies had been. "At that time we left everything else to go on week-long sparrow hunts. We crashed ironware in streets, courts, and squares. The children sat on roofs and trees, yelling and howling, so that the birds could find no place to light. Finally they were no longer able to fly and fell down exhausted. Then we beat them to death," I was told.

The following year it was apparent that the sparrows had devoured more than rice; they had gulped down caterpillars and other insects, and with the disappearance of the birds these multiplied alarmingly. Thereupon the campaign against sparrows was ended. During my travels in China I noticed plenty of them.

Other tests of the power of numbers involved more important projects. Peasants were mobilized by tens, often by hundreds and thousands, to build dams and irrigation canals. Officials, students, doctors, and businessmen left the cities to work on these large-scale projects.

Even the class struggle was organized on lines like those of the anti-fly campaign. Millions upon millions of Chinese were encouraged to criticize their neighbors, to expose bourgeois tendencies and capitalistic sentiments to the public. It was finally decreed that people had to confess their own faults voluntarily. In line with the nature of their offense, they were then subjected to ideological reconditioning, and the "serious" cases were sent to labor camps to be re-educated.

But all these campaigns were mild compared to what was to come in 1958. Party and government had convinced themselves that the thesis "hands instead of machines" could be put into practice in China. Now they decreed the "Great Leap Forward."

11

The "Great Leap Forward"

My first impression of Peking, as I have already mentioned, was of a huge village. Except along the wide streets that had been laid out recently, almost all the houses were built close to the ground, even lower than in other Chinese cities. The Emperor, the Son of Heaven, had not permitted the building of two-story or ordinary one-story houses in the city where he lived. Everything had to bow low before him. Even the appearance of the Western powers in Peking, the military depots of the Japanese, and Chiang Kai-shek's reign had not changed things significantly.

But in 1958 and 1959 the communist government decided to provide Peking with a series of large buildings. Like so many other modern structures in China, they were put up during the "Great Leap Forward."

Today we know that serious discussions must have taken place within the inner circle of the Chinese leadership, to determine whether the "Great Leap Forward" could possibly succeed and whether China could afford such an experiment. Unlike their opposite numbers in the Soviet Union, those who spoke against the "Great Leap" were not removed from their posts. Prime Minister Chou En-lai and his deputy, Vice-President Chen Yi, are said to have been among them. Among the advocates of the "Great Leap" was the present head of the state, Liu Chao-chi, who was re-elected to office in January, 1965, even though in 1958 he had supported what proved to be a wrong decision.

Not least among the factors that goaded China to take the "Great Leap" was its difference of opinion with the Soviet Union. This had been going on since 1958. The awaited help from the Soviet Union had not been given in a spirit of altruism, as the communist leaders had initially hoped. They felt burdened by their dependence on Moscow, and so they found the courage to translate into action a concept that would give them equality on the world scene.

Of course I had heard a great deal about the "Great Leap" and had read even more. But what it really meant, what sacrifices it demanded of the Chinese people, how great their accomplishments had been, and what immense reverses it brought about I could only grasp when I stood before the visible results of the "Great Leap."

First let us consider Peking.

Within a year ten large buildings went up under the slogan of the "Great Leap Forward." I visited some of them.

There is the railway station, big enough to accommodate 200,000 passengers a day. Modern but with the traditional curving Chinese roofs, it was finished in nine months.

On the square facing the imperial gate, Tien An Men, stand two huge buildings: the Museum for Chinese History and Revolution and the so-called People's Hall. Each of these structures, which face each other, was built in about ten months. They are approximately the same size.

The People's Hall was designed to serve several purposes. Here the People's Congress, the Chinese version of the Supreme Soviet, and the People's Council meet. Great assemblies are held here when it is impossible to stage them in the open air. Foreign guests are wined and dined here, surrounded by a horde of functionaries. The building has an overall surface of 1,853,568 square feet—more than all the buildings of the old imperial residence, the Forbidden City.

The entrance is reached by climbing a flight of granite steps more than three hundred feet wide. Here there are twelve columns, each almost a hundred feet high and more than seven feet in diameter. Beside them, the two soldiers standing guard in plain sand-colored uniforms look Lilliputian. The portal they guard is nearly sixty feet high.

Entering, I found myself in a foyer paved in red marble, which can hold ten thousand people. The walls are paneled in green marble and illuminated by a dozen chandeliers in the style of those once found in the Russian czar's palace, each weighing more than a ton. To left and right are wardrobes designed to hold ten thousand coats. Between them stand porcelain vases almost as tall as a man.

Inside is an auditorium seating ten thousand, with a main floor and two balconies. The stage holds five hundred persons. All of this is illuminated by thousands of electric bulbs. To the left and right of the rows of seats are dozens of spotlights which can be turned on when the proceedings are to be broadcast on television or filmed for the newsreels. There are built-in television cameras as well.

In addition to this gigantic hall, the building contains thirty salons furnished by the different provinces of China. Up to one hundred persons can be seated comfortably in each. The floors are covered with costly carpets and there are dozens of large easy chairs. On the walls hang Gobelin silk tapestries, and ivory carvings. Glass cases hold costly replicas of birds and landscapes in pure gold and silver, all commissioned and completed in 1959.

One ivory carving attracted my attention. On an elephant tusk about a yard long a ship of the former imperial flotilla had been carved, carrying no less than seven hundred figures—"people representing the former social classes." Even the dragon pennant of the Emperor had been meticulously reproduced. This expensive *objet d'art,* too, had been produced since 1959. Many of the other objects on the walls, derived from China's past, honored the classics or celebrated the nation's culture.

Many of the pictures are painted interpretations of Mao Tse-tung's poems. Some of the poems themselves have been affixed to the walls, lettered in gold. Naturally there are also political quotations from Lenin and Mao, with a preponderance of themes from the Long March.

I was led further into a banquet hall where five thousand people can be served at once. It has enormous columns and a podium that holds three hundred musicians. And so it went. The kitchen was equipped to prepare ten thousand servings in the shortest possible time. The largest carpet and the largest landscape painting in China adorn a foyer, together with a poem by Mao Tse-tung celebrating the Chinese landscape.

All this, the building itself and its furnishings, was completed in ten months, within the framework of the "Great Leap Forward" in 1959.

These dimensions were nearly duplicated in the other new buildings that rose in Peking during the "Great Leap": the two museums, the post office and telegraph bureau, the House of National Minorities on the principal thoroughfare. Hundreds of thousands of workers toiled day and night to meet the planned deadline.

Too, many a factory which I was to visit later had been built during the time of the "Great Leap." A textile factory with 100,000 spindles and three thousand looms, a factory for the production of lathes and another for machine tools were among them.

At first glance, then, one gets the impression that superhuman achievements resulted from the "Great Leap Forward."

"In those days the workers never went home," the manager of a machine tool factory in Peking told me. "They stayed at their machines twelve, fourteen, sixteen, or twenty hours at a time. They had only one goal: to do all they could. That's how enthusiastic we were about the proclamation of Chairman Mao Tse-tung. That's how determined we were to disprove the counter-revolutionaries."

And that's the way it was. Mao and the Party had called on the Chinese people to work unceasingly, to increase production not 50 or 100 but 300 to 400 per cent. With some projects, especially with those that are pointed out to foreign visitors today, they were successful. A number of structures went up in record time despite their huge dimensions. A number of factories seemingly sprang from the ground in a few short months.

What is not officially admitted, but what is more than merely hinted at in conversations, even by communists, is that goading the people to unheard-of achievements actually brought severe reverses.

For example, in factories where the workers tried to increase production by 300 per cent the expensive precision machines, brought from abroad, were so badly overused that they broke down within a few weeks.

Drill presses which were supposed to have a five-minute cooling-off period after each operating cycle were used without pause until the drills broke. The same thing happened to many other industrial installations newly delivered from the Soviet Union, Poland, and East Germany.

The demand for enormously increased production was not restricted to the factories. In an unprecedented campaign the people were urged to smelt iron. In every back yard, in the streets, in front of office buildings, and in villages small "people's ironworks" sprang up. Officials, students, doctors, and writers as well as workers and peasants abandoned their regular work in order to smelt iron, day and night.

Part of the coal and ore were supplied by the state, but often people denuded the hills and avenues of trees, collected household utensils and melted them down over wood fires. The result was a low grade of iron from which, if it could be used at all, only household utensils could have been made.

At the same time, millions of trees were planted in the name of the "Great Leap." At the Great Wall near Peking I saw dozens of hills on which those trees had grown to a good height. Nothing had grown on those mountains for thousands of years. In the Greater Nanking district twenty million trees were set out, so it is estimated, and the city does seem to disappear in a huge park.

But the negative results of the "Great Leap" surely outweigh the positive. This was especially the case with agriculture. Incredible demands were made of the peasants. Harvests were to be tripled; rice, wheat, and corn were to be planted three times as thickly. And it would be necessary to plow deeper, to bring good earth to the surface.

Almost without pausing, without resting at night, the peasants of China went to work. In many areas they plowed to a depth of four and a half feet. Thousands of irrigation ditches were dug to supply the necessary water, without careful planning and without analyzing the soil. Then came the threefold sowing.

The harvests were smaller than ever before. The deep plowing

had buried the humus soil and had brought to the surface unpro-
ductive soil which would remain infertile for several years. Too, the
newly dug ditches laid bare harmful minerals which the next rain
spread over the fields.

The "Great Leap" created further upheaval: the whole population was dangerously exhausted. Families were broken up because
of the separation of married couples and of parents and their children. Everyone was constantly on the move.

However, these negative social effects were insignificant compared with the political damage that was done. Until then, the Communist Party had the reputation of never making a mistake;
Chairman Mao and his Party had always won. If they held up a goal
to the people, that goal was reached. The communist cadres performed tremendous tasks, whipping up enthusiasm for the "Great
Leap." But this time the victory was not realized. The overnight
industrialization, the vast increase in agricultural production, the
acquisition of capital for industrial development—all failed. The
"Great Leap," which dwindled to a finish some time in 1960, left
behind it a spent people, disillusioned cadres, and an impoverished
China.

It is too soon to evaluate the psychological consequences of
this failure. I could not rid myself of the impression that even today
a lingering fatigue pervades factories and communes. It seemed to
me that in China, where people are famed for their industry, work
progresses more slowly than in other countries.

Is it a rest period, which, having become necessary, has been
ordained from above?

I talked with a Chinese authority on economics. He expounded
for hours on the economic measures taken in China from 1949 to
the present. But not one word about the "Great Leap Forward"! He
talked about the First and Second Five-Year plans as if they had run
their normal course. Finally I asked him about the "Great Leap."
He replied, "The 'Great Leap' contributed greatly to the over-fulfill-
ment of the Second Five-Year Plan. But we also made mistakes. It
was like jumping into the water to learn to swim. When you do
that your head goes under at times, you choke and have to swallow
bravely. But then you learn to swim, and that's good. In part, we

have learned through bitter experience, but it is experience that teaches, just the same. Now we know what is possible and what is impossible. That gives us renewed strength to plan both the present and the future. The next Five-Year Plan will be worked out on the basis of our experiences in the 'Great Leap.' It will correspond absolutely to concrete conditions in China."

That meant that the next Five-Year Plan would not overtax the people, industry, or the communes. It would be a return to the original cautious policy of the government.

At present, China works without a plan. The Second Five-Year Plan was organized for 1957 to 1962. The "Great Leap" clashed with it, although that is not officially admitted. The failure of the plan is credited to other causes, including the catastrophic weather of 1960-61 when crops were ruined by flood and drought.

Not one of my Chinese acquaintances failed to mention what official Chinese propaganda assigns as the principal role in the reverses of the early 1960's: the "treason of the Soviets."

"The Soviet Union tore up its treaties with China overnight and threw them away like so much waste paper. In the space of a single week the Soviets withdrew all their experts and advisers from China. They took with them factory blueprints and dismantled machines so that they became useless. More than that, the Soviet Union stopped delivery on industrial parts that were important to us, in violation of their treaties; they left us in the lurch in the middle of our greatest expansion. Because they behaved like this, all our plans were destroyed. But we overcame even these large unexpected reverses out of our own strength."

It is certainly true that the sudden departure of the Soviet experts and the cessation of their emergency deliveries, even in part the stoppage of normal exchanges of goods, contributed to the failure of the "Great Leap." But in my opinion the basic failure was inherent in the Chinese concept itself.

12

How the hundred blossoms wilted

At a street corner in the middle of Peking a saying of Chairman Mao Tse-tung's has been immortalized in gold letters: "Friendship between the Chinese and the Soviet peoples will endure forever." Next to it are large showcases filled with reminders of that friendship. Naturally, they refer back to the past, to the days of Lenin and Stalin.

Not far from this corner I found the House of Sino-Soviet Friendship, built by the Soviets in the Stalinist pastry-cook style. Such buildings are to be found in most large Chinese cities.

In one of Canton's most beautiful parks there is a monument erected to those Soviet diplomats who were killed while fighting with the Chinese Communist guerrillas.

But to find out what has really happened to Soviet-Chinese friendship in our time, it is necessary to visit a certain exhibition hall which the Soviets built for the industrial city of Shanghai some time ago as a gesture of friendship. This gigantic structure, crowned by an imitation Kremlin tower, bears an inscription in the Russian language and the cyrillic alphabet to "the unbreakable friendship of the Soviet Union with China." In the foyer stands a large plaster statue of Mao Tse-tung. Behind it is the exhibition hall.

"All the machines shown here were built by Chinese tech-

"Let a hundred flowers bloom, let a hundred ideas compete," reads the sign on this building at Peking University. The slogan can still be found in China today, but it no longer applies to destalinization.

nicians without foreign help, out of their own strength, and they are being produced today on Chinese assembly lines," the female guide explained as she set one machine after another into motion to prove that these were not just models.

"Out of our own strength!" Wherever one goes in China, all conversations include this formula. It means: we have learned to do without Soviet experts and engineers, we no longer need foreign advisers, we manage even without Soviet help. "Out of our own strength" is China's answer to the break with Soviet leadership. But is it true that the Chinese economy has recuperated from this break?

I visited northeast China, which is the Ruhr Valley or Pittsburgh region of the country. Here, close to vast deposits of coal and iron ore, the great industries have been established. True, the foundations of the iron industry were already laid by the Japanese after they conquered northeast China and made it an independent state called Manchukuo. Here too, since the area was inaccessible to American bomber squadrons, they built up a part of their war industry during the Second World War.

The Japanese in Manchukuo were disarmed by the Russians in 1945, and their industries were dismantled before the Soviets ceded Manchuria to Chiang Kai-shek's troops and left. But not all of the installations could be moved to the Soviet Union. Some remained; and when the communists took this part of China in 1948 they began to rebuild it. After 1949 the Soviet Union gave a great deal of assistance. In fact, the Soviets found themselves in a situation much like that of the Americans in Germany. What they had destroyed, they now replaced with new and modern machinery.

On my visits to the various steel plants, coal mines, refineries, and machine tool factories I repeatedly asked to what extent these works had been dismantled by the Soviets after the Second World War. Some of the managers quickly said, "Not at all." And then they added, "The Soviet Union at that time was under the leadership of the great Stalin, and all he did was help us." Other managers hesitated, with a glance at my traveling companion, the gentleman from the China Travel Service, and at my interpreter, and after some hesitation replied, "Nothing, here."

The Soviet Union under the leadership of Stalin is considered to have been a good Soviet Union, a Soviet Union that never harmed but always helped China.

The results of this help are still visible. On every large machine, especially in heavy industry, the four cyrillic letters CCCP (USSR) were stamped. But quite a few of these machines also came from Czechoslovakia, Poland, Hungary, and East Germany. The aid given by the Soviet bloc was undeniably great. Its cessation must have been a heavy blow to China.

In almost every factory I visited, some departments, often the largest, had been "reorganizing" for some time and were therefore closed down. I assumed that these were departments for which Soviet machinery was designed and that it had never arrived, or that they contained Soviet machinery for which there were no spare parts.

A typical example was the railroad car factory in Changchun. Built during the First Five-Year Plan, that is, between 1952 and 1957, it was designed to turn out 1,600 passenger cars a year. The plans called for 5,000 different machines and a work force of 12,000. "At present the annual rate of production and repair is 500 coaches," the manager told me frankly. That means that not even a third of the planned capacity has been reached. Instead of 5,000 machines, so far only 3,100 have been installed, as the manager admitted; instead of 12,000 workers, the shop employs only 4,500.

"Most of the machines are Chinese," I was told before I made my tour of inspection. That was correct. All the smaller machines were Chinese, and these were naturally in the majority. But the few big ones in use were Russian. And the curtailment of production may have been due to the shortage of heavy machinery. Consciously or not, the manager indicated as much when he said, "The Khrushchev revisionists tore up their treaties with China and recalled their technicians and their kith and kin overnight."

In several cases I was able to see for myself just how difficult it is for the Chinese to fill the gap left in their economy by the withdrawal of Soviet aid. In the industrial city of Fushun I visited a factory that produced mining lamps. The production had been "undergoing reorganization" for about a year. Instead of mining lamps, which were used in the nearby pits, the factory had been ordered by the state to produce heavy-duty batteries for electric trucks. "The USSR, the GDR [German Democratic Republic, or East Germany], and the Poles, who formerly supplied us with these batteries, no longer do so. Our electric trucks are all of East German make. Now we are supposed to manufacture these batteries," the manager said.

Apparently the planners realized too late that batteries, too, have a limited life span. Perhaps they had hoped for continued deliveries under a new trade agreement. Now this factory was trying to retool to a new line of production.

But it wasn't going rapidly. I saw one shop after another where most of the machines stood idle. One manager was obviously embarrassed. "We have far surpassed our quota and are on vacation, to clear the factory," he said. He wanted to show me some other factories, but my two companions declined the offer.

After I had visited a number of Chinese factories it was easy to understand why this one, like many of the others, couldn't change over as quickly as the economy required after the loss of Soviet aid. The Chinese don't like to take risks. They know that their planned economy has its disadvantages, especially where timely delivery of parts is concerned. They have designed their factories so that each is almost 100 per cent self-sustaining. All the components used in the finished product are made right on the spot.

For example, the factory that made mining lamps had a chemical department for the manufacture of acids, a department for producing the synthetic rubber that was used as insulation, a department for making plastics, one for wire, and so on. It can't be easy to convert such a factory to the production of totally different items.

In Fushun I also visited the "western open pit." It is one of the most extensive surface coal mines in the world, more than four miles long, almost a mile wide, with a 738-foot pit from which the coal is taken. Dozens of terraces line the walls, each with tracks along which electric locomotives are supposed to pull the full cars up to the conveyor belts, which in turn carry the coal to the top. The manager of the "western open pit" led me to a terrace where the manager's building stood and gave me a pair of binoculars so I could get a better view of the huge installation. He told me:

"Formerly the Japanese exploited not only the coal but the

people. Nothing was mechanized. Ten thousand coolies had to haul the coal from the bottom. To get to the seams of coal as fast as possible, they drilled into the walls. In other words, they didn't even try to work the mine systematically. Today everything is different. The 'open pit mine' is 100 per cent mechanized, everything is terraced, and removal goes on simultaneously on all the terraces. Hand labor has been replaced by machinery."

It was eleven on a weekday morning, a time when I might have expected to see the work in full swing and all machines in operation. With the binoculars I looked from terrace to terrace, expecting to find machines moving on each. There were big steam shovels, and although I couldn't read the name plates from that distance, even with binoculars, they looked very much like a type of Soviet steam shovel with which I am familiar. I counted eleven. One was in use. The others were standing idle.

We stayed on the terrace for about half an hour, and I kept looking to see if any of the other machines were working. They weren't. When I asked, I was told that perhaps the workers had decided to take a break or were repairing the machinery. That could have been the case. But then the question arose whether they had the necessary spare parts or, if not, whether each part could be made "out of our own strength."

Above the coal seams were veins of petroleum-bearing slate, which was also being mined. At the edge of the pit stood a plant for the production of synthetic gasoline. Here the slate was liquefied. Most of the installations were of Soviet or East German origin. They also produced ammonium sulfate, diesel oil, and gasoline. The highest octane they made was sixty. The factory was in full swing; not a wheel was still. But here, too, they will eventually need spare parts that are no longer obtainable from the Eastern bloc.

From these examples it is clear that China was hard hit by the departure of the Soviet experts and the discontinuance of vital deliveries from the Eastern bloc. On the other hand, in many plants I found the Chinese trying to fill in the gaps. It is easy to deduce that many of the original production and expansion plans have undergone radical changes—and Chinese industrial development was not very strong to begin with.

With the cessation of deliveries from the Eastern bloc, factories originally meant for the production of new facilities or consumer goods had to be converted to produce whatever was immediately and urgently needed. Gaps are being closed, material is being salvaged wherever possible, but it is a gigantic undertaking. It could have a lasting effect on China's relations with the Eastern bloc nations.

If the Chinese are able to manage on their own, they will gain a self-assurance that ought not to be underestimated.

Just the same, in view of the idle machinery, the closed shops, and the sharply diminished productive capacity, one must ask what led to the sudden break between China and the Soviet Union.

What lay behind the conflict, and what major reasons led China to determine on a course of independent action at such cost to its economic development?

No matter where I went in China, or with whom I talked, the subject of the Sino-Soviet conflict invariably came up. So the differences with Moscow are not confined to government and party circles; the entire population has been drawn into them.

Until recently, "international imperialism" was China's first enemy. This was understood to mean primarily the United States. Now the fight against "modern revisionism" is given at least equal importance. And the "modern revisionists" are in Moscow, not Washington.

Even the fall of Khrushchev did not change this at all. After a few weeks of expectant waiting the accusations against the Soviet Union and its Communist Party rose again. The hope that the new leaders in Moscow might come to some agreement with Peking after Khrushchev's departure had to be abandoned, at least for the time being.

Prime Minister Chou En-lai, who had been sent to Moscow for the October anniversary celebrations immediately after Khrushchev's ouster, and who tried there to discover how the new Russian leaders visualized their future relationship with China, came back to Peking disappointed. Ideological and political differences between the two parties had outlasted Khrushchev. The attempt of the Chinese to make the deposed leader their scapegoat had been in vain.

I was surprised by the strong language used against "the leadership of the Communist Party in the Soviet Union." It sounded as if they were talking about common criminals. The Soviet "revisionists" were "the arch-enemies of humanity," "traitors," "lackeys of imperialism," "vermin."

All of the anger of the masses has been mobilized for the battle against a "revisionism" that is supposed to stem from Moscow. That seemed paradoxical, since the reception rooms where I was hearing about all these misdeeds had been built and furnished with Soviet help a few years earlier. The machines before which I stood when listening to tales of the "traitors" came from Soviet factories and bore Russian name plates. The car in which we were riding when the talk turned to the "malignity" of the Soviet leadership was a Volga or a Muscovich. Many of those who denounced the present Soviet leadership to me had attended Russian universities. Some had grown up in the Soviet Union.

Even the outer forms of Chinese life are shot through and through with Soviet customs. Young Pioneers with red kerchiefs, soldiers carrying Soviet weapons, a Soviet-style bureaucratic setup, hotels, planes, and railroads organized on Soviet models—these are all part of China.

On the scene, the Sino-Soviet conflict thus seems much less reasonable than it may look from, say, Europe or America.

It took me only a few days to realize that the causes of the conflict are many and varied. It took much longer to discover some of them. Let me explain them as briefly as possible.

To begin with, communism has been in force in the Soviet Union for forty-eight years; in China, only sixteen. Soviet communism has thus had a longer time in which to become incorporated into the thinking of the Russian people. Today it is solidly entrenched. Khrushchev called the Communist Party "a party for the whole nation." In fact, during my travels in the Soviet Union I realized again and again that everyone takes the existence of the Communist Party and the government for granted, as though no other had ever existed or could ever exist.

In China it is quite otherwise. The Chinese are still engaged in the class struggle. The question is whether communism is the only feasible social form for China, how it will develop, and whether current communist practices will remain as they are. Communism in China is not solidly entrenched and does not feel secure.

Western observers have used this fact to back the opinion that an overthrow of the system is still possible. I do not think it is. The continued existence of Chinese communism depends on the power held by the state, and that is indisputably great.

Neither do I believe that the Chinese communists meet with decisive resistance. What they have to fear is not opposition, or sabotage, or counter-revolution—not bloody strife, but a slipping back into the old way of life is the danger.

That is why the Chinese communists must keep busy, must beat the drums, must spread terror when this seems advisable.

The primary difference between the Soviet Union and China may be summed up thus: communism in the Soviet Union no longer has to maintain the class struggle; communism in China faces the fear that any relaxation in the class struggle could soften and destroy it.

This is no mere theory held by the Chinese leadership. When Khrushchev settled accounts with Stalin and Stalinism at the Twentieth Party Congress in 1956, when he advocated more liberal methods for world communism, the Chinese as diligent disciples of Moscow fell into line. Mao Tse-tung himself introduced the new liberal policy to China with these words, "Let a hundred flowers bloom, let a hundred ideas compete!"

With these words the Chinese were encouraged to criticize Stalinism and its excesses, the mistakes made by cadres and Party functionaries, even police injustice. It looked as though the Chinese were determined to put into practice in their own country the same liberal policies that were becoming effective in the Soviet Union and in European communist countries.

The Chinese people, still numb from the reign of terror, did not trust these exhortations at first. Only hesitant and trivial criticism was offered. Then the highest Party functionaries took the lead. They waged a merciless campaign against the remnants of Stalinism. Now the intellectuals, the writers and professors and doctors, dared to make their voices heard, and the dam burst.

But what a difference from the criticism the leaders had expected! This was no mere factual criticism that could be utilized to improve the workings of the Party and liberalize the government. This was a volcanic eruption. Not only were the excesses of Stalinism condemned, but communism itself was criticized and there were demands for democracy and freedom. Not a few advocated the formation of democratic parties that were real parties, rather than puppets of the communist leadership.

It is said to have been much worse in the villages and more remote towns. Revenge was taken on Party cadres and functionaries, Party headquarters were besieged, police stations were stoned. In the people's communes the peasants tried to get back their former holdings for distribution to private families.

The fate of the government of China hung in the balance.

Moreover, this development came at almost the same time as the Hungarian revolution. But the developments in Hungary went at a much faster pace and in a more spectacular fashion. The Hungarian revolution was at first hailed by Peking. It was seen as a salutary process in line with developments in Moscow. Then it became evident where the developments in Budapest were leading, and the Chinese leaders began to make comparisons with their own country.

Now Peking reversed its tactics. It not only condemned the Hungarian revolution, it also rescinded the liberal measures it had taken and fought for weeks and months to regain complete control in its own country.

It must have been at that time, around the end of 1956, that the leaders in Peking came to the conclusion that liberalization in the Eastern bloc, and especially in China, must not be permitted for a long time, if ever. Undoubtedly they reached this viewpoint after careful analysis of events in Europe and China.

After the Hungarian revolution, Moscow, too, moderated its course, but without abandoning the general liberal trend. The fight against Stalinism continued, along with the gradual liberalization. But in China the course had been changed for a long, long time to come. Seven hundred million Chinese, almost all of them reared in the old ways, are not like 200 million Russians, only the oldest of whom can remember the pre-revolutionary days. In particular, the Chinese mentality is not like that of the Russians. Two thousand years of Confucian thinking, two thousand years of Taoism (or rather fatalism), and eighteen hundred years of Buddhism cannot be uprooted from the minds and hearts of the Chinese in sixteen years.

Today the leaders in Peking emphasize that they warned Khrushchev as early as 1956 against initiating destalinization. They claim that in the course of many talks with the Soviets they considered the struggle against Stalinism to be the beginning of the end of communism. "But the Soviet comrades did not want to listen to us."

In Moscow the Soviet leaders went on insisting that the communist system and the Soviet state were, as they had always been, the best and greatest and most beautiful that humanity had been able to produce in its search for happiness and well-being. Stalin was responsible for the fact that Soviet citizens had not been able to appreciate this for many years. He had departed from socialism, had scorned socialist justice, and had brought pain and misery on the Russian people. Not a bad explanation, this was surely designed to assure the Soviet leaders, then and now, of the confidence of their subjects.

Not a bad explanation for the Poles, either, or the Hungarians or Rumanians. They had suffered a great deal from Soviet intervention, and it was all right with them if the new Soviet leaders wanted to hold Stalin solely responsible. They didn't care whether it was true or not, so long as Moscow continued to follow a more liberal course with the East European people's democracies and was willing to concede them national freedom of action.

This aspect of the anti-Stalin campaign had surely found favor in Peking as well. A greater equality with the Soviet Union must have been a burning ambition of the Chinese leadership. But as I have already explained, destalinization was not feasible in China.

In Moscow there was a change in leadership. The new leaders could win popularity at Stalin's expense. In Peking the leaders remained in power. Furthermore, their grip on the country was not yet secure.

In other words, whereas in eastern Europe a small measure of freedom ushered in by the liberalization policy had made the people happier and more tractable, the liberalization period in China ("the epoch of the Hundred Blossoms") brought a lapse into the old ways which threatened to end Chinese communism.

So Peking could not keep step with Moscow in this important new phase. It had to take a different road.

This conflict finds its sharpest expression in the economy. The Soviets have recognized Yugoslavia as a "socialist country." The Chinese regard that move as a sin against Marxism. Peking believes that communism in Yugoslavia has totally degenerated. The Yugoslav factories do not belong *de facto* to the state but to the workers. It is they who administer the factories and buy and sell all the products. Thus control over the economy has "slid back from the hands of the state into those of private individuals." The condition of Yugoslav agriculture is "even worse." The soil is the private property of the farmers, who are allowed to hire as many as ten field hands. "There, man once again is exploited by man."

The leaders in Peking insist that such a development cannot lead to socialism or communism, but only back to capitalism.

Insofar as the Soviet Union accepts the Yugoslav way as socialistic, it seems to recommend, in effect, a "relapse into capitalism" for world communism.

The harsh reaction becomes understandable when one visits China. In earlier chapters I have described the strength of Chinese individualism, the strength of Chinese egoism, and the manner in which, for hundreds of years, the Chinese placed their personal well-being above that of community and state. If the communist government should allow the Chinese to follow the "Yugoslav way," the communist economy and ideology would be much more seriously threatened than would be the case in East Europe.

The inclination to own land or a business, to accumulate goods and money, is ingrained much deeper in the Chinese than in Europeans. The communist government might be able to hold its own even under a "Yugoslav system," but the ideology as well as the economy of the nation would suffer.

So, even in this respect, there is an essential difference between the East Europeans and the Chinese: 2,000 years of Christian moral and social ideology against 3,500 years of the Chinese attitude toward life, the state, and the economy.

The latest official Chinese pamphlet attempts to show that the Soviet Union is no longer a socialist country. The pamphlet bears the title, "Khrushchev's Pseudo-Communism and Its Meaning for the World." It appeared a few weeks before Khrushchev's overthrow and continued to be distributed all over the world even after the removal of the Soviet leader.

The pamphlet cites example after example. In the Soviet Union social classes have again begun to form the same bourgeois classes that exist in capitalist countries. Factory managers and high Party functionaries, with their families, already belonged to the bourgeoisie. But these classes did not come into being in the face of state opposition; the government knowingly promoted them. Now the Soviet Union again embraces the privileged and the underprivileged. The people strive for goods and chattels; ownership of private property on a large scale is again permitted; and the Soviet leadership encourages this passion for private ownership.

The Soviet kolkhoz system—"always inadequate in comparison with the people's communes"—has broken down completely. The kulaks, or large-scale farmers, have practically taken over the property of these collectives, and the market is being supplied with produce from privately owned fields. Prices are governed by supply and demand. The trade unions are only nominally under state control; they are really the private domain of privileged managers and functionaries. Private deals are made for machinery and other goods, and real estate is privately owned.

Interestingly enough, these statements are documented by quotations from Soviet newspapers and magazines, most of them the reports of trials conducted by the state in order to punish the "abuses." But the mere fact that such "abuses" occur was all the Chinese needed to point out the decline of socialism in the Soviet Union.

This is the conclusion they draw: the Communist Party of the Soviet Union is leading that country backward into a bourgeois society based on capitalism.

What does this bitter criticism of Soviet communism mean?

In my opinion, it reveals first of all the fear that the leniency practiced in the Soviet Union may also affect China—a China dominated by communism for only sixteen years, with a relatively small number of communist cadres trying to wean 700 million people away from their old customs and ideas and to teach them socialist discipline. That task could not be accomplished if China followed the more liberal methods of the Soviet Union.

This was explained to me by the use of a simple example. In the fly-extermination campaign, every Chinese was expected to kill as many flies as possible. Rewards were offered. Now, some Chinese are said to have bred more flies in order to kill and deliver them and get the rewards. I was told, "If the leadership relaxes its rule, it can no longer keep down the 'spontaneous capitalistic tendencies' of the Chinese people."

But there are many other reasons for the Sino-Soviet conflict.

13

Peaceful co-existence and world revolution

The tombs of the Ming emperors are a half-hour drive from Peking. Until 1958 a breath of eternity lay over this quiet, secluded valley, and only when it rained did the small stream that meandered through the valley turn into a raging flood that covered the land on both sides. Today the river has been tamed. As a prelude to the "Great Leap Forward," the government ordered a dam erected at the point where the river leaves the valley of the imperial tombs.

Everything was lacking: machinery, cement, lime, steel, trucks, and cranes. But that was no obstacle. The people of Peking were called upon to build the dam voluntarily, with their bare hands and feet. They left Peking by the hundreds and thousands—officials and university students, doctors and professors among them, in compliance with the command.

They worked without stopping in eight-hour shifts, day and night. They scratched the dirt off the nearby hills with their fingernails, split stones with the most primitive tools imaginable, and carried the dirt and stones to the riverbed in small baskets slung across their shoulders on poles. Here thousands more were waiting to tramp the stones and dirt with their bare feet. Party cadres with megaphones encouraged them and urged them to work harder.

Mao Tse-tung and the other members of the Politburo also worked on the dam. Even the diplomats of countries that had recognized China and been accredited by Peking were asked to help the Chinese people with the project. European ambassadors and envoys could be seen working alongside the scratching and stamping Chinese.

The dam was completed in six months. It is about 1,800 feet long, 85 feet high, and about 600 feet across at the base.

In appearance it is quite unlike similar structures in Europe and the United States, because it contains no concrete. It is a pyramid of earth and stones. But it works as well as any concrete dam in Europe or the United States. It holds back the floodwaters in a lake now many miles long, provides water for irrigating the fields, regulates the flow of the river, and drives the turbines of a power plant.

The Chinese cannot suppress their enthusiasm when they talk about the dam or show it to foreign visitors. To them it proves that the Chinese people "out of their own strength," without foreign help, without modern tools or materials, can perform feats equal to those achieved by highly industrialized nations. Western technologists and economists will shake their heads over such claims. But to the Chinese, the proof is there.

This dam and the principle it stands for, and the uses made of the principle, illustrate still another reason for the conflict between China and the Soviet Union.

Moscow insists, with increasing vigor, that the communist revolution can take place only in highly industrialized countries. The Soviet leaders reject the possibility of communist insurrections in underdeveloped countries.

Two-thirds of the human race, more than two billion people, live in areas that have yet to be industrialized. They are peasants and day laborers. This is true in large parts of Asia, Africa, and South America.

According to Soviet theory, national, bourgeois, and democratic revolutions must take place in these countries, culminating in the establishment of bourgeois governments that would build up a stock of capital. The emerging capitalists would then industrialize the country, which in turn would create a proletariat. Only when the proletariat had been politically schooled could a socialist-communist revolution develop.

Although Russia was industrially underdeveloped, at least she had the foundations of industrialism and a city proletariat. Therefore Lenin and the Soviet leaders who came after him held to the basic tenet of Marxism: revolution only where there is a proletariat.

The Russian revolution followed this pattern—but not the Chinese. Against Moscow's advice, Mao Tse-tung led the peasants into revolution, and to victory. This struggle, and especially the Long March and more than twenty years of guerrilla activity, convinced the Chinese communists that their system was the only valid one to bring about world revolution. Marx and Engels overlooked the fact that the twentieth-century peasant is a sort of proletarian. If the Soviet pattern were followed, the world revolution would have to wait for a long time—perhaps hundreds of years.

It follows that world communism has only one chance: to pin its hopes on the vast populations that exist in the underdeveloped countries. And that chance is better today than ever before.

The Soviet Union cannot agree with these Chinese theses, for several reasons. First, they run counter to Soviet history and also to the edicts of Marx and Engels. Second, the communist countries now in existence simply cannot afford to exhaust themselves in support of revolutions all over the world, and especially in the underdeveloped areas. In addition, they would have to support the economy of such governments. Even tiny Cuba has become a serious supply problem for the Soviet Union.

Third, to follow such a policy would automatically trigger a conflict with the Western powers, especially the United States. Peaceful co-existence under these conditions would obviously be impossible.

But Peking paid no heed to these considerations. The Chinese example has proved that successful revolution without a proletariat is possible. As for problems of support, Peking points out that the Soviet Union ignored the Chinese revolution until 1949. It even made pacts with enemies of communism—Chiang Kai-shek, the

Japanese, and the United States. Did not the Chinese revolution actually take place in a poverty-stricken country, without foreign aid?

In my opinion, Peking overlooks the fact that communism in China could not have triumphed if the Soviet Union had not come forth with massive support immediately after the victory. Further, the atomic power potential of the Soviet Union protected China and, in spite of that country's own first atomic experiments, still does so.

But Peking spurns these arguments. China today, say its leaders, gives proof that it can manage without Soviet help and that it can build industry under its own power. Moreover, they insist, it could have done so even if it had received no Soviet aid at the beginning.

Among the evidence offered in support of this contention is the dam near the imperial tombs. Was it not built without any help, without using Western methods—and in record time? Are not the hands and feet of millions of people worth at least as much as foreign aid and technical advice? Cannot the people of other developing countries follow the Chinese example?

In Peking no one even asks these questions. The leaders are convinced that the masses must follow the Chinese route to socialism and communism. Since this idea comes from Peking rather than Moscow, the conclusion is self-evident: China, not the Soviets, is in the forefront of world communism.

It is easy to see that we are no longer dealing with questions of practice, or even of ideology. The bid for world leadership has been made. The chasm between Peking and Moscow can scarcely be bridged.

With this in mind, it is easy to understand why the Chinese leaders began the "Great Leap Forward" in 1959. It was an attempt to make China economically independent of the Soviet Union in one mighty effort. The Soviets followed suit by recalling their technicians and experts and discontinuing deliveries to China.

But still this does not entirely explain the conflict. The Soviets argue that communist power could only have developed under the protection of the Soviet Union. Peking officials laugh at this notion. China, they say, bore the main burden of the Korean War and managed to "deal effectively with the Americans." They never considered that the Americans failed to advance into China only because they did not care to risk a nuclear war with the Soviet Union. Instead, Peking points out that an "infinitely vast" China with its masses of people would have been unconquerable even by the Americans.

Beyond that—and this is what seems to make the biggest impression on the Chinese—the Russians were not willing to share their atomic secrets with China; they were not even ready to supply the Chinese with medium-range bombers, let alone long-range bombers and missiles. "That's how the Soviet Union protected China!" I was told.

This unwillingness on the part of the Soviets to give their Chinese brothers atomic information and weapons is highly significant, touching as it does upon the core of the Soviet policy of "peaceful co-existence." The Soviet Union wanted to be the only nation to arbitrate with the West, especially the United States. War was to be waged only if Moscow found it inevitable—not, for example, if China decided to re-conquer Formosa or invade Korea or Viet Nam.

It could be argued that the Chinese took this for a sign of distrust, an inexcusable deviation from the principles of socialist solidarity, a heavy blow to the socialist principle of equal determination among nations.

But the policy of "peaceful co-existence" hit them even harder. China strove and still strives for recognition from the rest of the world. The United States and many other nations, including some of the emerging countries, deny it. More, the United States leads a long list of nations that are boycotting China economically. The great "Middle Kingdom," the center of the earth and of civilization, is today a pariah among nations.

Under such circumstances, Moscow proposes a policy of "peaceful co-existence" with precisely those nations that refuse to recognize Red China; above all with the United States, which supports Chiang Kai-shek and which has incorporated a Chinese province, Formosa, into its own defense perimeter—the same United States whose troops are now stationed in Korea and fighting in Viet

Nam, whose Seventh Fleet cruises along the Chinese coasts.

How can Peking consider such a "peaceful co-existence"? In any case, the Chinese conclude that the Soviet Union, having already feathered its nest, is making peace with the enemies of China and of communism without the least regard for the legitimate interests of the Chinese.

I was told in Peking that at least two European satellite nations shared the Chinese viewpoint: Albania and East Germany. The Albanians interpreted the flirtation of the Soviets with Tito as a real threat to their country and were afraid that Moscow would eventually give Tito a free hand, letting him draw Albania into the Yugoslav orbit. Some still believe that the original conflict between Stalin and Tito developed because Tito and Bulgarian Prime Minister Dimitroff had plotted to establish a Balkan federation under their leadership. The fear of Yugoslavia has driven Albania into the arms of Peking.

Some Chinese claim that East Berlin had to be considered in a different light. The East German communists had openly sympathized with Peking's view. Peaceful co-existence with the West would destroy the last hope of East Germany's Walter Ulbricht for including West Berlin in the GDR (German Democratic Republic) in the near future. It also ran counter to the conviction of the East German communists that all means should be utilized to bring about the collapse of the West and, above all, the collapse of the German Federal Republic. They believe that the re-unification of Germany must one day take place, and under communist auspices. Of course that is mere wishful thinking. Berlin poses a more immediate and a more practical problem. West Berlin is for Ulbricht what Formosa is for China.

These people believe that Khrushchev was forced to issue his famous ultimatum against Berlin mainly because of the Sino-Soviet conflict. Otherwise, he risked having the East Zone come out in favor of the Chinese position. Although the East Zone had nothing like the freedom of movement enjoyed by the Albanians, because of the presence of Soviet troops and its close economic ties with the Soviets, a weakening of relations between East Germany and the Soviet Union would have occasioned some discomfort in Moscow.

Khrushchev himself traveled to East Berlin to confer with Ulbricht, to show him that the destiny of the East Zone was tied to that of the Soviet Union, for better or worse; and that "peaceful co-existence" would not cause the Soviet Union to give up the struggle for West Berlin.

Khrushchev was playing both ends against the middle. On the one hand, he met with President Kennedy at a summit conference in Vienna, in the course of which he emphasized peaceful co-existence; on the other, he issued his ultimatum against Berlin. The opinion in Peking is that he would not have done this except for the pressure exerted by the "one and only true" Chinese argument branding peaceful co-existence as a capitulation to the West. The Berlin Wall was Khrushchev's means of evading his ultimatum without losing Ulbricht's good will.

A similar situation, according to Peking, was precipitated somewhat later by the Cuban missile conflict. Fidel Castro must have had serious misgivings about the Soviet policy of peaceful co-existence. He too feared that he might become its victim. That would have meant more to Moscow than the loss of Cuba's friendship, because then Cuba would not merely have been drawn into the Chinese orbit, it would have become an example for all the revolutionary movements of Latin America, and perhaps Africa and Asia. Again in consideration of the Chinese stand, Khrushchev was forced to give Cuba an incontrovertible sign of the Soviet Union's protection; to make clear that Cuba would not be sacrificed in the name of peaceful co-existence with the United States. The "incontrovertible sign" was the sending of Soviet atomic missiles to Cuba. Probably, I was told, the Russians hoped that the Americans would understand their strategy. But Washington "failed to understand that this step had been taken against China rather than against the United States." It was understood as a breach of the principle of peaceful co-existence and thus as a threat against the United States.

For that matter, the Soviets did not succeed in dispelling the misgivings of Cuba once the Kennedy administration had forced them to withdraw their missiles. Nor could they regain the full friendship of Fidel Castro. Since then, Cuba has stressed its neutral position in the conflict between Moscow and Peking. It stood with Albania and the Asiatic people's democracies as a social-ist country that values a good relationship with China—until 1966, when Peking tried to force Cuba into an open stand against Moscow by withholding rice.

The Chinese were quick to turn the Cuban incident to an ideological advantage. "Have the Soviet comrades not told us that peaceful co-existence is a necessity, that any warlike incident could unleash a Third World War, which must result in the destruction of the human race?" I was asked in Peking. Those who posed the question gave an immediate answer. "And then the Soviets sent missiles to Cuba! Who was playing with fire, we or they? Who risked the outbreak of the Third World War?"

But they avoided mentioning what they must have known, far better than the West: that the ideological pressure exerted by the Chinese made Khrushchev resort to such a haphazard action.

The withdrawal of the missiles from Cuba provided the Chinese with still more material for propaganda. "After this piratical policy, the Soviet Union is now pursuing a policy of capitulation. An ultimatum from the United States was enough to make the great Soviet Union put its tail between its legs and run like a whipped dog."

Khrushchev's policy of peaceful co-existence, which has been confirmed by his successors, has thus contributed a great deal to expanding the conflict with Peking. In Chinese eyes, the policy has had other consequences, as the examples of Berlin and Cuba are supposed to indicate. For example, the Soviet Union has left in the lurch the communist movements in Western Europe and the U.S., and above all in the emerging countries of Asia, Africa, and Latin America. Moscow can only co-exist peacefully with the West if it no longer actively supports communist revolutions. Khrushchev was acting in accordance with this idea when he advised the communists of the world to further their cause "through parliamentary channels."

With that, did China not become the sole repository of the world communist movement? This question is asked in Peking and answered with a resounding "yes!"

There are other reasons for the conflict between China and

the Soviet Union, but these are the principal ones. The most decisive and weighty seems to be the question of the class struggle.

China has no reason to be grateful to Stalin. It was he who abandoned the Chinese revolution to its fate and collaborated with Chiang Kai-shek and the Japanese—he who had once been a personal foe of Mao Tse-tung. And yet the entire Sino-Soviet conflict began over destalinization. Stalinism was and is the only method that enables the government in Peking to dominate its huge masses of people.

Even in China, Stalin is openly criticized in talk and in print. "He was unable to distinguish between his friends and his enemies." But the principle of the class struggle for which he stood is considered by the Chinese to be the alpha and omega of communist power. Without Stalinism, the Chinese insist, the Soviet state would never have arisen, or would have perished in the thirties. And without Stalinism, communism would have had even less of a chance in overpopulated and underdeveloped China.

Not all the methods of the Stalinist class struggle are accepted. Even in the eyes of the Chinese, Stalin strayed at times from the path of socialist justice. In China, on the other hand, the class struggle has been conducted strictly on the basis of socialist justice. The secret police have not been used by the Chinese leaders against the Party and certainly not against ruling members of the Party, as was done in the Soviet Union under Stalin, but only against the people; or, as the Chinese say, "only against the enemies of the people." And the methods used in the class struggle have been perfected by the Chinese; they have become uniquely Chinese. These are the methods that the West refers to as "brainwashing." Naturally, Peking resents this designation.

14

How to wash brains

During the third week of my stay in China I was having a discussion with the manager of a factory. He not only explained the machinery in his plant but also talked to me about the lives of his workers. Through the translator I was able to understand everything he was saying. And then, suddenly, I caught myself using some of the same phrases—catch terms, flowery expressions—used in informal conversation by Chinese functionaries.

I was talking about the "living niveau" instead of the standard of living; about the "district of life maintenance" instead of housing developments, markets, and canteens; about "masses" instead of people; about "consciousness" instead of ideological training; about "your struggle" instead of economic efforts without foreign aid.

When I glanced over my notes at the end of this discussion, I realized how much of the official language I had absorbed.

At the Peking Teachers College I met old professors; in a heart clinic, a world-famous Chinese surgeon; in the venerable library in Peking, a well-known scholar. All had lived through the old times. But all of them used, as a matter of course, the vocabulary introduced by the communists.

That may not be significant in itself. What is significant is that each of these individuals had gone on practicing his profession, and —if they are to be believed—without interruption.

For example, the Peking Teachers College has a staff of fifty-eight professors. I was interested to see how many of them had been appointed after 1949, that is, after the communist takeover. Somewhat surprised, they told me that they had all been professors "before the Liberation." None of them was appointed after the Liberation. I couldn't believe my ears. All the professors in a university which trains new generations of high school teachers had been there before the communist regime.

In that case, had many of the former professors been dismissed? They denied that, too. "The college had fifty-eight professors before 1949, and it has them now. No one has been dismissed."

Now I asked a direct question. "Was that because the old professors agreed with the new ideas? Did they follow the new lines of the Party in their lectures?"

They answered that the Party adopted a policy of tolerance toward intellectuals, but it also practiced indoctrination and re-education. The "social conscience" of the teachers had been developed. They came to realize that their former opinions were false, that they had been exploited by capitalist bureaucrats and the lackeys of imperialism, that they had been used as tools. Now they were serving the interests of the proletariat.

I asked how and by whom they had been led to this insight. The answer was given by a lady who served as deputy dean of the college. She had been a professor long before 1949; the larger part of her professional life had been lived under the old regime. But what she told me hewed to the Party line. No one had to convince them. That came spontaneously. They were "convinced by the facts."

I got much the same reply in a secondary school in Peking, where the faculty was also made up of old-time teachers. And similar answers met my questions at the Peking library. "The Party and the state show great consideration for teachers and professors, for all intellectuals, scientists, and poets."

This consideration consisted mainly of moral suasion. "The new regime placed education and the educators at the forefront of its program. The specialists were wooed by the Party, but they were also presented to the people as sages who should be honored."

This may have been enough to induce some educators to meet the new regime halfway. In addition, the regime took pains to provide them with suitable living quarters. Schools and universities were ordered to put up buildings and to assign apartments to their teachers. Until then, only those in the highest echelons had decent housing.

But the new government went even further in upgrading and wooing the intellectuals. Teachers and scientists were given government posts, invited to join the people's assemblies. Nowadays there is hardly an event of any consequence to which they do not receive special invitations.

That was one side of the "practical re-education." The other side was exactly opposite. Openly and covertly, all intellectuals were suspected of clinging to the old ideas, of harboring counter-revolutionary tendencies. They were admonished if they used a wrong phrase during an instruction period, offered a bourgeois definition, or in a conversation inserted a casually worded sentence that was not ideologically correct, that could be held against them later.

The most opportune occasions for these reprimands were meetings introduced by the communists for criticism and self-criticism. From the beginning these have been among the favorite methods of communists for re-educating and "awakening" people. One might draw a parallel with the Catholic confessional, or with the rules that prevail in convents. Through confessing his faults, through sharing them with others, through penitence, one cleanses himself, obtains pardon, and is given the strength not to repeat his mistakes.

In a system that denies the existence of God, in which man can only be held to account here and now, self-criticism—the open acknowledgment of faults—is one of the most important means of enforcing morality. It is strengthened through a much sterner device —that of criticism by one's colleagues, Party comrades, close friends, and even relatives. They are required to disclose not only one's faults but also the political, social, and economic failings of which he has been guilty.

The system demands of all citizens that they supervise their nearest and dearest, that they keep a stern watch over all his actions and conversations, and bare him to public accusation if he has sinned in the moral and ideological sense. And finally, those who do not denounce such faults are declared equally guilty. Those who try to avoid denouncing their friends and relatives must fear that they will be denounced because they have failed to expose faults known to them. The harshness of this system is apparent.

The communists in Europe had enough trouble introducing and enforcing this system of criticism and self-criticism among their members and, more important, among the general population. But Europeans brought up in the Christian ethic have some understanding of such a system. Not so in China, where loss of face has played a large role for centuries. If one was guilty of something, he did his best to hide it. None of the different religions in China required a believer to confide in others. Confessions were made silently at the graves of the ancestors. If members of the family learned of some wrongdoing, the entire clan made sure that nothing leaked out. The family sat in council, pronounced sentence on the culprit—sometimes a very severe sentence—and tried to avoid legal procedures. It was considered a disgrace if the public learned about a misdeed.

Loss of face went beyond actual offenses. If one acted clumsily or stupidly, if one failed in business or was maliciously pleased by someone else's misfortune, or if one broke his word or failed to keep a promise, one lost face.

So we can imagine what the new system of criticism and self-criticism introduced by the communists must have meant to the Chinese, particularly to the Chinese intellectuals. They must appear at public gatherings where they were asked to bare their own "bad character traits" and their own failings. Naturally, the tendency was to offer excuses and explanations. But the Party was prepared for that. Excuses were not permitted, inferred faults were made explicit. And then began the criticism—by colleagues, by friends, by family. In the case of professors, there was also criticism by students. For days at a time they had to hear how dangerous and counter-revolutionary their lectures had been. Held up to public scorn, they not only lost face, but that "face" was thoroughly destroyed.

It is easy to imagine the dread each felt, not knowing how the criticism would end. Would he lose his position, and with it the assigned living quarters? Would he have to give up his profession and work as a peasant? Would he perhaps be put into a re-education camp or sent to prison? Would he be separated from his family? Even a death sentence seemed possible.

And then, when the intellectuals were told that they could free themselves of "false thinking" through sufficient self-criticism, that their guilt would be taken away, the self-criticism in many cases began to exceed all bounds.

That is how the intellectuals—and others, too—were "re-shaped" by an intensive process. There are many examples of this "reforming" of people whom the communists could not dispense with and were therefore eager to introduce to a "new way of thinking."

One of these examples, probably the most spectacular, is that of the emperor of China. Oh yes, he exists. He was six years old when the Manchu Dynasty was overthrown. He was the heir to the throne; his name is P'u-yi. When the Japanese invaded the imperial palace in Peking in the thirties, they found the dethroned pretender still living there. They decided to use his name and his person, and made him emperor of Manchukuo, the part of China they had conquered.

In fact, P'u-yi had become a collaborator, guilty of high treason—an enemy of the people. The Soviets took him prisoner in 1945. He begged them not to hand him over to the Chinese. But when the communists came to power he was indeed handed over.

There was no show trial. Between 1949 and 1959 the ex-emperor found himself in a prison in northeast China. On several occasions, when he was paraded before Western journalists, he said that he was beginning to see the error of his ways and that he was undergoing a "conversion of the spirit."

Then he was hidden in silence for a long time. In 1959 he was released and allowed to choose an occupation. He chose to become a gardener, a trade he followed for only three years. Then he asked to be admitted to a research institute for Chinese history. The request was granted. It was what the communist authorities had planned for him in the first place.

Nowadays Henry P'u-yi is not only a prominent member of

Bulletin boards on many streets, and particularly outside the
gates of factories, show the latest economic gains and
success in the class struggle.

the institute, he sits as a representative in the People's Congress, and he has written a book which is now being published in installments, especially in those propaganda pamphlets that are printed in Japanese.

In this book P'u-yi describes "the first half of my life." It is a guide for those who have not yet been converted, a detailed exposition of how conversion must take root in a person, especially in his mind. P'u-yi describes exactly where his thinking was faulty in the past, why it was faulty, how he came to gain a clearer understanding, why all that the communists say is true and irrefutable.

One thing emerges clearly from the book: a really determined effort to renounce his old ways of thinking, a sincere self-conversion; that is, a fresh start which is necessary to expel fear and replace it with the real joy of living. He hopes to live from now on in peace and inner equanimity. The difference is as great as that between heaven and hell.

I have already described an encounter with Chinese "capitalists." Their existence allows the communist regime to prove that Mao Tse-tung's administration is in line with Leninist principles. Marx and Lenin were convinced that no historical step could be omitted. But Mao Tse-tung had made a successful revolution in China without waiting for the intermediate stages of the bourgeois-capitalistic development of industry.

He helped himself, ideologically speaking, in that he did not call for a dictatorship of the proletariat but created a "people's democracy" to take the place of the intermediate stages. And here he needed the capitalists: for economic reasons, to help existing industries, and for ideological reasons, to prove his strict compliance with Marxist-Leninist principles.

Thus no opportunity is missed in China to point out the existence of the capitalists to foreigners. I asked to be allowed to talk with them and so was able to verify for myself the "conversion of man" in China.

I met the capitalists in Shanghai. While only my interpreter usually came along on these excursions, this time we were joined by a member of the People's Council's foreign office. I realized why he was there as soon as we sat down with the first capitalist. He spoke a fluent, flawless English, a language my interpreter did not know. I really had no need of an interpreter under the circumstances, but without the official there would have been no one to follow the conversation. For the "capitalist," although he began the conversation in Chinese, soon switched to English and paid no further attention to my companions.

I looked the man over carefully. No more than forty-five years old, he would have been a mere youngster in 1949. Even so, he had been the owner of a pharmaceutical house and a drug importing firm. He seemed to pay a great deal of attention to his appearance; he wore a silk shirt of fine quality, his trousers were faultlessly creased, his shoes were Chinese export models. His nails were manicured, and he wore his hair in a style unusual in China—not parted but combed back. Face and skin showed assiduous care. From his gestures and the way he moved it was evident that he came from an educated family.

He described himself as an industrialist, and from his stories it became evident that he had made deals with companies in New York, London, Paris, and Zürich. His business partners had offices all over the world.

He walked through the rooms of "his" pharmaceutical plant as if he were still the owner. But for two hours he explained to me how he had been self-converted. It was the same old story. The facts had convinced him. He saw the strength of the new China, how it helped the poor masses, how justly it treated its enemies (not all of them, by a long shot), how it had helped him and his family "to find the right way."

This "capitalist" was also a representative in the government of Shanghai, but "of course not a communist."

Why "of course"?

His conversion left much to be desired, although he was on his way to becoming a respected member of socialistic society. A proof: today he earns a salary as the employed manager of the concern he formerly owned. He makes three times as much as the manager the state installed alongside him, and he continues to receive 5 per cent interest on his original capital investment. Such a man could not be a communist.

I asked the Party functionaries present why such a policy of "concern for capitalists" was being continued, why it was necessary. They answered quickly, "If the payment of interest were abolished now or if the salaries of the former capitalists were reduced, they would harbor an inner grudge against the communists. They would say that the communists had not kept their word. They would regard us as swindlers."

"Would that really harm the regime?"

"Yes, it would be bad. These people have great capabilities. They put them at the disposal of the new China. We can rely on them. They should not be upset. The time will come when they will voluntarily renounce their high salaries and their interest payments."

"Have some of them already felt the urge to become members of the socialist society?"

"Oh yes, quite a few former capitalists have asked us to reduce their salaries and to stop paying interest. But as you can imagine, if we followed their requests all the other capitalists would say that we were using moral pressure on them to do the same, and the grudge would be there regardless."

I was told in Peking that the government will probably soon re-evaluate its stand on interest payments. The question is whether the capitalists' eagerness to work is now well enough established to survive the cessation of payment.

These few examples perhaps illustrate what is meant by the "conversion" of the Chinese people, a "conversion" for which the West has coined the term "brainwashing."

Of course, there are many other forms of brainwashing, such as those employed in the "camps for labor and education." I will report on these in connection with Chinese judicial procedures.

And yet, not all "class enemies" have been converted by the communists. As I have indicated, many were dealt with summarily after 1949, were given no chance to re-think but were executed. Some experts on China regard this as a logical sequence in the victorious course of a revolution. But one has only to read the works of Mao Tse-tung to realize that the Chinese leaders even at that time were thinking in uncannily clear terms. The "conversion" would not have been so effective if the threat of these horrible executions had not been ever-present to the millions of candidates for conversion. Only those who can be really frightened are ready for conversion. "A measure of terror is necessary," Mao Tse-tung wrote. And he knew why.

But to these direct conversion methods, which are aimed at the individual—criticism, constant anxiety, self-criticism, and more anxiety—comes the daily flood of propaganda slogans and explanations emanating from the press, radio, television, films and theater, opera, and so on. As I have already mentioned, even a foreigner finds it impossible to escape the repetition of slogans. How then can the Chinese? Remember the loudspeakers on the trains!

But the main emphasis of all the communist attempts to make "new human beings" of the Chinese is not focused on the adults, but, as a matter of course, on the education of the younger generation.

15

Mao's youth and the red banner

Those who read Chinese newspapers or translations of them, who attend a few meetings in China or view Chinese films and television, soon sense a peculiar obsession. But no, it is more than an obsession, it is almost an outcry. Sometimes one even has the feeling that it is a cry of fear, uttered by the old communist leaders of China. "Where are our heirs? Where are the young people into whose hands we can entrust the banners, tattered by sorrow and struggle, of the Chinese revolution?"

One appeal follows on the heels of another. "Make sure that our youth continues the revolution! Take care that their efforts do not lag! Do all in your power to strengthen the young with the examples of the Long March! Keep them from falling into the error of revisionism!"

In China today one campaign follows another under these slogans. The Communist Youth Association (formerly called the Comsomol, after the Soviet model; today you are corrected if you use the term) has after a long interval again held a full session of its Representative Assembly and has newly elected or re-elected its Central Committee, its Secretariat and Politburo.

News of the Congress has been reported thoroughly, as though the most important governmental body in the nation were in session and the most vital decisions were to be made. And that is probably true. China's leaders are all old men. Mao Tse-tung is seventy-three. Lui Chao-chi, the present president of the Chinese Republic, is seventy-four. Prime Minister Chou En-lai is seventy. Mao's oldest companion in arms, the real third power in the state, Marshal Chou Teh, is seventy-five. Vice-President and Foreign Minister Chen Yi is over sixty.

The handful of men at the top of the Communist Party of China, and thus at the head of the nation, have only a few more years to enjoy their offices and honors. They are different from the Soviet leaders, for example, during Stalin's regime and after his death. The purges brought about an unintentional rejuvenation of the Soviet leadership. At the time of Stalin's death very few old revolutionaries, those who had stood with Lenin on the barricades in the old days, were left. It is far different in China.

The Chinese Party leadership has known almost no revision since the time of the Long March; that is, since 1934. With only two exceptions since, all the leaders have held top positions within the Party and the government, without interruption.

That has a deep meaning: among other things, that these leaders, on the Long March or soon afterward, apparently entered into a firm alliance that has endured until the present.

On the other hand, this has kept younger politicians from growing into positions of real responsibility. There has been and still is a definite break in the continuity between the "old-timers" and the next generation. Have the younger ones been mistrusted, or was there simply no room at the top? However that may be, the present leaders are aware that there is no one to take over the banners of the revolution without an inevitable break in the leadership of China. That is a worry to the Chinese Communist Party. A much more serious worry concerns the cadres of the Party and the people as a whole.

The entire membership of the cadre that participated in the Long March is on the way out. I encountered them in communes and factories, where they are supervisors approaching or already beyond retirement age. The younger cadre members did not take part in the Long March. They have had no experience of the deprivations, the daily struggle for mere existence, the battles with the enemy. They may be fanatical communists, but will they be able to maintain the general line of continuous revolution?

If one reads the current appeals to youth, one cannot escape the impression that the old leadership simply does not believe in the ability of these younger cadre members. Again and again I read the plea: they must be "made to take over the banner." So they are not considered ready as yet.

A new aspect of the "Great Leap Forward" becomes apparent. Was this exertion also a mighty attempt to consolidate the communist system, to round out and to conclude the lifework of Mao Tse-tung while he and his colleagues were still alive?

It did not succeed. Today it is openly said in Peking that to consolidate the socialist order another hundred, hundred and fifty, or two hundred years will be needed. As for attaining the communist order which Khrushchev declared had been reached in the Soviet Union, nothing can be predicted. And apparently the leaders of the Chinese Communist Party are not quite certain what methods to use in order to achieve and consolidate their goals.

There is a tendency to suggest that the young should undertake a "Long March" even in peacetime, to undergo hardship and deprivation, to renounce possessions, to give up the search for material possessions and continue the class struggle in the spirit of sacrifice manifested by the original Long March.

I have seen half a dozen Chinese movies devoted to this subject: the renunciation of comfort and material possessions by young workers and peasants. They are exhorted to live like monks, penniless and dispossessed, serving only the idea. And yet the attempt is repeatedly made to offer youth material rewards and to hold before them the hope for a better life and a higher standard of living.

In a recent performance of the Peking opera, a young worker was persuaded by his mother-in-law to go hunting wild ducks to get money for a new suit of clothes. Because of his absence from work, the production quota was endangered. The dramatic climax came when the young worker realized that he had sinned against the common welfare and fallen victim to his mother-in-law's evil bourgeois ideas. A chaotic scene ensued in which his father, an old fighter, condemned him.

As an unprejudiced onlooker, I expected that the new suit, already bought, would be eliminated as the *corpus delicti* and that the mother-in-law would be banished from the home of her children, as she was the one who had suggested the forbidden deed. Denunciation to the police also seemed to be called for.

But no. Things work out quite differently. The son breaks down. The mother-in-law wants to flee. But the old fighter steps in. The hunting of wild ducks should be regarded as a beautiful sport, a recreation for the young worker. The sale of the wild ducks is not only legal, but will augment the diet of the people. The Party will certainly approve the purchase of new clothes because it wants the workers to be better dressed. So why all the uproar?

The old fighter answers his own question. The spirit in which all this was done was wrong, corrupt and dangerous. The ducks had not been hunted for sport, they had not been sold with the intention of supplementing the food supply, the suit had not been bought in the awareness that it was the reward due an industrious worker.

The spirit behind all these machinations had been corrupt and bourgeois. It had been a "spontaneous capitalistic sentiment" and the young man had yielded to temptation. He was unaware of the misery, the struggle through which the Party had gone in order to offer youth a better life. He had been ready to betray these achievements in spirit. But now that he recognizes his faults, he will be forgiven.

Now it's the mother-in-law's turn, I thought. Again, no. As she prepares to leave the house with her bedding on her back, the old fighter stops her. This is no way to atone for one's faults. On the contrary, she must go to the home of her children and be converted by them. The memory of her faults must be kept alive for a long time so that both sides can learn from them. The son, who has been ready to throw out his mother-in-law, is scolded again. "Honor your elders, and educate them."

What is one to make of that?

Girls studying in their dormitory at Peking University. When they finish their education they will be urged to "return to the village," where China desperately needs manpower.

Through the first three acts, property and trade are despicable. At the end they become an achievement of the new China. The ideological gap between the old and the young is shown; it seems nearly impossible to bridge, yet it is bridged.

A badly contrived libretto?

The theme appeared again and again in plays, operas, and movies. It was developed and brought to a dramatic climax in the same fashion and resolved in the same way every time.

What I had originally taken for a hopeless plot that could not extricate itself from its own paradoxes now presented itself to me as a guideline, born out of the fear that youth would depart from communist ways. This line seemed to reflect uncertainty. Of course it is the goal of communism to provide a better way of life for its people, to guarantee security and prosperity. But prosperity in China today is considered a sign of capitalism, a reminder of the rich "exploiters" of the bourgeois society. How does one reconcile the ultimate communist goal with the unremitting class struggle regarded as necessary by the government? And how does one teach youth not to falter in the class struggle, to practice communist asceticism and at the same time to work hard for improvement in the standard of living and the future?

I put these questions to a functionary of the Communist Youth Association, with whom I had an interview. He was the assistant editor of the central organ of the association, *The Chinese Youth.*

"The spiritual condition of our youth is good," he declared. "It is full of revolutionary spirit. But the class struggle goes on. The bourgeois and feudal influences on our young people are always present. We must continue to fight relentlessly against individualism and the bourgeois way of life, against pacifism, humanism, religion, and superstition."

"How does the bourgeois influence make itself felt?"

"It doesn't exist within the Communist Youth Association, but it does exist in private life. Therefore we must develop our proletarian ideology still further, to destroy the bourgeois ideology."

"How do you proceed with the destruction?"

"Through persuasion and education."

"Of adults by their children?"

"Yes. Adults educate the children, and children educate the adults."

"Doesn't that lead to quarrels within the family?"

"We try to avoid them. We urge our members to educate their parents gently. That is one of our guiding tenets. Parents must be respected and obeyed by their children."

"But if the parents persist in their opinions?"

"That's something else. There can be no co-existence with reactionary sentiments. We then recommend that the young person draw the line."

"By leaving the parents?"

"No, because children have a duty to provide for their parents. But an ideological separation is possible along with the duty to provide for the family. Within the family, a pure ideology must prevail."

"Do you go so far as to ask children to denounce their parents?"

"Only in cases of marked counter-revolutionary activity; not just for persisting in their bourgeois ideology. This problem cannot be solved by force. Since we are dealing here with an ideology, the struggle must be waged on ideological grounds. Denunciations are no help there."

"Do the young people long for amusements and possessions?"

"You mean the 'dolce vita'? Not within our association. So far they haven't shown any such tendencies, but we know that this presents a danger. That's why we guard against it. Outside the association there are young people who hunger for pleasures and possessions. The Youth Association numbers more than twenty million members. [There are more than a hundred million in this age group.] Through enlightenment and education we can counteract bourgeois tendencies even outside our group."

"What is the goal of the association?"

"To strengthen our young people, to educate them in the revolutionary spirit, to make them capable of receiving the revolutionary flag from the hands of the older generation, to forestall any faltering in their revolutionary enthusiasm by keeping the examples of the past before them as a model. In short, our youth must not be corrupted by peace and the rising standard of living. It must continue the class struggle. It must be strengthened against a revisionism that offers prosperity instead of struggle."

"How will you do this?"

"The great campaign we have started shows the apprehension of the leaders. They are determined to do everything in their power to keep our young people from going the way of the Soviets or, worse, the Yugoslavs. The Party organization can carry only half the burden. The other half must be carried by the kindergartens, elementary schools, high schools, and the colleges."

16

No need for a proletarian grandmother

"Let a hundred flowers bloom, let a hundred ideas compete," was the motto I saw in big red letters over the entrance to the library of the Peking Teachers College. I was astonished. Was this slogan still in force? When Mao Tse-tung made his "hundred-flower" proclamation it almost led to an insurrection among the intellectuals. After its suppression, rumors went around that the "hundred flowers" phrase had been devised to make enemies come forward so that they could be unmasked. Now I still found the "hundred flowers" in that very institute where the elite high school teachers are trained.

In this library I found the latest American publications in the field of education, the Encyclopaedia Britannica, and the Brockhaus. In fact, everything the Western world offered in the field seemed to be there. There were also books on natural history, general science, semantics, philosophy, etc.—in at least thirty languages.

It is true that this section of the library was open only to the staff, not the students. Nevertheless, it was easy to see that the Chinese university professors had not lost touch with the progress made by the rest of the world. What they passed on to their students is another matter.

It is much the same with the "hundred flowers" slogan. The motto has not been officially retracted, nor have the "Great Leap

Forward" and other significant general lines. The Chinese leadership does not make mistakes; therefore it cannot reverse itself or retract its decrees. But the meaning of the phrases can change mightily on occasion: the "hundred flowers" phrase has quite a different meaning now than when it was first proclaimed. Then it marked the beginning of the fight against Stalinism. Today it is supposed to indicate that all schools of thought may be cultivated in China. In fact, as is to be expected, all thinking is channeled into the Marxist-Leninist stream as interpreted by the words and actions of Mao Tse-tung.

The greatest emphasis in this program is placed on educating the youngsters, and it begins in kindergarten.

I visited several kindergartens in China, as well as primary and secondary schools and colleges. No doubt I was usually shown the best among them. But there is also no doubt that present-day China expends a great deal of time, money, and effort on the education of its young people.

The curriculum has two goals: to give the children as much factual information as possible and to direct them ideologically.

The head of a Peking kindergarten told me, "We try to give our little ones [between the ages of three and seven] knowledge about everyday life and to educate them morally."

"What does the moral education consist of?"

"Love for the motherland, love and respect for public property, love for the Party, love for Chairman Mao, and love for proletarian internationalism. In addition we instill respect for the parents, for honesty, courage, patriotism, and helpfulness."

A great deal of emphasis is placed on personal and household hygiene. And there is no pretense; the wall charts that show the children how to brush their teeth and wash their hands and feet show actual Chinese living conditions, with water being fetched from a well and used in basin and bucket.

The children do not wear uniforms but are dressed colorfully and—as everywhere in China—better than the grownups, reflecting a wealth of parental love.

The main ideological trend, already noticeable in kindergarten, is intensified in the elementary schools. School-entering age is seven. From seven to thirteen, attendance at elementary school is compulsory.

I often asked, "Are there really enough schoolhouses and teachers for the millions of Chinese children?" The answer came reluctantly. "In the city all children do have an opportunity to go to school—at least, to primary school. It's not always possible in the country. But even in the country they attend when they are eight or nine. It can be said that for the first time in our history all children learn reading, writing, and arithmetic."

I then asked about the guiding principle of the primary school curriculum. The answer came promptly: "Primary school education has to serve the cause of the proletariat. It has to supply information, moral guidance, physical culture; and above all it teaches love for work."

"Anything more?"

"Yes, the duty to the state. We have to turn out well-informed young people who can go on to the higher schools, as well as trained workers."

I found that from the age of thirteen on, Chinese children play a part in the "productive work process" as juvenile workers in the people's communes and apprentices in the factories.

Since 1963 vocational training has been required. Beginning in secondary school, children are called on to do practical work. They must spend some time in the people's communes, helping with the sowing and harvesting. In the factories they perform simple assembly-line operations. The schools also offer courses in carpentry and mechanics.

At elementary school age they may join the Young Pioneers, the children's branch of the Communist Party.

"Not all of them?"

"No, about 90 per cent."

"What happens to the other 10 per cent?"

"Either they don't qualify or they don't want to join."

"Are their parents against it?"

"Perhaps that, too."

In any event, all the children I saw in the classrooms were

wearing the red kerchief that marked them as members of the Pioneers.

"And do they practice criticism and self-criticism?" I asked. The answer surprised me. "No, they are just children. They should not be so heavily burdened."

In other communist countries children are expected to practice these disciplines. "We have not done that here. We do not want our children confronted with such a high level of reasoning at such an early age. They lack the necessary maturity."

"Is it possible to expel anyone from the Pioneers, and what are the results in school?"

The rules are very strict. "Expulsion from the Pioneers is equivalent to expulsion from school. There must be good reasons for such a disciplinary measure, reasons which the school cannot overlook, though the problem arises outside the school."

But my informants denied that the reasons could be of an ideological nature. "These children are simply hard to educate. They are then sent to a school for labor and education." From the description added by the teacher I gathered that this was a reformatory.

Now, how about enrollment in the high schools? Since the tuition fee is not very high and the state theoretically "gives each child the opportunity to become a valuable member of society," most parents would naturally want to send their children on to high school. How is the selection made?

I was told that selection on the basis of ability would be a "bourgeois survival," although that is the strict policy in other communist countries. Marxism-Leninism should be practiced more completely in China. Accordingly, one human being is as important as another. None must be given preference. I was told that all children who want to go to high school are enrolled. (High schools are divided into two sections, each with three grades.)

I found it hard to believe that such a long course of study under competent teachers could be available to all children. "Is the child accepted if he comes from a bourgeois family?" This of course would offer another basis for selection, without involving ability. But I had some trouble making myself clear. I explained as best I could. "But of course. Such children need education even more than the others.

We don't make such distinctions, we don't give any preference to the children of peasants or workers."

"What happens if a child expresses bourgeois ideas? Suppose it is apparent that his bourgeois upbringing continues at home?"

"We talk with the parents."

"Are they held responsible?"

"No, we can't do that. We can only advise. In most cases they follow our suggestions." They always follow, as I learned later in the conversation.

In any case, the relation between school and home is close. Each pupil, even in elementary school, has a notebook in which the teacher's comments on his studies and behavior are entered. The parents must sign it each week. In addition, his grades are entered in this notebook at the end of the term.

I asked if any pupils failed to pass from grade to grade. This question, too, missed its mark. I tried to explain. "Oh yes, theoretically a pupil might have to repeat a year. In practice it never happens. Children are sent to school to learn. Any human being can learn anything if it's presented in the right way. That is the teacher's job. If a child can't follow the class instruction, the teachers are expected to tutor him after school until he understands. In our system no one fails."

"But suppose you have children who are slow learners or who don't want to learn?"

"Then there is something wrong with them, and we have to analyze it. If it's a clinical case the child is sent to a special school. If the fault is ours, it must be remedied. If it's the home life, we speak to the parents." The parents are not summoned by the teacher, but the teacher goes to see them, perhaps to have a look at the conditions at home at the same time.

Even in the elementary schools the curriculum is no small matter. As early as sixth grade it includes Chinese (reading and writing), arithmetic, natural science, (especially chemistry and physics), agriculture, physical education, singing and dancing. By the end of the sixth grade the students must master 3,500 Chinese characters and the Latin alphabet, since efforts are being made to transpose the

Chinese language into Latin script and thus eventually to modernize it.

In high school, ideological training is increased. Two lesson periods a week are devoted to it. This curriculum, too, is interesting. "What ideological material are the children given?" Here are the courses for the different grades: First grade—communist morality, above all obedience to the Party, love for the Party, love for Chairman Mao Tse-tung, readiness to help one's neighbors, respect for public property, and so on. Second grade—a brief history of the development of society, including the development of democracy; this does not conform to any of the time divisions usual with us, such as the Bronze Age, antiquity, the Middle Ages, and the modern era. Their Chinese counterparts are primitive communes, slaveholding society, and the feudal era; then come capitalism, colonialism, imperialism, which is transformed through revolution into socialism, this in turn to develop into communism. Third and fourth grades— political science, consisting entirely of the thinking of Mao Tse-tung, whose works are read, discussed, and memorized. Only in the fifth and sixth grades are Marx and Lenin studied, under the title of "philosophical studies," but even on this level the works of Mao Tse-tung come first.

Ideology dominates all other subjects, too. This fact emerged when I asked the director about the teaching aims in the high school. He said, "We are educating our youth to take the flag of the revolution from the hands of the older generation. Education serves the interests of the proletariat and the advancement of productive labor. Our young people are brought up in the spirit of the classless society and thus in the spirit of class struggle. They have to think along revolutionary and collective lines, and they are trained in dialectical materialism, love of their motherland, dedication to the Party and to Chairman Mao Tse-tung, and they are taught to love all the peaceful nations of the world. We educate them to hate imperialism and reaction and to distinguish between right and wrong. They learn to sympathize with the oppressed nations, which we must help in every possible way."

From these answers it is easy to see that ideological indoctrination increases from kindergarten through the elementary school and again in secondary school.

I asked what subjects were used to teach the children to "hate imperialism and reaction." The response was passionate. *"All* subjects are full of this spirit, but especially the history courses. We use facts to educate our children. The daily crimes of American imperialism are easy to see. It is our worst enemy." "Hate for reactionaries" is inculcated by references to China's former social conditions.

I had been assured that the high schools are officially open to all children, but I was told that university enrollments are limited. One of the principal tasks of the high school is to keep pupils from seeking a college education. They are even discouraged from going into the factories as pre-trained workers. The slogan nowadays is: "Join the people's communes, go into agriculture."

One of the most acute problems in China today is what to do with all the high school graduates, to say nothing of the university graduates. There are not enough offices or civil service openings to go around, and too few factory jobs. The population flow is to the cities, but there are not enough jobs.

Youth in Our Village is the name of one of the latest Chinese films, done in East German Agfacolor. It starts with a girl and a boy of nineteen, both high school graduates, pedaling their newly acquired bicycles back to their village. As they approach, the production groups break off work in the fields, run toward them, and greet them enthusiastically. The youths are from "our village," and have actually done one heroic deed already—they have come back home.

They are returning to "our village" from the city. And what a life awaits them there! Since they are both high school graduates and thus have been studying for twelve years, they know more than the other villagers. The head of the commune and the Party secretary strike up long conversations with them. Plans are being laid. With two students on hand, it will be child's play to set up a small electric generating plant. The two graduates are experts, having had training in technology.

Days and nights are devoted to planning the power plant, and finally it is built. All the young people in the village are busy mixing concrete, laying brick, diverting the small river, etc. In short, the young man and the girl are the village heroes. Even the commune chairman and the Party secretary follow their lead.

But, as was bound to happen, in the course of their work they become guilty of deviation, to both right and left. To the right, they see a golden era opening up for the village. With plans and sketches they re-create the village as a well-to-do community flowing with milk and honey. Hereafter the villagers will live in comfort.

When they reveal these plans they are attacked vigorously. Criticism is heard, and they are required to practice self-criticism. "Naturally, conditions will improve in time, but it is wrong to promise too much too soon." Now we see that the Party secretary is really the leader of the village.

The deviation to the left comes when a turbine is needed and the manufacturer in Shanghai cannot deliver it on time. But they are familiar with the slogan, "Out of our own strength," so they build a turbine out of wood. With it, they are able to start generating power. The turbine falls apart and the machinery is badly damaged. The criticism and self-criticism that ensue are milder this time. Everyone recognizes that they were following Party slogans, to work "out of our own strength" and "create technical innovations," but they overlooked the fact that the slogans apply to the entire country and that they should have waited for the turbine from Shanghai. They would still have been using "our own strength," for the steel turbine would have been a Chinese turbine. "One must not rush ahead blindly even to build socialism."

On the other hand, it is of course a familiar fact (not in the movie, but certainly to the producers) that steel turbines are hard to come by and that young people have to be encouraged actually to create out of their own strength. So they are permitted to build a second wooden turbine. This time, because they have gained experience and are guided by concrete conditions, they proceed more slowly and plan the work more carefully. At last, everything works, even the wooden turbine. They have succeeded. The power station works!

The last part of the movie shows a number of electric machines which lighten the work of the peasants in the commune. The heroes who have accomplished all this are, of course, the two high school graduates.

In a communist state, and particularly in one as strictly run as China, there are no coincidences, especially not in the writing of scenarios. If the entire younger generation is made to see *Youth in Our Village,* there must be a reason.

The idea is to persuade high school graduates to go back to the villages. It is part of a plan to keep them from wanting to go to college, to earn diplomas, to win doctorates, and then turn to the state and demand that it find good positions in the city for them. China today faces the problem of over-education. It knows the dangers inherent in too much education and too little job opportunity. Steps are being taken to avoid producing too many intellectuals.

That is one side of the problem. There was and probably still is another side. Before the "Great Leap," and even more during it, the Party tried to withdraw as much of the work force as possible from agriculture and convert it into an industrial proletariat. They hoped to make this possible by establishing the people's communes. Through throwing fields together and mechanizing farm work they hoped to release part of the labor force from agriculture. The workers thus released were needed to build new industries. Hands instead of machines!

So they were brought to the cities; or, at least, no obstacles were placed in the way of those who wanted to go to the cities. In China, as elsewhere, the city lights are alluring. In China, as elsewhere, farmers' sons and daughters hope for a better life in the cities —regular working hours, plenty of leisure and amusements to fill it, however modestly. And so the cities were flooded with peasants and young people. The population of Shanghai increased by one-third— some sources say one-half. Despite all the attempts of the regime, it was impossible to find work for all of them. Some never went back. The aims of the "Great Leap" are said to have failed in part because the villages had insufficient manpower.

Now the government realized its mistake. But it was not easy to persuade the peasants to return home, especially the young ones who had been brought to the cities. Grotesque situations are reported. Some of the peasants became integrated into city life, and stayed. But the people's communes urgently demanded more manpower, especially when the mechanization of farm work failed to materialize. Work forces had to be provided; so regional officials prevailed upon students, officeholders, and intellectuals to give up their positions and their studies in the cities and go back to the country. There they seem not to have done too well. It took quite a while to establish any kind of a balance between the city and rural populations.

The motto, "Back to the Village," is now supposed to bring about a return to the soil of young people, most of whom have grown up in cities. There is an additional reason for this campaign. It is easier to feed people in the country—easier to bring people to the food supply than to take the food supply to the people.

Measured against the total population, estimated roughly at 700 million, the number of students is still insignificant. But measured against the number of good positions available, there are already too many. The original goal of the communists, to educate an army of technicians and intellectuals, has turned out to be a handicap.

At the Peking Teachers College I sat opposite the deputy dean. At that time 5,134 students of both sexes were being trained as teachers there. After attending the university for five years they receive their diplomas and become secondary teachers or scientists.

I asked how many high school students applied for admission to the university and how many were actually accepted.

"We take one out of every ten applicants."

"What happens to the rest?"

"They can apply to other universities or switch to productive work. They can also take home study courses or TV lecture courses."

About four thousand students are registered for television courses, which are given jointly by several universities. At the end of each course the students must take the final examinations at a university.

The fact remains that at least eight out of ten high school

graduates are rejected by the universities. At the technical colleges the number is not quite so high, but here too the tendency is to send the graduate back to the village or into the factories.

But the screening is not restricted to pre-college students; it continues after graduation. "Before the Liberation there were many unemployed academicians. This is no longer true. Formerly it was possible to win diplomas and still have no way to earn one's daily bread." The deputy dean told me proudly, "Today the state sees to it that all graduates are employed."

"Does that mean that the state places university graduates?"

"Yes, the state finds work for them."

"Can the graduate choose his own place to work?"

The deputy dean, the representative of the communist youth league, the woman who represented the teachers' union, and the assistant Party secretary, who were all present throughout this interview, now began to discuss my question among themselves. They agreed on an answer, which I was able to verify later. The state supplies the graduate with a list of available positions. He makes his own selection from the list.

The state, therefore, can direct educated young people where they are most needed. Nowadays the lists include openings in remote areas, in the border provinces, in provinces which are just being opened up, where exploration for oil and coal is under way.

Again and again I met people working far from their homes, who had been transferred to job sites by the state.

Two hours later I visited the university students in their dormitories. I had been told that none of the universities allows the students to live at home. For five years they live and learn in the same surroundings, which include not only lecture rooms but common rooms and dormitories.

I asked some of the boys and girls what they intended to do after graduation. The answer was unanimous. "We will work wherever our country and the construction of socialism need us."

Had they no ambitions of their own?

Oh, yes. "We'd like to be sent to the remote provinces, to the border country," was the immediate answer.

The border country is far from hospitable. There are no towns, almost no villages, nothing but gigantic labor camps. Conditions are like those in California during the Gold Rush or in Siberia when Khrushchev appealed to Soviet youth to go east. As in the Soviet Union, the aim is to open up an immense virgin territory and to discover its resources and found industries so that people will settle there. Almost half of China's territories have not been developed. They are known to contain large reserves of minerals, coal, and oil which young settlers can extract for the benefit of their country.

I also asked the students about their background. I assumed that the ones I met had been carefully chosen, although I went to visit them in their living quarters. There were nine, four boys and five girls, and each had a different background. College students may be the children of peasants, laborers, soldiers, government officials, artists, railroad employees, etc.

I asked whether any special attention had been paid to their family origins when they applied for admission to the university. At first they denied it. "Young people of all backgrounds are welcome here. Only moral, academic, and physical fitness matter."

"What do you mean by moral fitness?"

"A candidate's behavior must be faultless, and he must be politically and ideologically unobjectionable."

"So your origin does matter, after all."

This upset my companions. "Not at all! Why should the child of intellectuals not be perfectly all right, politically and ideologically?"

I said, "Suppose his parents were bourgeois and continued to harbor bourgeois ideas?"

"Even so, the child may be all right politically."

This question was argued for some time. What they were trying to make me understand was clear: "It is not necessary to have a proletarian grandmother. Children from former or even recent bourgeois background are at no disadvantage, so long as they themselves are unreservedly devoted to communism."

I tried a different tack. "Suppose two candidates have the same academic and physical qualifications and the same qualities of character, but one comes from a bourgeois family and the other from a worker's family. Which one gets preference?"

At first they did not want to consider this a valid question. Candidates with identical qualifications hardly ever appeared. Then I was told, "Let us accept this hypothetical case. The laborer's child would be preferred. And do you know why? Because it is our duty to help the proletariat, those on a lower educational level, and to make a higher level of education available to them."

The universities operate on the principle that students must become familiar with productive labor during their student years. They are taken to factories and people's communes to help with the work. Liberal arts students must spend twenty-five weeks at productive labor during the five-year course, and science students, twenty-two weeks.

Students have an additional task to perform in the people's communes. They are supposed to work with the peasants, live, eat, and sleep with them, and write down their family histories.

"What is the purpose of that?"

"The students must learn how miserable the peasants' former existence was, how they suffered from the tyranny of the big landowners, and how much better off they are today. Also, these recitals help the peasants remember the bleak times they went through. Their histories become part of the village records."

Obviously, the establishing of such village records is meant to contribute to the ideological conditioning of the peasants, and of the students as well.

Chinese university training is among the most intensive in the world. At the Peking Teachers College there are no less than 58 professors and 929 instructors as well as 226 proctors for a student body of 5,134. That works out to one faculty member for every four students.

Learning is not restricted to the lecture rooms but goes on day and night under the guidance and supervision of the faculty. The university is simply but adequately furnished. In the English language classroom, primitive headsets are supplied for each student: two large rubber earphones connected to a tape recorder with thick wires. It is not a fancy piece of equipment, but the headset makes it possible to hear recordings of English broadcasts meticulously articulated. The Russian room has a primitive projector connected with a loudspeaker. The pictures thrown on the screen show the tools of everyday living and scenes from everyday life in Russia, and the commentary is in Russian.

The other classrooms are much the same. Teaching materials are often of the do-it-yourself variety, but they fill the need. The library has more than 1,600,000 volumes, making the knowledge of the entire world available, although for the most part books dealing with the West are accessible only to the teaching staff.

The reading rooms and lounges for foreign students are considerably better furnished. At the time of my visit there were only two, both Vietnamese, at the university. But in other university quarters in Peking—extensive areas with dozens of schools—I saw Negroes, Arabs, and Latin Americans.

Since the universities are coeducational, I was interested in finding out whether this presented any problems, whether any marriage counseling or birth control was provided. "We don't know of any such problems. It's not our business to deal with them," was the surprising reply.

Which prompted me to investigate this aspect of young Chinese life.

When, where, and how do young Chinese meet their future husbands and wives? And what is the attitude of the government toward love, marriage, and birth control?

17

Guided love and planned parenthood

Love of country, love for the Party, love for Mao Tse-tung, love for public property—these are found everywhere in China. Love between man and woman, or boy and girl, is almost never mentioned.

In high schools, where students are as old as nineteen, I was told that love doesn't exist among the students. "Our young people grow up in the spirit of the Revolution and social progress, and they have no time for love or the problems of sex," the principal of a Peking high school told me.

"Legally, a man can marry at twenty and a girl at eighteen. Our male students don't reach that age before they finish high school; our female students just barely reach it. Therefore the question doesn't concern us," he went on.

Education is carried out on behalf of the motherland, and all efforts are concentrated on it; no one falls in love in high school. Love at that age is unknown in China.

Since the graduates are nearly of marriageable age, and the girls have already reached it, I asked whether young people in their senior year are not prepared for marriage in some way. The answer was a flat no.

In the colleges I got much the same answer. Only about 1 per cent of the student body is married, and these without exception are people who worked together and were married before starting college. Wives and children may not live on campus, so they are separated from the husband and father for five long years.

In the Communist Youth Association, whose members are aged thirteen to twenty-five, I asked about the attitude of the Party toward love and marriage. I was told, "For us, the main question is the young couple's correct concept of love and marriage."

"What is the correct concept?"

"Both parties must have the same political ideology, and t.ieir main concern must be production."

The first of these requirements was clear enough from a communist viewpoint, but what was meant by the second?

"Only what is good for production is good for marriage. Work must take precedence over love, and a married couple must show a proper understanding of this."

In other words, a couple must renounce love and even marriage if the government, the Party, the factory, or the commune so decides. They do so decide when they separate young couples by assigning them to different cities or villages. They decide when they require overtime, night shifts, and special assignments. From married couples they may demand total dedication, forcing parents to leave their children in kindergartens or boarding schools. In the opinion of the Communist Youth Association and the Party, only those who are prepared to go to these lengths have the correct attitude toward love and marriage.

"Work must never be disturbed by love and marriage," the youth official went on. "Also, the couple must be immune to feudal and bourgeois ideas."

I wanted to know what he meant by that. The answer was somewhat surprising. "Above all, the parents must not be allowed to arrange the marriage, or to sell the bride." That was still possible, he implied, as has been the custom in China for thousands of years.

Further, "It may not be a marriage of convenience, that is, a marriage contracted because one of the partners owns property." The word "property" must not be understood in the Western sense, since there are no longer any propertied people in China. No one owns any land (even the small plot a peasant is allowed to cultivate for himself actually belongs to the commune). But for that very reason, certain consumer goods are regarded as property: wristwatches, radios, TV sets, bicycles, perhaps even a motor scooter (although I saw only one during my entire stay). It is also possible to own a small treasure in clothes or textiles or several pairs of shoes. And it is not impossible that parents might try to arrange a marriage for the sake of such material possessions.

The Youth Association is also against another "bourgeois idea." "Marriage should not be entered into because the bride is beautiful. That would be a bourgeois prejudice. We are against it."

What traits, then, should the bride have?

"Both partners ought to be progressive, hard-working, sound in mind and body."

A sound mind means, in the first place, being a good communist or at least enthusiastic over the social program and the new China. Accordingly, the youth official said, "Socialism has to come first in the life of the people. Marriage partners, the family, and children must take second place."

"Does the Youth Association provide marriage counseling?"

"Of course, we help the young people to found a progressive and revolutionary family."

That was not what I had meant. I tried to be more explicit. "Does the Youth Association help the young couple solve any marriage problems that may come up? Does it give them any instruction in married life?"

"If you mean sexual problems, these are not within our scope. They are medical problems. Bourgeois questions are no concern of ours."

"Why bourgeois?"

"Sexual problems play a role in bourgeois prejudices, but not with us."

I asked whether the newspaper published by the Communist Youth Association did not receive letters on marriage problems. I had been told that the editor got between six and seven hundred letters a day. But the answer was, "No, we have not had a single inquiry on this subject."

It seemed useless to hope that I could learn anything about love and marriage in today's China from official sources, other than the extremely puritanical views of the administration. So I changed the subject to birth control, a question that has had a long history in China. Democratic politicians in earlier times had asked for a strict program of population control. They had never succeeded in putting it into practice.

In the beginning the communists also felt that China's high birth rate ought to be reduced. After they came into power they began to propagandize birth control. But the policy was soon reversed. "Birth control is the watchword of our enemies. They want the Chinese to become extinct."

According to the new policy, since every human being is a part of the work force, and each work force makes for progress by strengthening China's economy, people ought to bring as many children into the world as before, if not more. This appeal revived the "Yellow Peril" fear among the Western nations.

But in the last few years things have changed a great deal. The government has soft-pedaled its slogans and exhortations, and its unreasonable demands on the people. How does it stand today on the subject of family planning?

I put the question often and to many kinds of people. I got a lot of different answers, but one fact emerged: At the universities, in the Youth Association, in the factories and communes the consensus was, "The Party does not want young people to get married before the age of twenty-five." As the official age of consent is eighteen and twenty, the question arises why the Party wants this waiting period. There are two answers. "The Party wants people to be mature and to have some experience before they undertake marriage. This way their marriages will be better and there will be fewer divorces." And "Young people ought to postpone having children as long as possible. This automatically limits their number, and the mothers remain healthier."

A prominent member of the Chinese government went into the question more fully. "We have adopted several birth control measures. Our experts have studied all the available methods in England, Sweden, Switzerland, and Japan. Today we use many different methods of preventing conception. Equipment and information are available to everyone, and we advise people to use them."

The reasons behind this were stated frankly. "We have learned that a small family is more useful to the state and to itself. With fewer children, parents can give each child better training. Thus they become better workers and a better qualified productive force."

Are all these explanations merely designed to allay the fears of China's neighbors that an increasing population will mean new pressure?

Judging from what I saw and heard in China, preventive methods have not made much headway as yet, but the approved marriage age of twenty-five is generally observed. All my doubts that young people would be held back from early marriage were dissolved by one sentence: "They need a marriage license, which is issued before twenty-five only in exceptional cases." Illegitimate children are not an "exceptional case," so a marriage cannot be forced on that ground. On the contrary, because of the prevailing morality, parents of such children meet with contempt and derision.

In the institutions of higher learning the young people are urged through instruction and ideological training not to form any romantic attachments. Likewise, the plays, films, and operas produced by the youth groups, although mainly intended for adults, serve a twofold purpose. Love occurs everywhere (in one movie I saw, four couples were romantically involved), but marriage is always depicted as far in the future. A young couple love each other, but they never even hold hands, much less kiss. It is really platonic love that is portrayed, in a manner almost painful to Westerners.

For example, in one film a girl discovers her girl friend knitting a pair of men's gloves, obviously intended as a present for a young man. The embarrassed knitter buries her face in her hands, then runs and hides in a corner of the room.

In the next scene the young lovers meet in a park. They have important things to talk about; a difficult problem has arisen at work and has to be discussed. They arrive at a solution which will double production. Both of them are ecstatic. They bid each other farewell. At that point the girl holds out the gloves to her boy friend and leaves swiftly. The young man stares at the gloves. Then he gets the idea. Dumfounded, he looks for the girl, who has long since disappeared. After another glance at the gloves, he presses them to his chest and then hides them under his sweater. Interestingly enough, the audience got very excited during this scene. There were loud comments, and some of the women giggled.

There was one further reference to love in this movie. The young lady in question, twenty-five years old and an engineer by profession, discovers her friend after midnight in his office. He has fallen asleep over a weighty mathematical computation, the results of which will be required by the factory in the morning. Until dawn, she works out his mathematical formula and leaves before he wakes. This too is a sign of love. . . .

This sort of puritanical morality is widespread in China nowadays. It is noticeable when one strolls through the parks in the evening. I have seen many young couples, but never lovers kissing.

Chinese puritanism is especially striking to a visitor from the West. Not one poster shows the face of a pretty girl. In Shanghai I saw a poster advertising ladies' hosiery. It pictured a few flowers. Women's dresses are advertised with flowers and samples of cloth.

In the movies, girls are shown as one actually sees them on the street: in shapeless trousers, white blouses, and pigtails or simple pageboy bobs. All sex appeal is carefully avoided.

I noticed that no special lingerie was offered in the women's wear sections of the department stores. All that was on display was the same kind of cotton undergarments that men wear. Since Chinese women are not particularly curvy to start with, the kind of clothing prevalent nowadays is even less flattering to them, at least to Western eyes.

Female restaurant and hotel employees seemed uncommonly stern. Although I was almost always waited on by women, they did not even so much as glance at me or any other foreigner. When I greeted them in the morning or thanked them for unusually good service their expression remained austere and unchanged. Most likely, this is meant to eliminate any personal contact between foreigners and the Chinese if daily work happens to bring them together.

Needless to say, in present-day China no form of commercial love is allowed. Foreigners who knew China in earlier times are astonished by this; they told me that China formerly surpassed all the other Oriental countries in that respect. Today this is hard to believe.

After the communist takeover, prostitutes—there were hundreds of thousands of them, especially in the seaports—were put into reform schools. Most of these girls could neither read nor write. They were taught these essentials and also required to work. An attempt was made to inculcate them with a "socialist morality" that went far beyond morality in our sense of the word. They were not only supposed to desist from their former way of earning a living, which had been declared illegal and was heavily punished, they were also supposed to be integrated into the state and the new social structure. Foreigners who visited the training schools at that time were particularly moved when they saw how these girls were persuaded to quit their former calling on the one hand, and how they were fed Marxist-Leninist doctrines on the other hand. No one was permitted to leave these "homes" until pronounced cured in the ideological sense, and sometimes in the medical sense as well. "You must not forget how needy the population was in the old days. If a family was to survive, at least one of its members had to earn a living—somewhere and somehow," I was told.

Some of the girls are said to have relapsed after their release from these centers. They were sent to camps for "re-education through work." In any case, the problem seems to have been entirely solved. Nowhere in China is there to be found even a trace of prostitution.

The opportunities for young people to meet and get to know each other seem to be limited. "Nowadays you get acquainted with your future husband or wife where you work." I was told that now and then dance music is played in the cultural centers and restaurants, but during my stay I never heard it in one of these places. Such entertainment seems to be rare.

While no one can get married in China these days without the permission of the state, in the old days it was not even customary to legalize the marriage contract. The marriage ceremony was a private affair between two families. Well-to-do Chinese announced the engagement in the newspapers. Marriage contracts were concluded between the families, and these documents were legally recognized.

To get divorced, an equally informal ceremony was sufficient. Man and wife or even just one party declared themselves divorced. This too might be announced in the papers by one of the parties if, say, the husband feared that his wife might still regard herself as married and contract debts in his name.

Although monogamy was legally enforced under Chiang Kai-shek, wealthy Chinese could and did own concubines until 1949, and the practice was overlooked. But since most of the wealthy Chinese who remained in China lost the greater part of their fortunes, or were forced to buy government bonds, which amounted to almost the same thing, they found it almost impossible to support the concubines and their children. In any case, polygamy is illegal and severely punished in today's China.

Equal rights, self-reliance, and independence for women are underscored by a decree according to which a girl need not assume the name of the man she marries. The propaganda urging young women to show their dedication to communism by retaining their maiden names is so intense that most of them do so. This complicates matters for a foreign visitor. When one is introduced to a married couple, two entirely different names are mentioned. If it is not expressly stated that they are husband and wife, one might guess that they merely live together. Also, husband and wife are never designated as such. If they mention the marriage partner to a third person they speak of him or her as "my beloved." This is the intent of communist colloquial usage, for to say "husband" or "wife" would indicate a condition of dependency that "exists only in bourgeois marriages."

On the other hand, I was often told—and later saw for myself —that it is relatively difficult to obtain a divorce in present-day China. Marriages today are officially registered; they are no longer a private transaction. Divorces must be sought by petition from the courts, which make a thorough investigation. The free love that some leaders endorsed in the youthful days of the communist movement does not exist in China any more than in the Soviet Union.

I got the impression that the family life of the Chinese is again intact, or as intact as it can be when husband and wife both work and have to turn their children over to grandparents, nursery schools, and kindergartens. However, this arrangement seems to intensify the parents' efforts to dedicate the evening hours and the free day to the children and the family.

As the Chinese people are now being granted a respite, as an eight-hour work day is scrupulously maintained, as the city population is given a day off each week, I asked how the Chinese spend their leisure time. I was soon to learn a great deal about it, especially in Shanghai.

18

Structured leisure

"Oh, so you're going to Shanghai too. You'll like that city. It's entirely different from, say, Canton or Wuhan or even Peking. There are other kinds of people there—cosmopolitan, if you know what I mean." This was my Chinese interpreter speaking, in Canton. He was a native of Shanghai, and his enthusiasm for that city was easy to understand.

But there was more to it than that. Shanghai really is something special among Chinese cities. No other has as many European and American traits, no other emanates such an international aura as does Shanghai to this day, even though its population no longer has much contact with the rest of the world. Naturally, ships still tie up in Shanghai's harbor: from Korea, Albania, now and then one from the West. But most ships with freight from Europe unload at the British crown colony of Hong Kong. On the Huang-po there are more junks than ocean liners these days. And yet thousands of people throng the quays every evening, just to get a breath of fresh air. They lean against the railings and look out over the water that once kept them in hourly touch with the rest of the world.

Behind the wide street along the river front, formerly known as the Bund, once lay the international European quarter. There were great hotels, banks, stores, business offices. Nowadays they are all owned and run by the state. But the people who work in them, it seemed to me, have retained much of their enthusiasm and animation, their international outlook. Many of them speak English or French, even if they are out of practice and approach foreigners hesitantly. They are proud of their city.

At first Shanghai was the stepchild of the new communist government. Before the communists came to power it had been the center of European, American, and Japanese activity. It was from Shanghai that the foreign powers and General Chiang Kai-shek directed their separate trade and China's economic development. And for the same reason it was the only truly modern industrial center in China. Hundreds of foreign firms had opened large and small branches there, and if the Chinese today insist that these were merely auxiliary or service branches, they cannot deny that Red China's large and complex industrial supplies were first obtained from the factories that remained.

Today the big buildings look gray and somewhat dilapidated. They have not been repaired for several years. But they are clean, and their elevators, switchboards, bank counters, and reception desks are still in good working order. I could tell that the bank employees were pleased to change foreign money again, to make use of their knowledge of English; they seemed to enjoy their "internationalism" when I changed a few dollars and pounds sterling.

The pedestrians even walked differently from their counterparts in other cities. They walked like cosmopolitans, briskly and busily. When I asked someone in English how to get to the post office, I was not stared at in surprised reticence but was immediately directed to the right street. Someone once offered to take me there. He wanted to know where I came from, what I was doing in China, whether I liked the country in general and Shanghai in particular.

In Shanghai there is still a British consulate general, the last trace of a large English enclave in this city. Some East bloc nations, too, have consular representation here. The Yugoslavs have left, the Soviets have closed their consulate—that is, they had to close it. On the other hand, I met many Albanians in Shanghai.

On the second day of my stay I discovered what particularly

A "coffee break" at Automobile Factory No. 1. Some of the workers play feather ball.

distinguished these people from the Chinese of other cities. They all seemed to share a joy of living, if expressed only in something so small as an extra bow in the hair of a young girl. But it goes without saying that communism has permeated even this city and controls the life of the twelve million inhabitants of Shanghai. Here too the day begins between five and six in the morning. And as in the other cities of China, it begins with morning exercises.

It's odd. In the large squares of Peking, in the parks, in front of the low village-type houses, the many people doing their exercises didn't seem as disturbing as in the narrow streets between Shanghai's tall buildings. Shanghai is the only Chinese city that has a European-American air; all the others have remained Chinese. Since the sidewalks in front of the tall buildings are too narrow to hold all the inhabitants at once, the exercises take place in the middle of the street.

In large groups, men and women are lined up in rows. Each is directed by a leader using a megaphone. He announces the exercise and then—"One, two three!" In the large squares, loudspeakers are turned on and the exercises are done to music. These morning gymnastics don't last just fifteen or twenty minutes; they usually go on for an hour and sometimes longer. Traffic comes to a standstill except on the main streets. I also saw columns of young men in gym suits running along the sidewalks; their morning exercises looked like a cross-country run.

Another group has no leader or loudspeaker. It practices another sport, shadow boxing, which has nothing to do with boxing but is almost the opposite. Slow, graceful movements are performed with the feet and legs, the arms, hands and fingers, with head and torso. It is like a slow-motion dance performed on one spot.

The shadow boxing is done alone or in groups. As it is an age-old form of exercise, there are people who have mastered its hundreds of forms perfectly. Others who practice it are beginners, and, it is said, they will need ten years to master it. Those who achieve mastery refuse to perform in a group. I could see how differences of opinion might arise in such a group, if one or another party departs from the established ritual. Apparently, the individual movements must be harmonized with one another. I watched youths and old men with bald heads and long, thin Chinese beards going through these difficult dance exercises together.

Mao Tse-tung urges people to perform gymnastics not only in the morning but at intervals during the workday and in the evening. Ordinarily a recommendation from Mao is as good as a command. But participation in the morning exercises, like so much else which the Party demands of the people, is voluntary. A few students told me that they did not participate; they even repeated the excuses they resorted to when teachers and friends asked where they had been during the morning exercise period.

Nevertheless, I got the feeling that for the most part the people enjoy taking part in these exercises, particularly the shadow boxing. In the factories, too, I often saw workers gathered for their exercises in front of the workshops during their "coffee break."

In general, sports are popular in China. The Chinese are famous for their first-class table tennis players, and I saw many large and small halls in which ping-pong was played on a dozen or two dozen tables. Basketball is another popular sport. Baskets are mounted at almost every street corner, and there are small basketball courts in many back yards. Soccer is also favored, and I saw many soccer fields, but it is a poor second to basketball. Chinese spectators go wild at matches, cheering for their teams and celebrating their victories with enthusiasm.

Formerly the East bloc countries sent their national basketball champions to China. Nowadays the international sports matches are restricted mostly to entrants from Albania, Cuba, North Viet Nam, and North Korea. In Peking, as in other cities, the government has built large stadiums for basketball and soccer, and games are scheduled frequently.

Those who do not care for sports have other ways of amusing themselves in the evenings. I shall say more about the theater and cinema in chapters to follow. The Chinese are passionately devoted to films, theater, and especially the opera. But there are other entertainment possibilities. Acrobatic performances are extremely popular and China is famous for its acrobats. Many large groups of them come to the cities to perform and also appear in the villages. Their feats are often breathtaking.

I attended several such performances. At home I am indifferent to variety shows and don't care much for acrobatics, but I found these Chinese performances rather enjoyable. I soon discovered why: it was the only form of amusement which did not subject me to the constant propaganda barrage. No film, no stage show, no opera in China is without tendentiousness; actors recite whole passages that make them sound just like Party functionaries, endlessly repeating the slogans of the state and Party. The acrobats are silent. When they open their mouths it is to imitate the voices of birds or other animals.

In Shanghai, before the communists took over, there used to be a great amusement center called "The Great World." It was famous all over the Far East; everyone who came to Shanghai simply had to see it. But even then it was, of course, the exact opposite of "the great world." It offered amusement for the little man, the lower classes. There were cabarets, operettas, songs in the dialects of the many provinces, something for the people from out of town. There were shooting galleries, refreshment stands, and all the rest. Because "The Great World" attracted tourists, it was also known as a marketplace for the city's lesser vices.

The real "great world" took its pleasures in the nightclubs of Shanghai, which are said to have had no equal anywhere in the Far East. Hong Kong's bars always had British closing hours— eleven P.M.—and those of Tokyo, which today rank with those of Paris, were just getting started.

Today one searches in vain for a nightclub or even a bar in Shanghai. The best British hotel, the Cathay, which is now called the Peace Hotel, has closed its bar, once the largest in China. In contrast with the hotel for foreigners in Peking, the Hsichiao, even foreign visitors are not served.

"The Great World" has now been renovated and reopened after several years of disuse. Yet like the people, it has changed. Outwardly it looks the same: there are six opera stages, two theatrical stages, an open air movie theater, and various innocent amusements, such as a fun house with distorting mirrors, a ball-pitch, shooting galleries, and chuck-a-luck. Interspersed among these are refreshment stands and snack bars. Although wine and spirits are available, most people drink beer; the price of anything stronger is too steep for the natives.

Here as in other Chinese cities the main attraction is the acrobats, who perform in the largest open-air arena. When they are due to appear, the crowds on the other floors thin out and the operas and theaters are almost deserted.

There is still a cabaret in "The Great World," but I heard no satirical comments on the government or, God forbid, the Party, or even about the daily routine. The jokes were confined to human weaknesses and everyday family happenings, and there was only a small audience.

Large chessboards were set up on one of the terraces. The best players in Shanghai come here night after night to use these huge squares. The boards are big enough so that the spectators can follow the moves, and they follow them on their own boards, which they bring along for that purpose. The game is played Chinese style, without chessmen but with round counters on which the value of the pieces is indicated in Chinese characters. Otherwise it is not very different from our chess.

"The Great World" is unique in China; no other city has so many facilities for amusement under one roof. But all cities have a similar institution: the cultural park. Upon payment of a small admission fee, the visitor finds several stages, merry-go-rounds, and usually a tent for acrobatic performances.

But the greatest innovation communism has brought to the worker's leisure is the culture palace, built and run by the unions. "Our palace of culture was opened in 1958. It is an expression of the Party's and the union's interest in the cultural life of the workers," the director of one such center in Shanghai told me. Ideology has first place in the culture palace. "It is the duty of the Party to educate the workers in the spirit of socialism by giving them scientific and cultural knowledge, raising their intellectual and ideological level." Only when all this is provided does the culture palace try to "enrich life during the hours of leisure."

The terrace of the "culture palace" I visited has an area of more than sixty thousand acres. "Here we have three theaters, an ice-skating and a roller-skating rink, a basketball court, three exhibition rooms, sixty recreation rooms, a library and a tea-house."

There are said to be twenty-one such culture palaces in Shanghai alone, all about the same in size and facilities. I went through one. First came a hall labeled "Palace of Knowledge," equipped with large blackboards covered with drawings and Chinese characters. What purpose do they serve?

The first dealt with superstition, including religion; but not overtly. An "explanation of man's dreams" was given, how dreams originate, what they express and why. In yesterday's China people must have had a strong belief in dreams and their interpretations, but today's Chinese communists must not be influenced by such superstitions.

The second board dealt with common illnesses prevalent at that time of year; the third with the effects of exposure to strong sunshine. The fourth was slightly ideological in tone: it concerned eating and the chemical processes of digestion that go on in the human body, and the ailments engendered by a bad diet. A part of this, too, was directed against superstition.

Other boards described the functioning of the brain and nervous system, and the origin of the mental processes. Finally there was one dealing with foreign countries. At the time I was there it showed a map of Pakistan and described the land and its people. Pakistan is in high favor in China as a friendly neighbor. That it is also a member of two Western defense alliances was not mentioned.

Shortly before leaving the "Palace of Knowledge" I received an enlightening explanation of the relation between quality and quantity in productive work. The purpose was to show precisely the limits within which a man can get maximum production without endangering quality. As ordered by Mao Tse-tung, the aim seemed to be to use creative intervals to increase production.

In the next room there was a storyteller. There used to be tens of thousands of storytellers in China, wending their way from village to village and telling beautiful old tales about emperors and princes, nobles and courtiers, or about knights, robbers, and brave peasants. Their appearance in the village was the signal for a celebration.

Here in the workers' culture palace was a representative of this age-old institution. He talked animatedly, and the listeners were spellbound. "What is he saying?" I asked my traveling companion. "I don't know if you are familiar with it, but to us it's a famous book, *The Daughter of the Party*." I was familiar with it. It is one of the great standard works of the new Chinese communist literature, intended especially for young people. We went on and passed the library, which functions on a very simple level. There are no catalog files. The books stand on shelves behind panels of glass that are slitted. If a browser finds a book he likes, he pokes a finger through the slit and pushes the volume so that it falls on its side. The librarians bring the designated book and charge it out.

We came to the practice rooms for amateur artists. These were humming with activity. In some, dance groups from different factories were rehearsing dances that dramatized modern themes, such as the revolution, running a blast furnace, homage to Mao Tse-tung. In another room a harmonica band practiced.

In another room workers' paintings were exhibited; the next displayed photographs of exemplary men and women workers, all with medals on their chests.

Another exhibition preserved Shanghai's past. Old photographs, photocopies of newspaper clippings and documents depicted "the miserable lives of Shanghai's workers under the yoke of imperialism." There were pictures of workers on strike, street battles, many dead bodies, and much blood. Also shown were buildings of the English, French, and American firms formerly located in the city. In the middle of the room were busts of once prominent communists who had been executed.

We now entered a theater with room for an audience of 1,350. It was air-conditioned, and in contrast with the outdoor temperature of 100° in the shade, it was cool. This was the only place in Shanghai where I found air-conditioning. An opera was in progress, starring "an agent of the Chiang Kai-shek clique" and an elegantly dressed lady—a type no longer seen, in China's theaters or elsewhere.

"When we liberated Shanghai, the reactionaries thought the Red Army would soon be demoralized," my companion said. "This opera shows the attempts of the imperialists to corrupt our soldiers. It goes without saying that these attempts failed miserably."

We visited yet another auditorium in which amateur magicians were doing their tricks. And in the sports square of the culture palace a film was being shown under the open sky. Next to it the ubiquitous acrobats were performing, and here too they had the largest audience.

In the teahouse, refreshments were served. "Every day we have several thousand visitors in our culture palace." The expenses of the culture palace are met by the union. They amount to 500,000 yuan ($200,000) a year in round figures. Seventy-two full-time officials administer the palace and see to it that there is always a richly varied program. Lay groups are engaged without remuneration, but the ensembles of the Shanghai opera and the theater, who appear quite regularly, are paid.

In principle, even the culture palace is a medium for the dissemination of propaganda, but in addition to the activities I have described, hobby groups are organized for the workers and there are do-it-yourself groups for assembling radios, operating short-wave equipment, building models, and collecting stamps. Stamp collecting is very popular in China; on Sundays hundreds of people congregate at postal stations to trade duplicates and buy special issues.

Leaving the Shanghai culture palace, I noticed a large statue of Mao Tse-tung in the vestibule. In front of the door my rented car was waiting. Hundreds of visitors surrounded it. When I got in, they applauded. Wherever there is a car, there is usually a visitor from abroad; and, true to the guiding principle of "proletarian internationalism," he is welcomed.

19

A visit to China's Hollywood

In the foyer of a movie theater in Peking—just as at home—hang numerous portraits of familiar film stars. I asked my interpreter whether movie stars were very popular in China. Instead of answering, he wanted to know what I meant by "popular." "Do young girls hang portraits of film stars on the walls of their rooms, or do young men own pin-ups of stars?" He bridled at this idea and rejected it. "Nothing of that sort happens in this country. No such honors are accorded an actor."

Indeed, until now, in all the homes, canteens, and students' dormitories that I had visited, I had seen nothing but pictures of political leaders or photos of relatives. And yet the film is one of the communist government's principal means of spreading propaganda. Even so, audiences are supposed to admire the roles being played and not the actors, in such parts as, for instance, a wise Party secretary, or fearless heroes of the army or the labor force.

In Changchun, in northeast China, I was invited to inspect a movie studio. Thus I came to visit one of the small Hollywoods of the new China. Here, as everywhere else, I was ushered first into the reception hall, with its large, overstuffed furniture, lace tidies, and teacups. Here, as everywhere else, the first thing I heard was the history of the enterprise.

I was told that the studio was founded in 1945, forced to evacuate by Chiang Kai-shek, and moved to a coal mine by the communist underground. "At that time, all we turned out were documentaries about land reform and the War of Liberation. Only in 1949, after the Liberation, did we try to produce feature films. To date we have shot 167 such features. This year, the government has given us a quota of nine films; we believe that we can put twelve in the can."

The studio head recalled the first film: "It was called *The Bridge* and was a sensation. For the first time in China the laboring class was portrayed in a film."

He cited the various guidelines for the production of movies as promulgated by Party Chairman Mao Tse-tung: "Art and literature must serve the workers, peasants, and soldiers." They thus serve the sole representative of the Chinese worker, peasant, and soldier—namely the Communist Party.

Hence, only films that follow the current Party line are produced. Movies lacking such a message, let alone comedies, are nonexistent (although humor is often used). Each movie studio in China has a regular staff of actors, scenario writers, directors, camera-men, technicians, etc.

"Are there enough good leading actors so that each studio can produce full-length films?" I asked.

"In China, there are about a hundred actors who are especially good and are well-liked by the public. They are apportioned to the various studios, where they remain. Our staff here is roughly 1,500 people. They all live in quarters owned by the studio. This is their home; their children attend school here, and even the schools were built by the studio. If another studio wants to borrow a performer from us for a particular role that he alone is able to do well, we lend him out gladly. There is no rivalry. The studios exist to serve the people, and so each studio's only concern is the progress of all of them."

I asked whether there were stars—actors especially popular and sought after by each studio. "I know exactly what you mean," he answered. "I am aware of the star system in Europe and in America. I know that the promise of high salaries in America has lured

A movie studio in Changchun, one of the small "Hollywoods" of China. The scene is from a film which focuses on the class struggle in the villages.

French and Swiss stars to Hollywood. No, nothing like that exists here. A movie actor is a worker just like any other. He serves the country and the Party."

Just the same, the wage scale for "creative artists" differs from that of other workers. There are sixteen wage categories. Those who have just graduated from a high school for drama or for the film arts (and there are such schools) belong in category ten or eleven (category one being the highest). They receive roughly 60 yuan ($24) a month. In the studio I visited, the principal actors were in category five and earned 325 yuan ($130) a month. With this, they were as well paid as the manager of a large factory or the chief of staff of a hospital.

"But earnings are not governed by the type of roles an actor plays or by how popular he is with audiences," said the studio head. "Seniority and performance are the determining factors. We have some actors who play many leading roles and are popular. But they are still young and belong in categories nine and ten."

I suggested that this didn't seem equitable; a leading player in a leading role, even if young, contributes more than a supporting player in a supporting role, though he may be older.

"You're looking at this the wrong way," the studio head replied. "The role has nothing to do with it. Everyone works in the service of the nation. Therefore, only the years of service count. There is no such thing as the star system."

And then the studio head said something that illuminated the present relations between China and the Soviet Union. "Our system is very good. It would be impossible here for a leading performer to receive 20,000 rubles for a role while other performers receive a mere 300 rubles, as is customary in certain countries today. Such a system leads to the creation of a bourgeois class, is detrimental to an ordered society, and in addition damages the relations among performers." He did say "rubles," smiling meaningfully.

We got back quite soon, openly this time, to the subject of the Soviet Union. The movie studio not only turns out its own films; it also dubs in productions from foreign countries. Altogether, this studio dubbed in, from 1949 to 1965, 590 foreign films.

"Most of these originated in other socialist countries, but

we have also dubbed in some progressive films from capitalist countries."

Most of the films from the "other socialist countries" were Russian. Formerly the studio dubbed in thirty-five Russian films a year, but the number had decreased lately. In 1964 there were only seventeen such films. I asked why.

The studio head became animated. "Revisionism is prevalent today in Soviet art and literature. The Soviet Union is turning out films that distort the heroic picture of the Soviet people. The Chinese public does not want to see such things. They used to like Soviet films, especially those of the thirties, and they have learned to admire the Soviet people and their heroic armies. Our people do not want this impression destroyed."

I asked which Soviet films could lead to disillusion. The studio head had the titles down pat. "For example, *The Ballad of a Soldier,* or perhaps *The Cranes Are Flying.* How is Soviet man depicted? The Soviet soldiers are shown to be cowards. The Chinese people cannot understand how the Soviet army could have ever achieved victory if such cowards had been in its ranks!"

In my opinion, it is not the aspect of "cowardice" that prompts the Chinese to reject Soviet films. Rather, it is because a basically more liberal viewpoint is expressed in these films, a desire for property and a humanism that run counter to Peking's Stalinistic concepts.

Who decides whether a film is ideologically pure? Naturally, none other than the public. Or so stated the studio head. "Initially we did not limit the importation of Soviet films. We continued with our dubbing-in. But the public protested; we were asked why we imported such films. So we acted on the wishes of the public."

Now I turned to the "progressive films from the capitalist countries."

From the United States, naturally enough, no films at all are imported, not even "progressive" ones. At the top of the list are films from France. Unfortunately, only the Chinese titles were available, but some of these could be translated, for example, *Forbidden Games, If the Nations of the World Act Thus,* and *Without Address.*

From England: *Laughter in Paradise* and *The Millionairess.*

From Italy: *11 o'Clock in Rome* and *No Peace Under the Olive Trees.*

From Japan: *Street Without Sun, 24 Eyes,* and *The Last Women.*

From Switzerland: *Heidi.*

Other films, whose titles were not mentioned, were imported from Egypt, Spain, Greece, Mexico, and Argentina.

Each film is shown almost simultaneously in the movie houses and on TV. Because the Party wants a particular film to evoke a particular reaction in the public at a particular time, distribution must be as broad as possible.

I was also conducted over the grounds of the movie studio. A small Hollywood, it encompassed 325,000 square yards, of which one-sixth was occupied by the studio itself. Besides the studio grounds proper, the layout included the living quarters of the studio personnel, approximately 48,000 square yards. Although not all of the 1,500 people employed by the studio live there, the allotted space did not come to more than five or six square yards per inhabitant. "The actors do not receive any more room than anyone else," it was emphasized. Apologetically, the studio head added, "As you know, our level is still low." By level, the Chinese mean standard of living.

I scrambled through a great deal of scenery, most of which represented living quarters and inns. There was not one room without a picture of Mao Tse-tung hanging on a wall. Even in the basement of the studio I found many pictures of Stalin and a number of gilded busts of Mao.

In one of the courts of this movie city, a dozen women were busy making artificial trees. It was Saturday afternoon. "Those are office employees. On their day off, they help with production work," my guide explained.

I said good-bye and left the studio. In the driveway leading to the main entrance was a sort of monument: the group of figures that is invariably shown, spotlighted, before each main feature, somewhat like the MGM lion—a peasant, a female laborer, and a soldier.

According to Chairman Mao Tse-tung's precepts, art and literature must serve the Chinese peasants, workers, and soldiers.

Just at that time the newspapers of China were featuring government-sponsored editorials and lead articles under the headline, "A Great Revolution on the Cultural Front." They referred to the Peking opera. Thus, fifteen years after the communist takeover, one of the most effective cultural forces in the country was pressed into the service of the Party.

20

The dragon king as commissar

Upon arriving in Peking I immediately asked to have tickets for the Peking opera. But I had to wait ten days. The opera houses were reported to be sold out and the theaters jammed. Frankly, I didn't believe it. I thought there was some reluctance to let me see the opera because it had nothing to do with the new China or with communism. The Peking opera has a tradition hundreds of years old, and is not, as I thought at first, just one opera house. That is, there is no Peking opera in the sense of La Scala or New York's Metropolitan. Peking opera is a dramatic form. It is by no means confined to one opera house in Peking, but is performed in various theaters and culture palaces all over Peking and in other Chinese cities as well. There are dozens if not hundreds of groups performing Peking opera.

In China, there are significantly more opera performances than movies or plays. Shanghai, for example, has only forty movie houses and more than one hundred opera stages. That indicates the popularity of this art form with the Chinese people.

Certain figures are always present in classic Peking opera: emperors and empresses, princes and princesses, dukes and mandarins, demons and spirits and famous heroes. The costumes are unsurpassed for beauty and color. The orchestra uses only traditional Chinese instruments, mostly stringed instruments (with one or two strings), drums, and cymbals. To our ears, the music seems atonal and merely serves as background for the actual performance. An authentic Peking opera often lasts four, five, or six hours. The dramatic content is conveyed by the movements and gestures of the actors, rather than by the lyrics.

One morning my Chinese interpreter showed up beaming. "We have two tickets to the Peking opera!" That evening we drove to a culture palace. We had scarcely reached the area where the palace was located when I noticed a number of policemen in white uniforms and tropical helmets on the streets. The usually thin automobile traffic had multiplied astoundingly. When we arrived at the culture palace there was an impressive line of cars reaching up to the entrance, especially large Soviet-made sedans with the curtains drawn.

I thought this was a special performance for some high officials. But I saw peasants in their patched shirts and pants, workers with calloused hands, and Young Pioneers leading blind people to their seats.

From one of the Soviet cars emerged an elderly woman, white-haired, wearing a silk blouse and gold brooch. An usher jumped up and by elbowing people aside cleared a path through the crowd for her. "She is the wife of one of our great poets," my interpreter said in an awed voice. But she did not get a seat of honor; she sat down among the peasants. The same was true of all the other officials.

The spectators talked animatedly, with many gestures, often across several rows. When they saw someone they knew, they would stand up, wave, and call out. There was hearty laughter. There were no refreshment stands in the foyer, but street vendors were selling ice cream in front of the opera house, and some of the audience entered with ice-cream sticks and popsicles. In Europe they eat bonbons during intermissions at the theater and movies; in the United States, soft drinks and popcorn, but in China all the spectators eat cloves of garlic. During the performance and intermission my neighbors devoured this wholesome vegetable while fluttering their fans, since there was no air-conditioning and the temperature was about ninety-five. Under these conditions it was all I could do to hold out for the entire performance, which lasted between three and four hours.

The curtain rose, the music sounded, but the audience was not to be diverted from its own conversations. It was about five minutes before silence prevailed in the auditorium and the voices of the singers rose above those of the audience.

I was astonished by what I saw on the stage. There were no emperors, no princes, no mandarins or demons, but instead, workers, peasants, Party secretaries, soldiers, and "Chiang Kai-shek bandits."

The orchestra still plays the old tunes that were traditional in Peking opera, where the melodies were always the same, only put together in different sequences to suit the action. If I had been unable to see the performers it would have been exactly like the old Peking opera, especially since nobody understands what is being sung. The notes are drawn out to such length that the words are completely lost. For this reason the libretto is projected onto a screen alongside the stage, so the audience can read what is being sung. My interpreter supplied a running translation.

In this story, a prisoner of a village tyrant has fled and meets in a forest some prisoners of the Chiang Kai-shek government who have also managed to escape. They decide to form a band to fight Chiang Kai-shek and the rich landlords on behalf of the poor peasants.

But they make one mistake after another and soon begin to realize that they need strong leadership. Learning that a communist commissar is to be executed in a nearby village on the following day, they decide to prevent the execution and ask the commissar to assume leadership of the band.

In the next scene, the "Chiang Kai-shek bandits" are seen preparing for the execution under the direction of a big landowner. But no man is led to the gallows. Rather it is a woman, sore and bleeding from the tortures inflicted on her. In an aria sung under the gallows she prophesies the fall of the Chiang Kai-shek clique, and the rise of a new China in which the peasants and workers will be happy. As the noose is being placed around her neck, the band of escapees appears and in unparalleled acrobatics, with somersaults and leaps, they join battle with the soldiers and win.

Now they ask the lady commissar to take over the leadership of their band. But that is impossible. The communist guerrillas are under discipline. They must obey the orders of the Central Committee. A band of escaped peasant convicts is not capable of doing so. They are still filled with the bourgeois spirit, as the lady commissar explains. However, she is willing to give them advice. But she keeps coming up against the peasants' lack of understanding. They want to attack where reason would indicate retreat. They want to kill the well-to-do peasants, whereas these should be "reformed and turned into new human beings." In other words, the men cannot really "distinguish between friends and enemies." Also, some of them are not really interested in establishing the dictatorship of the proletariat but are merely out to enrich themselves through robbery and theft. Thus, the lady commissar finally declares herself willing to travel with the band and teach them discipline —that is, to train them ideologically.

This disciplinary training continues for four acts. The dramatic climax comes when the men decide to attack a village in which Chiang Kai-shek's troops are quartered. The Central Committee of the Communist Party sends a messenger to ask them not to attack. But the lady commissar, who wants to follow the committee's instructions, finds herself talking to deaf ears. The men will not obey.

In desperation, the lady commissar practices self-criticism and sings an aria lamenting her failure. But then she acts. While the band rushes to its doom, she brings reinforcements from a nearby unit of the Red Army. The tide of battle turns in the nick of time, the class enemies among the fighters are unmasked, the band repents its lack of discipline and demands to be accepted into the Red Army.

The audience followed all this avidly, cheering and applauding when the Red Army attacked and wildly elated when the class enemies were exposed.

Later I attended several other Peking operas. The music was always the same, but the action varied considerably.

There were the vain young men who worked only to obtain material comforts. Their behavior resulted in damage to public property (machinery) and danger to their fellow-workers. There were the village youths who had learned new methods of raising livestock but had to fight their elders' insistence upon traditional methods.

There was the young girl who was tired of the heavy work in her village and wanted to move to a richer village. She married a young man who lived there, even though she was not really in love with him. Retribution followed, and she realized that her place was really with the peasants in her native village.

One opera was even based on a firemen's unit that comprised both competent and lazy firemen. The lazy ones almost caused a catastrophe, thereby endangering the bride of one fireman, who was rescued at the last minute from the burning house. Thus the lazy firemen were led to realize how badly they had behaved.

I noticed that in all these operas no one ever called on the police or the courts for help. It was always the Party secretary who intervened with help or advice, and it was he who graciously forgave the gravest faults. He was always eager to save the souls of idlers, daredevils, and even those who had rejected his advice, the tenets of the Party, and the law. And he was always successful.

Everybody was converted in the last act. They all became new human beings and took their stand for socialism and communism, without any reservations. Even those who had appeared as class enemies in the first act, who admitted that they were opposed to the Party, and who pursued the "old bourgeois goals" for three or four hours, were "re-educated."

These Peking operas were also broadcast on television and radio. Above the stage there was always the new Party slogan: "Weed out the old so that the new can grow."

Thus the Peking opera has been drafted overnight into the service of the Party. Gone are the classic plots, gone are the colorful old costumes, gone are the emperors and princes and demons. The transformation is complete.

Outwardly, the change was accomplished in a day. The central organ of the Chinese Communist Party demanded in a lead article that the Peking opera should serve the "workers, peasants, and soldiers," in accordance with the instructions of Chairman Mao Tse-tung, and on the following day the new-style Peking operas were being staged.

How many months or years it had taken to prepare for this transformation behind the scenes is another matter. Dozens, perhaps hundreds of new librettos had to be written. The singers and actors had to learn and rehearse their new roles, the new costumes had to be made, new scenery had to be built. But no one talked about the great commotion that was taking place behind the scenes of the Peking opera.

The change occurred at the touch of a button, and, incidentally, not without a sly dig at the equivalent changeover in the Soviet Union. The same lead article that gave the signal for the transformation of the Peking opera had this passage: "We have already seen, in the literature and art of modern revisionism, how they spread bourgeois theories of human nature, humanism, pacifism, and so on and so forth; how they do their utmost to oppose revolution, to attack the dictatorship of the proletariat and try to ruin the socialist system. To their stages they bring the decaying and degenerate modern art of American imperialism, spreading propaganda for the American way of life and poisoning the minds of the masses in the socialist countries, particularly the younger generation, whose will power is weakened and becomes spiritually and morally corrupt."

I was told that old-style Peking operas will still be presented now and then, but only those "of a progressive character." None of the old-style operas was performed while I was in China. Groups of players were urged to take the new operas into the villages and back country, to bring the cultural revolution into every home throughout China.

All other forms of opera in China, and there are many, had to be adapted overnight to the new style. After a fifteen-year wait, and having already converted the films and the theater, the communist government has now placed the most popular of all art forms at the service of the continuing revolution.

I was told that the old-style Peking opera was poorly attended during the last few months of its existence. "The masses were no longer interested in that old stuff." Now people fight for admission tickets, and those who must return a ticket to the box office are likely to have it torn out of their hand in front of the culture palace. The Party can point to this as evidence that "the masses have given their vote of approval to the new Peking opera."

21

In Automobile Factory No. 1

Like other communist countries, China must surely have a "new class"—that is, a stratum of high Party and government functionaries whose standard of living differs substantially from that of the rest of the people, a group that enjoys a number of special privileges. In the Chinese cities and in the country as well, I was on the lookout for indications that such a "new class" existed. I found them—and then again, I did not.

In the cities of the Soviet Union, particularly in Moscow, a visitor soon notices that the center strip of the street is marked by two white lines and is set off from the other traffic lanes. This center strip is the lane reserved for cars that have priority; for example, fire engines, police cars, and emergency vehicles such as ambulances. It is also used by official Party and government vehicles. There is no such arrangement in China. It would be superfluous in any case, since those who travel by car automatically belong to a privileged class, if we overlook the few private capitalists in Shanghai who can still afford cars of their own. Hence cars have the right of way everywhere.

As I mentioned before, the traffic signals switch to green at the approach of a car if the driver honks his horn at the policeman in time. Although in principle traffic keeps to the right, drivers are free to make their way through clusters of bicycles and tricycle rickshas, no matter which side of the street they are on. Cyclists and pedestrians make way when a car approaches, and to make sure that they do, drivers honk their horns almost constantly. But I never saw a pedestrian who, reaching safety, cursed or shook his fist or gave vent to his feelings. It is evident that the privilege is respected.

Not far from the Hsinchiao Hotel, where I stayed in Peking, there is a large new building; incidentally, it was the most modern structure I saw in Peking. It is the headquarters of the Communist Party. The first time I walked past it, a Mercedes was just coming out of the driveway, its rear windows covered by curtains.

Because passenger cars are a great rarity in China, passersby eye each one and try to identify the occupants—hence the drawn curtains. But the make and model of a car serve as clues to the rank of the passenger. An old Muscovich means a middle-echelon official. A Volga means a higher official. Then come the older Soviet luxury cars, the Zim and Zil, and finally the cars made in China—"Phoenix," "The East Glows," and "Red Flag."

In northeast China, formerly Manchuria, I was chauffeured for three days around the countryside bounded by Shenyang, Fushun, and Anshan. This is the great industrial center of China. Again and again, smokestacks emerged from between the hills and I saw workshops and the terraces of surface mines. Railroad tracks crossed our road. While China does not yet boast many concrete roads, in this section of the country they had all been blacktopped and were in fine condition. They were just wide enough for two trucks to pass.

There were hours on end when I saw no trucks, and during the entire three days we did not meet a single car. But the roads were not empty. Long columns of workers and peasants walked along them in single file. Innumerable hand-drawn carts passed, as well as those pulled by horses and donkeys. The people who rode in these carts often had the strangest appearance. When it was raining, they wore overcoats of reeds or bamboo leaves, with wide Chinese straw hats on their heads. That seems to be the rainy-day gear of the rural Chinese; in the cities I saw plastic raincoats, although they were of poor quality and all the same color.

These reed-covered columns blended into the Asiatic landscape, where, between industrial centers, little plots of earth are tilled and broad irrigation ditches cut through the fields. There are hundreds of mulberry and willow trees, and green hills softly break the horizon. And the village houses with their curved thatched roofs harmoniously complement those wide straw hats worn by their inhabitants.

Only when we approached a large city or industrial plant did the greenery give way to the black of coal and soot. Instead of bamboo coats and straw hats, the people here wore blue overalls and visored caps.

The workmen's housing projects skirting the plants made a desolate impression on me. For the most part they consisted of low one-story huts, the walls made of mud with corrugated tin roofs arching over them. "Those are left over from the time of the Japanese occupation," my interpreter told me. "We are in the process of replacing all these with new housing projects."

Some of the new housing projects soon came into view. Although they had just been built, they looked as if they had been standing there fifty years or more. Exposure to weather and smoke had aged the brick façades. Most of the buildings were four or five stories high and spaced about one hundred to one hundred fifty feet apart. "Social greenery" was not much in evidence when I saw them, although efforts were being made to supply it. In Anshan thousands of trees had been planted between the buildings, and they seemed to be doing well. "Not everything can be done at once. The expansion of industry comes first. The workers have had to make do with temporary accommodations. Now we have built the projects, and in time we'll be able to beautify them," my interpreter hastened to explain.

But whether in Peking or Nanking, Fushun or Anshan, I looked in vain for better houses or villas in which officials might be living. Nowhere else, in all my previous travels through remote corners of the world, had I been conscious of such a lack of what we in the West could call a "cultural oasis." A lonely, almost forlorn feeling crept over me. Although there was always a hotel with neat, pleasant rooms (and most of them even had private bathrooms), it made me uncomfortable not to see a single house behind the windows of which I could imagine people living what we consider a normal life. Present-day cities in Africa, South America, the rest of Asia, and the countries of East Europe undoubtedly have their share of rundown neighborhoods and their slums, but they also have modern sections that are pleasing to our eyes and meet our standards of housing. These are lacking in China. Here I found myself in a milieu that we know only through descriptions of the early period of European industrialism, without being really able to imagine such a way of life.

I have been told that top Chinese Party and government functionaries are well but not luxuriously housed nowadays. Mao Tsetung, for example, whose residence in Peking looks from the outside like a small palace, occupies only a one-story house in the courtyard. It is said to be furnished in simple East European style and devoid of all luxuries. His former fellow-campaigners and the politicians today are said to live in equally unpretentious quarters nearby.

Even in the old days there were only a few villas in the European style, and those few were situated on the outskirts of the large port cities. Well-to-do Chinese lived in compounds similar to our country estates. "Most of these buildings have been turned into children's homes, culture centers, or libraries," my interpreter explained. But I suppose that the mansions formerly occupied by ministers, high-ranking army officers, state officials, and politicians of the Chiang Kai-shek government are still available to the same types of persons in the present regime. It is just that they are not in evidence, since they are located on estates or behind high walls. This seems to be typical of the urban Chinese generally; he likes to have his own house surrounded by a wall and thus cut off from his neighbors.

It is also probable that special sections in the department stores, where foreigners can buy imported merchandise and consumer goods of deluxe quality, are also open to high dignitaries. I have been told that they also have special stores such as are found everywhere in Eastern Europe, stores carrying a much wider and better selection of merchandise at low prices. But these shops are not to be seen, at least by foreigners.

At airports I noticed some people who, unlike the other Chinese in their shirts and pants, wore uniform-like suits and seemed usually to be saying good-bye to wives and children. They obviously occupied high positions and so could afford the expensive suits, and their wives and children were also well dressed. I was unable to find out whether they were government, Party, or business officials. But even they had to wait in line at the ticket counter, the same as everyone else, and they did not get reserved seats on the planes. However, upon arrival they were met by large cars.

The people who shared my first-class sleeping car had also been brought to the station in cars and were met by other cars.

In the restaurants, which in other communist states are often frequented by the privileged classes, I saw no tables reserved for such persons. But as there are no waiting lines in any restaurant, and free tables are plentiful, they find seats just as others do. To eat in a restaurant is quite expensive in terms of a Chinese income. It costs from 3 to 10 yuan, which, on an average income of 60 yuan, is quite a large sum. So it is safe to assume that all the guests in a restaurant belong to the higher income group.

On just one occasion I thought I had discovered a sign of special privilege. It was in a special hospital for cardiac diseases in Peking. During the inspection I was shown a room with private bath, toilet, and nurse's cot. The patient was not very sick—he jumped out of bed to greet me. This man was from the cadre in charge of railroads, evidently a Party official. But I was subsequently shown a dozen equally well-equipped rooms and told that "these rooms are for patients whose illness does not allow them to leave the room." That the not-so-sick official was occupying one of them was probably just a courtesy.

So the only sign of the existence of a privileged class discernible to a foreigner is the car.

I had asked for permission to visit a Chinese auto factory because the automobile industry is an index of technological development and a measure of the living standard. "You must see China's Automobile Factory Number One," I was told.

Apparently, this is the only automobile plant that is willingly shown to foreign visitors, perhaps because the others are busy turning out armaments; perhaps, too, because their installations are less impressive than those of Plant Number One.

Changchun lies in the northeast of China, in what used to be Manchuria, halfway between Shenyang (formerly Mukden) and Harbin, near the Soviet border. Changchun is one of the tidiest cities in China. The larger part of it was built by the Japanese, who made the city the capital of their satellite state Manchukuo. Many of the large buildings, now about thirty years old, were formerly occupied by ministries and their offices. The communists, under whom Changchun reverted to the status of an ordinary provincial city, have converted most of these buildings into universities; with over thirty thousand students, Changchun is now one of the largest university cities in China.

We drove along a wide street named Stalin Avenue, lined on either side by ancient trees. At the end of the street is a small park, in the center of which stands a memorial to the liberation of Manchuria in 1945 by Soviet troops. It is an obelisk topped by a replica of a Soviet dual-engine war plane, "because the paratroops were the first to land here," I was told. We went on, past the memorial and through several university neighborhoods to the edge of the city. Crossing a bridge, we found ourselves on a highway that boasted a streetcar line. It led to the automobile factory, although many workers lived on the site.

A few minutes later we were there. Plant Number One is no mere factory, it is a city. The housing quarters came first, then squares and parks, and finally we drove through a great archway and to the factory proper. I remembered other automobile cities— Detroit and the Volkswagen plant in Wolfsburg—and was impressed by one striking difference: here there were no cars. In this Chinese city where so many cars are manufactured, traffic consists entirely of streetcars and the two-wheeled horse carts that bring vegetables to market and materials to building sites.

But we were in one of China's most modern industrial plants, and I was impressed by my first look at it. There were at least thirty big workshops, each about a thousand yards long. Between them ran strips of grass and wide driveways. Electric trucks and fork-lift trucks were running between the buildings, all of them handled by women. Our car stopped in front of the administration building. A small man in a simple uniform-like suit stood waiting for us at the entrance. He was introduced as the plant manager.

As usual we went directly to the salon, and as everywhere else, the Party secretary and the chairman of the union were waiting for us. We began our interview by sipping green tea and smoking Chinese cigarettes.

I asked why we had not met a single passenger car on our way or in the city itself. The director smiled politely, even a little condescendingly. "We do not have private cars."

"Then cars are only for the privileged?"

"A car is not a luxury but a necessity, meant to serve a cause rather than an individual," he explained. "The cause requires that government and Party functionaries, city administrators and business executives have access to state-owned vehicles. None of these vehicles can be used without restriction, even by officials. They have to be requisitioned from government car pools, and the purpose of the trip must be stated." He added, "In this country, private cars are driven only by former capitalists and in Shanghai."

However, he seemed aware that Americans and Europeans measure the prosperity of a nation by the number of cars its people own. "We are not opposed to the ownership of cars by anyone, including workingmen," he said. "But it will not do for some to have cars while others don't. Everyone should have a car; any other way would be wrong."

Again the sly dig at the Soviet Union: "There are brother nations, socialist countries, where this principle is no longer followed, but that's a revisionist policy."

I asked how this policy of "cars for everyone" could be achieved except step by step. He had no answer.

Now it was clear to me why I had seen no gas pumps or service stations in China. All cars, without exception, are serviced by government car pools. Nor are the cross-country roads suitable for driving. A few main highways are indicated on the map, but I was told that most of them were in bad condition, with long stretches that could hardly be traveled by trucks and tractors. The government has given priority to extending the railway network.

Just the same, I had been told that Automobile Factory Number One manufactured not only trucks but also passenger cars. I asked about this, adding that I would like to see the assembly plant for passenger cars and that I myself would like to drive a Chinese car.

This request embarrassed my hosts. At that time the factory was turning out nothing but trucks. The passenger cars they had made were unsatisfactory.

"Why?"

"We didn't like the body. It was an attempt to combine modern design with the traditional Chinese style. The shape was wrong. We have commissioned our young technicians and art school graduates to come up with a new body design. Until then, production will be at a standstill."

The car that had been produced here was a large model, two hundred horsepower. It was called "Red Flag" and was larger than the other two Chinese cars, the "Phoenix" and "The East Glows." Even these two have six-cylinder engines and 150 horsepower.

"Are there no Chinese compact cars?"

"No, what for? Private individuals can't buy cars, and a compact is too small for government use."

I asked how much the "Red Flag" cost. The answer explains why any car in China is beyond the means of the individual. The "Red Flag" was priced at 30,000 yuan ($12,000).

At that, we wouldn't regard the "Red Flag" as a luxury car. In performance it is about equivalent to a small Chevrolet, in spite of its high horsepower. Maximum speed is about 100 miles per hour and it has three forward speeds and no overdrive.

But I did get to drive the "Red Flag," after all. When we emerged from the last workshop, after a two-hour inspection of the factory, a brand-new "Red Flag" with a chauffeur in a white duster at the wheel was standing before the door. The upholstery was protected by nylon seat covers and the car was marked with the numeral 9.

"We produced fifteen of these cars for the Party anniversary, and one is still here."

I was invited to get in, and we took a trial spin. "As you can see, the car is still too noisy. It is our aim to create a Chinese Rolls-Royce. You know what the English say about the Rolls-Royce—that inside the car you can hear only the ticking of the passenger's watch. Naturally, that's an exaggeration. But I must say that we would like to produce a car without noise."

I didn't think the car was that noisy, but when I said so, the chauffeur repeated that it was scheduled to become the Rolls-Royce of China, and that there would be no further production until they could achieve that goal.

The shop where the "Red Flags" had been produced was shut down, and production was at a standstill. On the other hand, the other shops were in full swing. Two types of trucks were being produced, a four-ton truck with a 90 horsepower engine and a two and a half ton truck with 110 horsepower and overland four-wheel drive. Both of them were copies of Soviet trucks, which in turn were copies of American models. Thus American design had entered Automobile Factory Number One via Moscow. The layout of the factory is also largely based on Soviet designs, which again follow the American pattern.

The plant was equipped with conveyors and assembly lines, but they were not in full operation. Not every motor or chassis that comes along the line to the mounting area is taken off the line; it stays on if the assembly work previously undertaken is unfinished. Eight trucks an hour is the production rate. But this plant works only one eight-hour shift; there is a shortage of skilled workers and apparently also of material, making more than one shift impossible. "The factory cannot meet the needs of the country."

Not by a long shot. I was unable to find out whether there is a number two or three plant in China. Visitors who saw this factory a few years ago have written that they did not know why it was called Number One, as there was no other in China. I am not so sure that a second or even a third factory hasn't been built, because the manager said, "We are in a position to produce not only trucks but also the machinery for outfitting other automotive plants."

In any case, there must be several other factories for the production of vehicles for the armed forces.

Plant Number One, in terms of capacity, is enormous. Not

only are there the twenty shops I mentioned earlier; it has its own power plant for electricity, gas, and heat, and, like almost all factories in China, it produces its own component parts. Nothing is delivered to the factory except the raw materials. The manager told me there was one exception: the tires came from other plants. At the same time, he figured that each truck had 160,000 parts, apparently all manufactured on the spot.

Therefore I wasn't surprised to see gears being molded, screws turned, and rivets produced in most of the workshops. Only in the last two, where all the parts are brought together, are motor and chassis assembled.

Altogether, 21,000 workers were employed in the factory. As in all Chinese factories, the workers' housing section was built by the factory and made up part of the industrial city.

Considering the production figures, it is understandable that passenger car production has been discontinued for a time and that all efforts are concentrated on producing light trucks. Although I had been shown the "Phoenix" passenger car produced in Shanghai and "The East Glows" produced in Peking, neither of these comes off an assembly line; they are produced piece by piece.

It is not surprising, then, that the cars of Chinese officials are still foreign models, mostly from the East bloc countries. Now they are beginning to buy German and, above all, English cars. In Canton, where a yearly exposition is held especially for foreigners, it seemed to me that English cars already predominated. They were put at the disposal of Western business executives during their stay.

22

Needles and centipedes

I had been shown a series of new and modern hospitals. In each I had talked with the chief of staff, the doctors, and the patients. During these talks I had noticed how often the term "Chinese medicine" was used, often in apparent contrast to the kind of medicine being practiced in the hospitals. I had previously read and heard a great deal about Oriental doctors. Now I began to wonder whether the Chinese medicine mentioned by my companions was the kind practiced by these doctors. This was immediately verified.

Actually, it is not surprising that China, which for three thousand years of recorded history had no contact with Europe or the rest of the world, inevitably produced its own school of medicine. Now I learned that this differed fundamentally from the European kind. I asked to meet some Oriental doctors, which led to several invitations, starting with a visit to the "Institute for Research of Chinese Medicine" in Peking.

Four doctors sat facing me. All four had graduated from medical school, had studied Western medicine for five years and Oriental medicine for two and one-half years. The state had appointed them to find the "scientific basis" of Chinese medicine.

To begin with, they told me a little about the history of Chinese medicine. There had been times when doctors were held in low esteem in China, owing to the old Chinese philosophy and outlook.

Illnesses were thought to be the workings of supernatural forces which, in the opinion of the sages, should not be tampered with. In addition, ancestor worship forbade dissection. Those who died must not be disfigured, for people believed that their spirits lived on and that bodies must remain intact. There were few medical centers and doctors had to depend on their natural talents and instincts. This encouraged quacks and charlatans, so people could not have much respect for the medical profession.

Nevertheless, some remarkable achievements were recorded in ancient China. The causes of infectious diseases were known before they were discovered in Europe; even if the existence of bacteria could not be proved, a medium for infection was assumed. Plagues and pestilences were fought by killing rats, which transmit the diseases; in rabies epidemics, all dogs were killed. Skin diseases were treated with mercury and sulfur two thousands years ago, with good results. Chinese doctors also had medicines to combat leprosy when it was still regarded as incurable in Europe. Even immunization was practiced after a fashion. Buboes were cut out of persons stricken with bubonic plague, dried, and pulverized. The powder was then blown into the nostrils of the healthy, who were slightly ill for a while and thereafter were immune. Smallpox was treated in the same way. Although Chinese physicians were not permitted to cut open cadavers, they calculated the position of the internal organs by observation and touch. Three thousand years ago they had a fairly correct idea of the human anatomy.

The doctors tried to explain that it was impossible to compare Western and Oriental medicine. They described them as two "totally different systems." I found this hard to understand. After all, I objected, all human beings have the same organs. Those organs are subject to the same diseases. Then the means of healing those organs couldn't be materially different.

Finally they gave up their attempts to enlighten me. "Come through the institute with us and see for yourself."

The first stop was a lecture room. Here stood a model of an ancient Chinese bronze figure representing a naked human being. It was pierced by many small holes, so small that only a needle could enter them.

This type of figure has been used for hundreds of years to teach one aspect of Chinese medicine—namely acupuncture. It was coated with wax or lacquer and filled with water. The medical student was given a diagnosis and told to stick pins into the holes showing where needles should be inserted for treating the disease in a real patient. If he hit the right spot on the first try, water ran out. Most candidates needed years to develop sufficient skill to pierce the correct spots with absolute accuracy.

Next to the figure lay eight hands, deceptively like real human hands in appearance but made of a special rubbery plastic. They seemed real to the touch, and electrical pumps simulated a pulsebeat. These are among the most modern teaching aids used in Chinese medicine. With these hands Chinese doctors learn to feel a pulse, by an entirely different method from that used by Western doctors.

A hospital is attached to the institute. We went into a section where a few patients were being examined. It was here that I began to learn the fundamental concepts of Chinese medicine.

To return to the pulsebeat: "A human being has not just one pulsebeat, but many. Depending on where and how the pulses beat, a traditional Chinese physician can determine which part of the body is sick and sometimes the degree of illness. Therefore he must be master of a whole range of possible pulsebeats. Western doctors merely ascertain the rhythm of the heartbeat. We arrive at a diagnosis on the basis of the pulsebeat."

But that is only a partial diagnosis. In the next step, the patient's tongue is examined. "The Western physician looks to see whether the tongue is coated, whether it is coated heavily or lightly, and possibly what the color of the coating is. The tongue offers us a sort of X-ray picture of the patient. We give a long and thorough inspection to the several spots of the coating, which way it runs on the tongue, where it is thick or thin, all the gradations in color, and so on." This is the second part of the diagnosis.

The third consists in letting the patient talk. As doctors in the West know, he can best describe his own symptoms. But this is of only marginal significance to the examining physician. He observes the patient as he talks. He notices whether the patient stretches at certain times, whether he bends over, and whether the patient coughs or clears his throat and how he does it.

The fourth part consists of an examination of the entire body. "Chinese medicine knows no isolated illness; the disease of an organ is merely the expression of the illness of the whole body, and the cause can often be outside the diseased organ. The illness is the result of the total constitution of the patient," I was told.

It is useless to ask a Chinese doctor for further explanations, for at this point he assumes a Chinese-scientific air which is meaningless to a Westerner, especially a layman.

Taoism and Chinese mysticism were incorporated into the structure of Chinese medicine; concepts from philosophy and the "world view" became part of it. Lao-tzu taught that the Tao is the origin of all being. Neither he nor other Chinese philosophers fully explained the Tao, as I mentioned before. But Lao-tzu spoke of the Yang and Yin concept, which the Chinese can and do represent visually. The Tao is shown as a circle, and within the circle are two curving almond-shaped figures which fill the circle and complement each other. Usually one of these shapes is shown in black, the other in red. One is called Yin, the other Yang.

The bright red Yang represents initiative, the sun, the day, the male principle, the external, the thick. The dark Yin balances this by representing passivity, the moon, the night, the female principle, the interior, the thin. These concepts have always played a large part in Chinese mysticism and also in Chinese medicine.

If the patient coughs at night, but not during the day, he falls into the Yin category. If his tongue is thickly coated, this is a sign of Yang. If he is reticent, quiet, and introverted he is classified under Yin. If he gestures a great deal and is volatile, talkative, and extroverted, he falls into the Yang category.

If a patient comes under the sign of Yin, his illness stems from his lungs, heart, liver, kidneys, spleen, or organs ruled by them. If he comes under the sign of Yang, the cause of his illness can be found in the gall bladder, large or small intestine, stomach, or their subordinate organs. A fast pulse indicates Yang; a slow pulse, Yin.

According to the Chinese doctors, Yang calls for a weakening or decreasing therapy, Yin for a strengthening or increasing one.

Chinese medicine is divided into specialties, but on quite a different basis from ours. They are: (1) Li, or theory; (2) Fa, or methods; (3) Fang, or prescriptions; and (4) Yan, or medications.

In general, treatment falls into two classes: acupuncture, which is also practiced in some parts of the West, and the administration of Chinese medicines, which have always been categorically rejected by Western physicians.

I have seen both methods of treatment. The results achieved by acupuncture were amazing. This method consists in sticking thin needles of gold, silver, or steel in varying lengths, from about a third of an inch to more than two feet, into certain spots on the body. There are 365 such spots, discovered in the course of thousands of years by Chinese doctors.

The spots are connected by so-called meridians, which have nothing to do with the nerve or vein systems. The existence of these meridians was determined merely through experience.

Most of the meridians run from the head to the toes or the ends of the fingers. After careful diagnosis, the doctor must determine which meridian should be punctured, where the precise spot is to be found, and what type of needle and method of stabbing must be used.

The effects of such punctures at certain points are well known to the Chinese doctors. I witnessed the arrival of a pregnant woman who was transferred from a clinic where Western medicine was practiced. She was suffering from appendicitis, and the Western doctors refused to operate because of her condition. She was punctured with two needles: near the shinbone and near the big toe. The pain went away in a few minutes, and the doctors told me that she could be discharged after five more treatments.

In most cases the punctures do not hurt at all. I saw a patient being treated with a needle about 27 inches long. The heel was punctured and the needle worked in a complicated manner through the entire leg. I talked to the patient while this was being done; he assured me he felt almost nothing.

"Manipulation of the needle by the physician is one of the most delicate problems of the treatment," the doctor explained. Much depends on whether the needle is inserted deeply or just under the skin, in what direction it is pushed and whether it is rotated during insertion, and—once it is in the body—whether its direction is changed.

"As we have already explained, sickness is merely a symptom that the whole body is ill. That's why every patient is ill in a different way. It cannot be said that, given a certain illness, the same spots are always to be punctured in the same manner. We punctured this woman's leg. With another patient who has appendicitis we might puncture the arm or the neck. It's all a question of diagnosis."

In addition to acupuncture, moxibustion is sometimes used. In that case herbs are stuck on the needles and ignited. Although the fire does not even touch the body, many recoveries are said to have resulted.

I saw patients who had ten to fifteen such packs burning on inserted needles. I kept asking how the treatment worked, but even the doctors were not able to tell me. They themselves do not know. It is supposed that electric currents flow through the human body, probably along the meridians, and that their strength and action are changed by illness. Through the insertion of the needles the currents are "normalized" and the illness is healed. But as yet there is no proof of this theory.

One of the first books of Chinese medicine to give exact instructions about acupuncture and moxibustion was compiled by the physician Haung fu Mi in 256 B.C. Even at that time the healing effects of these two treatments were well known.

But in old China no one asked for scientific proof. The healing effects were known, and that was enough. In the nineteenth and twentieth centuries the Chinese doctors who had traveled in America and Europe turned against the traditional Chinese medicine. They demanded scientific proof, but there were no research institutes where such proof could be worked out.

Only lately have the Chinese tried to discover just how the healing effects of acupuncture and moxibustion are produced. The institute in Peking which I visited is dedicated to this task. Many modern instruments are used to measure and record the brain waves, heartbeat, etc., of patients during treatment. The instruments react immediately to the effects of the acupuncture, but even they cannot account for the effects produced.

"We are working on it; we are progressing slowly, but we shall know some day," the doctors said. They are drawn largely from the ranks of those who practice Western-style medicine, to discover the secrets of the traditional cures by using Western methods.

Finally, I asked what diseases could be cured or ameliorated by acupuncture. There are too many to list here, but some of the most important are: gastritis, infantile paralysis, rheumatism, arthritis, urticaria, sciatica, asthma, neuralgia, neuroses and psychoses, meningitis; paralysis, especially of the facial nerves, the eye muscles, the arms, and the diaphragm; urinary troubles and female disorders; eye diseases such as glaucoma, lack of night vision, and color blindness; skin diseases, high blood pressure, goiter, tonsillitis, and inflammations of the throat, nervous hiccups, eclampsia, St. Vitus dance, even deaf- and dumbness and malaria.

The most amazing cures are those of infantile paralysis. "If treatment is begun during the acute stage, while the patient is still feverish, we can almost always prevent paralysis," the doctor declared. "Even six months after the onset of the disease, we can remove the paralysis in 90 per cent of the cases. And we are still able to ameliorate the condition within ten years after the onset of paralysis," a Chinese doctor claimed.

The percentage of cures in cases of rheumatism, arthritis, sciatica, and asthma is also impressively high. I was shown patients who had hardly been able to move their arms and legs, whose spines had given them acute pain at the slightest movement. After several weeks of acupuncture they were able to do calisthenics.

Marked improvement is supposed to take place even in cases of epilepsy and angina pectoris. The intervals between attacks are said to increase appreciably and the attacks themselves are shorter and milder. Immediate improvement results if acupuncture is performed during an attack.

In the cure of all sorts of nervous troubles, acupuncture has had miraculous results. Toothaches are eliminated by a single puncture, although only for a certain length of time. Most other nervous complaints can be cured permanently.

Even the enumeration of all these cures left me skeptical, but numerous Europeans in Peking and Hong Kong assured me that acupuncture actually does, in many cases, effect a cure which could not have been accomplished by Western methods.

In Nanking I visited an academy where Chinese physicians are trained, and the connecting hospital. Here I was shown medicines that were used (and had been used for thousands of years) in the treatment of disease. It is only today that they are being systematically used and their healing powers examined scientifically.

The academy has existed only a few years. Traditional Chinese doctors received no scientific training. They passed their knowledge on from generation to generation. For this and other reasons, traditional medicine was dismissed as quackery by modern doctors. No doubt there have been some quacks among Chinese doctors, and some may have had a rather sketchy knowledge of the healing art; there were neither scientific training centers nor examinations, nor were diplomas granted.

But the great mass of Chinese peasants were dependent on the traditional doctors, since the modern ones seldom came to the villages. Thus traditional medicine was kept alive in the country. There can be no doubt that the communist government would like to raise traditional medicine to a place of honor, for in twenty years of guerrilla warfare the communists were dependent on it. No other help was available in their strongholds. The few modern doctors who joined their ranks could not cope with so many soldiers and their families. So it may be assumed that the esteem of the communists for traditional medicine was born during the partisan struggle. Most of the training schools for Chinese doctors were established after they came to power. Today there are colleges for traditional medicine in almost every large Chinese city. However, modern medicine has not been slighted as a result. It goes without saying that the universities have their modern schools of medicine and, now as before, many more modern than traditional doctors are being trained in China. But candidates for a degree in modern medicine are required to dedicate a year to the study of traditional

Chinese medicine after completing their five-year course. Similarly, students of traditional medicine must devote two years to studying modern methods.

"Physicians of both disciplines must know the advantages and disadvantages of both, and they may not compete against each other. When Western medicine fails, traditional medicine must be applied; and when traditional medicine fails, modern medicine must be consulted," I was told at the Nanking academy.

Here, too, the two great techniques of traditional medicine are studied—acupuncture and moxibustion—as well as treatment with medications. I was shown through rooms where the raw materials used in the preparation of traditional medicines were exhibited for educational purposes. Among them were thousands of plants from every corner of China. Many were labeled only with Chinese characters, without the international Latin nomenclature.

"For four thousand years Chinese doctors have studied the curative values of these plants. Now we are cataloging them and listing their effects. Although there are fragments of records from former times, there is no comprehensive catalog. It will take us years to compile it," the superintendent said.

We inspected some large showcases. "Here are the mineral and animal ingredients used in our medicines."

I could understand why modern doctors reject traditional Chinese medicine as quackery. In the showcases were tiger claws, reindeer antlers, snakeskins, shells, stones, pearls, animal skins, and some objects I couldn't identify. I asked, "What are those large balls?"

"These are deposits formed in the stomachs of horses. They're hard as stone."

"Are they also made into medicine?"

"Yes, of course. They are especially valuable. We use them in treating mental diseases. They are pulverized and mixed with other medicines."

I asked him how some of the other raw materials were used. Pulverized pearls are used against vertigo and in the treatment of certain eye diseases. Shells are a specific against swellings, snakeskins against rheumatism, tiger claws against paralysis, animal horns against nervous conditions. Tiger bones are also used in treating rheumatism.

But the best was yet to come. I was conducted to the pharmacy of the hospital that is connected with the academy. "We have more than five thousand medicines in storage here, besides thousands of raw materials used in their preparation."

They opened a few drawers and jars for me. I could hardly believe my eyes. There were dried bugs, centipedes, spiders, and other insects that I didn't recognize. I swallowed and asked what they were used for. The answer was given with medical objectivity. "Centipedes are good for all kinds of rheumatic pains. Tree bugs reduce swellings. Cockroaches are used as plasters on wounds to promote faster healing."

I must admit that it was I who put a stop to any further inspection of the pharmacy. But it wasn't the different insects that drove me away; it was the unendurable smell that emanated from the dried "raw materials."

We continued our talk in the tearoom. "All these raw materials will be pulverized. Often, several of them are combined and given to the sick in tea or soup," I was told.

I was unable to hide the skepticism which I share with modern doctors in regard to Chinese medicine.

"Well, let's go into the infirmary."

One section was devoted to patients who suffered from a severe disease of the blood vessels; many of them had already undergone partial amputation.

"They have all come from hospitals of modern medicine. We don't perform amputations here," the chief of staff told me. "They had been under treatment for months—in some cases for years. The treatment ended in amputation. Most of them can't undergo further amputations. That's why they have been transferred here."

"And what happens to them here?"

"We treat them with Chinese medicines."

"Successfully?"

"Oh yes, with amazing success. Many of them had lost all sensation in their limbs. It comes back to them after a one- to two-week course of treatment. The blood again begins to circulate in the affected limbs. Even if further amputations could be performed, they are no longer necessary."

I talked to a few patients. They confirmed the doctor's diagnosis.

Then we met the head of this department. He is a doctor of the modern school who had practiced Western-style medicine for fifteen years before he began his study of traditional medicine. "I was so fascinated that I asked to be transferred to a traditional hospital," he admitted. "I believe we can achieve maximum success only by combining both schools. Traditional medicine is useless in many diseases which can be helped by modern medicines and surgical methods. For example, traditional medicine has no cure for cancer. All we can do for certain forms, such as cancer of the throat, is ameliorate the discomfort. The same holds true with several heart diseases. In this area, modern medicine can sometimes achieve a total cure by means of surgery. Surgery is seriously underdeveloped in traditional medicine, because no one ever believed in it. But even there, certain techniques exist that are superior to Western methods—only a few. On the other hand, we do better in several other spheres than modern medicine, such as diseases of the blood vessels and certain liver and kidney disorders."

I saw patients suffering from those diseases who had supposedly been given up by Western-style practitioners. Their bodies were swollen almost past recognition. "Water," the attending doctor explained. "In the Western hospitals, nothing could be done beyond assuring constant withdrawal of fluids. The disease was not cured; on the contrary, the patient declined from month to month. We do not withdraw the water, we cure the disease."

"Successfully?"

"Yes, almost incredibly so. Look at that man over there. He was dying when he came in here. He is already better."

At this point, let me make clear that I understand too little of medicine to be able to testify to the efficacy of Chinese medicine from mere observation. I can only report what I was told. I talked with the patients and let them tell me how they had been before and how they were feeling now. Their reports agreed with what the doctors had told me.

I asked about the rules governing the admission of patients to both types of hospitals. "In the first place, the patient has free choice. Some come here. Others have more confidence in modern medicine. Once a patient is in any hospital, the doctors determine objectively how he can best be helped, and they recommend a transfer if it seems to be indicated."

In addition, doctors of each discipline make use of some branches of the other. Thus, Chinese medicines are issued in some hospitals of modern medicine, while the traditional hospitals nowadays use electrocardiograms, X-ray apparatus, electrical massage, etc. The goal seems to be a fusion of both systems.

Near Anshan in northeast China I visited a sanatorium for the treatment of rheumatism and sciatica. The doctors there were already utilizing all the methods of both modern and traditional medicine that were available to them. Modern medicines were dispensed, mud packs and baths were prescribed, acupuncture and moxibustion were used, and these, interestingly enough, were augmented by electrical apparatus of modern design.

The communist government, by the way, places great emphasis on the development of public health. Every commune is required to build its own hospital, since Chinese villages had previously been almost totally without medical facilities. Many new hospitals have been built in the towns and cities, and in Peking I was told that more and more were being equipped for specialization.

For instance, I visited a clinic where general surgery had been performed only six years before. Now it was almost exclusively confined to surgery of the heart and blood vessels. Several mature, experienced doctors head the staff of this hospital.

They immediately asked about internationally known European doctors, whether they were working at this or that clinic, how research in their specialties was coming along. I was not able to answer all their questions. "We meet each other repeatedly at international medical congresses," the doctors said. "We are allowed to leave the country for this purpose, and the government pays all our travel expenses. Formerly, Chinese doctors had to pay for themselves, which many of us could not afford to do." But when I asked them whether there were more Chinese doctors traveling abroad today, they were unable to answer.

There were three heart and lung machines in the Peking heart clinic. I was told they were made in Shanghai; they bore Chinese labels and firm names. I asked whether complicated heart operations were undertaken with the help of these machines and whether they were used on "blue babies." "We are increasingly successful, but the beginnings were very difficult. We couldn't experiment for long; we had to operate here, since there was no way to send our patients abroad, for instance to Sweden. The mortality rate was high. But today we carry out the most difficult heart operations. With blue babies, the mortality rate is still not as low as we might wish, and there's one thing we haven't mastered yet: we can't install artificial heart valves. On the other hand, we replace every sort of blood vessel, and these operations turn out very well."

The doctors asked me to go with them to a lecture hall. Here a screen had been pulled down and a projector set up. For three hours I watched films of difficult heart operations. They had been taken in the clinic, and showed the entire surgical procedure from the moment the patient was put on the operating table until the wound was stitched. Pictures of the healing process were included. The patient is shown before the operation and upon leaving the hospital, and these pictures appear at the end of each film segment.

"We made these films primarily for our medical students, but also for doctors who are to be trained as specialists. Every manipulation, each cut made during the operation has been recorded."

Although I am not a professional in this field, it seemed to me that all of the surgical procedures had been carried out competently, at least on film. I was especially interested in the operations on various blood vessels and the replacement of heart arteries by artificial arteries.

The explanations were given in fluent English.

The accent of the professors indicated that they had studied in the United States many years ago. They receive all the scientific journals in their field from all over the world, and they pass their knowledge on to their students. This heart clinic is said to have trained nine hundred doctors as heart specialists in the last five years. Undoubtedly the work of the clinic itself suffered, but the training of specialists took precedence.

As everywhere else, a Party secretary sat with the professors. I asked if he was also a doctor. No, he was an old soldier. I asked whether, in that case, he was in a position to advise experienced doctors. The professors came to his rescue. "Cooperation with the Party is necessary and good. It builds our political morale and teaches us to serve the masses. It has given us a new morale. Formerly we thought only of material gain. Today we know that our greatest reward is the success of our medical art. The Party has taught us that. The Party helps us beyond that. Its campaigns raise the standard of national health. Once China was the dirtiest country in the world. Today it is clean. The extermination of flies and mosquitoes was a Party feat. The Party teaches the people to be hygienic and to use disease-prevention methods."

I asked how much the director of the hospital earned. "My monthly salary is 350 yuan [$140]," he said. This for a man who stands at the operating table ten to twelve hours a day.

This excursion into the field of medicine showed me how much the government wants to maintain traditional Chinese knowledge and methods, to incorporate them into contemporary Chinese life. But medicine is only one of many fields where this tendency is noticeable. There are many others: art, music, literature, agriculture, building construction, even propaganda. Party and government are conscious of tradition. They claim for themselves entirely the greater part of Chinese tradition, although with ideological reservations. This includes Confucianism and imperialism.

23

Mao and the ancient emperors

The Tien An Men, the "Gate to Heavenly Peace" in the center of Peking, is the entrance to the so-called Forbidden City. The Forbidden City was the Peking residence of the emperors of China. Their might and magnificence found expression in the Tien An Men. Perhaps no other ruler's residence in the world has an entrance gate as large as a palace. For that reason, the Tien An Men is Peking's most outstanding symbol. The communist government has had it renovated. Today it bears two large inscriptions, slogans of the Mao government, in Chinese characters: "Long live the People's Republic of China!" on one side; "Long live the great unity of the nations of the world!" on the other.

The square dominated by the Tien An Men (Tien An Men Square) serves nowadays as the stage for the huge mass rallies of the Communist Party. It has been greatly enlarged at the behest of the Party. Here stand the three most important buildings of the new government: at the right of the Tien An Men, the Great Hall of the People and the two museums for history and revolution; on the left and exactly opposite the Tien An Men is the Monument to the Heroes of the Revolution. This is a square structure 155 feet tall with various scenes of the revolution in bas-relief.

On each of the four sides of this edifice is a Chinese inscription in gilded letters. These do not look, however, as if they had been made to order by sign painters or stonemasons according to conventional models, as would be the case with our monuments. "Mao Tse-tung, Liu Shao-ch'i, Chou En-lai, and Chu Teh themselves wrote these inscriptions. These are in their personal handwriting," my guide told me. And that, too, conforms to tradition. Inscriptions on monuments and memorials have always been written by the Chinese emperors or high dignitaries themselves. The communists are merely carrying on the tradition.

Of course, this is not only true of the Monument to the Heroes of the Revolution; I came across the personal handwriting of the highest Communist Party leaders fairly often in China. Even the airline names on the passenger planes of the only state-run Chinese airline are not in Latin letters but in Chinese characters, originally inscribed by Premier Chou En-lai.

But the square in front of the Tien An Men shows even more clearly than most things in China the continuity that the communist government has tried to maintain with China's past. When the mobilized masses march across the square on national holidays, Mao Tse-tung and the highest leaders of the Chinese Communist Party review the troops from the terrace of the Tien An Men. They stand exactly where the Chinese emperors stood when their commanders-in-chief brought them glad tidings.

I could not help making a comparison between this square and Moscow's Red Square. It did not seem to be entirely without symbolic significance that while the high Soviet leaders review their parades outside the Kremlin walls, they do so from the new Lenin mausoleum. These parades pass in review before a communist shrine, a sort of sanctuary of Soviet power. Here, in Peking, Mao stands on the terrace of the imperial gate.

The Forbidden City stretching out behind the Tien An Men was for a long time the target of attacks by democrats and later also by the communist revolutionary movements. Because no citizen of Peking had been allowed to approach this sector of the city, those hastening across Peking had to make enormous detours around the Forbidden City. And so the imperial sector was looked upon as a tyrant's citadel by democratic revolutionaries.

A statue in front of the Ming tombs.

Today great care and effort are expended to maintain the imperial palaces in the Forbidden City.

When you first enter, its sheer beauty leaves you breathless, confronted by a magnificence beyond description: the vast courts paved in marble, the regal bridges spanning artificial canals; the bronze lions, dragons, phoenixes, turtles, and cranes, all larger than life; the marble statues on the bridges and stairways.

Yellow was the imperial color. The rooms of the emperor were done in black and yellow. That is why all the roofs are covered with glazed yellow tiles. The gables are curved in typical Chinese style.

The first four buildings stand one behind the other, separated by courtyards. They are The Gate of Supreme Harmony, The Hall of Supreme Harmony, The Hall of Perfect Harmony, and The Hall of Enduring Harmony.

There is an imperial throne in each of the three buildings. These become more beautiful and ornate as one progresses. Here the emperor retired to meditate or to confer with the sages. The interior has not only been preserved, it has been renovated and restored by the communist government. Even today dozens of craftsmen are at work in the Forbidden City trying to replace the intarsia on the smallest doors and to repair the imperial furnishings.

The extent of the Imperial City is vast. The structures are almost too many to count. They served as accommodation for the emperor and empress, the numerous concubines, the highest courtiers, the hundreds of eunuchs and thousands of servants. Between them are temples, monuments, and everywhere great statues of bronze horses, colored dragons, fabled creatures of all kinds. The individual buildings are separated by courtyards, gardens, and parks.

One would need weeks really to see all the details of the Imperial City. Most of the large buildings have been turned into museums. The imperial paintings are on exhibition, and so is the old imperial treasure house. The imperial porcelains, as valuable as jewels, the sculptures, the tapestries, the clocks, the hand-crafted art—all have been placed in separate exhibits in the various palaces.

The treasures stored here can no longer be evaluated. In the treasure house alone there are art objects of gold, jade, and jewels of inestimable value. Naturally, the placards explaining the articles are in keeping with the times. There are many references to "immeasurable exploitation of the people," "gluttonous life of the emperors," "wastefulness at the expense of the people." But frequent mention is also made of the cultural value of the art objects and that "through this labor from the workshops of China, the world has been given invaluable works of art."

There are many other imperial buildings in Peking. One of the most famous is the so-called Temple of Heaven. The emperors offered thanks for a rich harvest in its "Hall of the Harvest Sacrifice," or pleaded here for rain in times of drought. Even the emperor was not admitted to the Temple of Heaven itself. Its throne was meant for God alone. No one was permitted to accompany the emperor when he approached the threshold of the temple to commune with the heavens.

The "center of the earth," which I mentioned earlier, is also situated within the grounds of the Temple of Heaven. If you stand on the round stone which marks this mid-point you can hear your voice amplified a dozen times. Clever architects constructed the marble balustrade that encircles the plateau in such a fashion that the echo bounces back precisely to the center of the earth.

A similar marvel has been performed in the fore-court of the Temple of Heaven, which is surrounded by a high round wall. If the visitor stands against the wall his voice is carried all around the court, even if he speaks in a whisper. In the middle of the court are three stones. On the first, the echo is single; on the second, double; on the third, a triple echo can be heard. The emperors used these architectural features to claim heavenly and supernatural faculties.

The attitude of the communist government toward these imperial buildings is best reflected in an entry I found in the official *Guide Through Peking:* "The feudal rulers made use of this marvelous architecture to confuse the minds of the people and force them to subordinate themselves. On the other hand, the creation of such artful edifices by the workmen of our country under the conditions of that time is not only an important event in the history of Chinese architecture and a valuable inheritance, but also a contribution to world culture."

Another construction regarded in present-day China as a contribution to world culture is the Great Wall. I was surprised when I learned, at the Museum for Chinese History, that the Emperor Shih Huang Ti, who had the Chinese Wall built, is now considered a "good" emperor in historical accounts. Nevertheless, peasants by the hundreds of thousands were forced into slave labor for years, made to work on the Wall through torrid heat and icy storms. No building materials were provided. The interior of the Wall, which is twenty to fifty feet high and roughly twenty-seven feet wide, is made of earth and stones which the laborers had to dig and break on the spot.

Neatly cut stone blocks make up the outer surface. Man-high barricades, placed on both sides of the Wall, are pierced by broad embrasures through which archers and lancers could attack the enemy. Watchtowers are located about a thousand feet apart all along the 1,500-mile Wall.

An excursion to the Great Wall is on the weekend program of every visitor to Peking. A three-hour drive brings one to the Wall at a point where the government has had it renovated exactly as it was originally. The road has been blacktopped and a parking lot built near the Wall, and several small teahouses offer refreshments to the tourists.

On the way to the Wall we passed a number of buses of modern design from the various East bloc countries. When we arrived, there were about twenty cars in the parking lot, likewise of Soviet and Czechoslovak manufacture. My interpreter was very excited. "Look, look, so many cars! I've been here many times, but I've never seen so many cars." Most of them bore the large red sign of the diplomatic service.

"This is the only excursion we are permitted to make," a European diplomat told me later. "Otherwise we may not leave Peking. Consequently, we drive repeatedly to the Great Wall. This prevents claustrophobia and keeps us in touch with nature."

One can climb the Wall and walk along on it. On the breastworks I encountered many Europeans and Japanese. For the first time since arriving in China I heard familiar languages: Czech, Hungarian, Polish, but also Swiss-German, Danish, and Swedish; and for the first time I saw European children. But here too the custom of not getting too involved with other travelers prevailed. I tried to start a conversation with one or two, speaking in English, but after a curt reply each turned away.

At the end of the renovated section, a striking view of the Chinese landscape presented itself. Blue and green, the hills and mountains stood before me, yet I could see valleys that merged to the north into a broad plain, itself bordered on the far horizon by dark-blue mountains wreathed in haze.

"About 200 B.C. the territory of China ended here," my guide said. "At that time it had not by any means reached its greatest expansion."

Now I learned why the founder of the Wall, Emperor Shih Huang Ti, is said to have been a good emperor. "It's true that many workers perished in building the Wall. And the people were badly treated. In many cases the food supply was inadequate and housing non-existent. Many poems and stories in Chinese literature tell of the misery and desperation of the workers on the Wall. But you see, it was a necessity. This Wall protected China and repulsed hostile attacks so the people could live in peace. From a historical point of view the Wall performed a very important task, and the victims it claimed can be considered as sacrificing for their homeland. Perhaps the sacrifices could have been avoided; but then, it was a time of slavery."

A remarkable explanation, which I found again in Chinese history books. As I have said, Communist China has not broken with the past but claims the past as its own and makes use of it to imbue the people, especially the children, with national pride. Although the former emperors are today measured with the yardstick of socialism, not a few of them stand up well even according to that measure. The Chinese communists with whom I talked often quoted Confucius, citing his sayings and rules of conduct. On a flight, the stewardess explaining the historical significance of the landscape over which we were passing recited from memory a long passage from Confucius celebrating the beauty of this landscape. With lifted finger, she added, "The Master said when he climbed this mountain, 'Only now do I recognize how small is man.' "

This is in obvious conflict with the political slogan, "Tear Confucius out of every nook and cranny of your heart." When I pointed out the contradiction I was told, with a smile, "That is merely directed at the social teachings of Confucius. No one denies that he was a great man, a sage to whom the Chinese people are much indebted. Confucius erred grievously in his obsequiousness toward feudal rule, but at the same time he gave wings to our culture and civilization. Our evaluation today is just. Even Chairman Mao Tsetung has often quoted Confucius in his works."

As an expression of its bond with tradition, the government also gave orders that the secret of the Ming emperors, hidden for many generations, should be revealed: the secret of the Ming tombs.

At the end of the fourteenth century, the first of the Ming Dynasty emperors commanded that the construction of grave sites for the Chinese rulers be started near Peking. Those who were sent out to find a suitable place chose one of the most beautiful valleys of China.

I have seen that valley. It is enclosed on three sides by wooded hills, divided by a stream; a broad road winds through the bottom of the valley. This is the road along which the funeral processions of the Ming emperors once made their way. Pictures of it are often seen in the West. At its beginning stands a large imperial gate, beyond which lies the first stone temple. In its center stands a large marble turtle about ten feet long and almost as tall as a man. On its back a marble tablet sixteen feet high records in hundreds of characters the names, dates, and deeds of the Ming emperors.

From the temple the crooked road runs into the hills. Along both sides of the road stand gigantic stone figures: kneeling camels, standing camels, kneeling elephants, standing elephants, horses, unicorns, and other fabled creatures. These statues stand in long rows at intervals of fifty to sixty-five feet. They are followed by more-than-life-size mandarins, soldiers, and other types of that time. "All the world lined the road when the emperors were borne to the grave."

Nowadays this region is known as the Valley of the Tombs.

On each of the hills stand main temples and ante-temples, indicating the grave site of an emperor. Most of these are built of wood with large round columns, lacquered red. "The columns are of one piece. Such large trees grow only in the south of China. They were brought here over a distance of about 1,300 miles. This could have been done only during the winter, when snow covered the roads. The columns were pulled on sleds and transported on rollers through the cities. Thousands of people were required to haul these gigantic trees."

In this valley are buried thirteen Ming emperors with their wives and concubines. In keeping with the ancestor cult, the tomb of the first emperor is the largest and most beautiful, and that of the last and youngest is the smallest. Sons must always be more modest than their fathers.

Although the sumptuous temples and palatial structures in the Valley of the Tombs were known for almost six centuries, no one knew the exact location of the tombs themselves. According to Chinese custom, they would be dozens if not hundreds of feet underground for safety from robbers and vandals. It was partly assumed and partly known from ancient manuscripts that innumerable treasures were hidden in the tombs. Archaeologists from many nations have tried to find them. When the Japanese occupied Peking they made an all-out effort to open the Ming tombs. They, too, failed to locate them.

It was only in the 1950's that Chinese archaeologists succeeded in locating one of the burial sites, commissioned by the new government and using methods which have not been divulged to this day. They managed to penetrate the tomb of the Emperor Chu-I-chin, who was the fourteenth emperor of the Ming Dynasty. It is one of the smallest graves, and lies buried about 1,400 feet deep in the middle of a hill.

But if finding it was difficult, opening it was even more difficult. It was supposed, rightly, that the emperors had safeguarded themselves against intruders and that any careless penetration would cause the tomb to collapse. Months were spent studying the mechanism of the doors to the grave. Then the explorers burst in, only to find themselves in an antechamber.

They stood before two more huge doors, each cut from a single slab of white marble. These could be opened—but only from the inside. They were equipped with a mechanism that caused an immense bolt to fall into place on the inside when the doors were slammed from the outside, thus locking them.

Weeks were required to reconstruct this mechanism, invisible from the outside, and to reverse its motion. When the marble doors opened, the archaeologists entered a marble hall, in which stood three thrones: two for each empress and the third, much larger and decorated with marble dragons, for the emperor. In front of it were huge vessels filled with precious stones, vases, and implements used in sacrifices.

The largest of the vessels contained oil. Here, in honor of the emperor, an eternal flame should have burned. The supply of oil would actually have been sufficient for many years; what had not been considered was that the flame would also need oxygen. Deep in the earth the light soon died, and the oil remained.

But the dead were not in this marble hall, nor in the two side chambers that were opened next. Here too were found only funeral offerings of rare value.

Then the third door, behind the marble hall, was opened. The sight that presented itself to the archaeologists must have been overwhelming. Three large red sarcophagi stood on a platform surrounded by innumerable treasures—gold and silver bars, ceremonial objects of precious metals studded with hundreds of gems, jade figures of singular beauty, and jewelry of all kinds, especially diadems.

Yet all that was as nothing compared with the treasures found in the caskets. The bodies of the dead had not been embalmed, or the embalming had been done badly. But in the headdresses of the empresses there were dozens of gems of almost unimaginable splendor and, in addition, wigs made entirely of jewels.

And that was one of the smallest Ming graves! I visited that grave, named "the subterranean palace." Today it is lighted by electricity. One descends into its depths by a broad, circular flight of stone stairs, enters the antechambers, goes through the marble gates, and stands before the thrones. In the sepulchral chamber itself, the sarcophagi have been reconstructed, because the originals disintegrated when they were opened.

The treasures were divided among several museums. Some can be seen in a museum standing at the foot of the hill at the grave site. Whatever was transferred to museums in Peking has been replaced here by copies, so that one can see what the precious objects looked like.

Driving back to Peking from the valley of the Ming tombs, one comes to a reservoir. The dam, which holds back the water of the river, was built—as I have already mentioned—at the beginning of the "Great Leap Forward." In the center of the dam a pavilion has been erected, from which the lake and the dam can be seen in tranquility. The pavilion was designed in the style of the ancient imperial structures. Instead of the usual communist slogans one finds miniatures of the traditional Chinese paintings: mountains, streams, valleys, trees, people, and animals.

At the edge of the artificial lake stands a monument dedicated to the workers who built the dam in a few months. It bears an inscription in the imperialist manner, but in the handwriting of Mao Tse-tung.

A column bearing a decorated marble hook stands in front of the monument. Identical columns stand before the hills containing the tombs of the emperors. The emperors had them erected so that important news and announcements could be hung on them, and they have been considered tokens of imperial might since time immemorial. But the column with Mao's signature was erected in 1958.

Many of the imperial edifices in China served a religious purpose. Visiting them, one is often amazed that the communists have renovated religious sites and altars. It hardly seems consistent with the reports about the persecution of priests and the suppression of religious groups after the rise of the communists to power. So I tried to discover the attitude of the communist regime toward religion and religious freedom.

24

Religion — target and weapon

I visited a people's commune in the vicinity of Nanking and saw the village, the new irrigation system, then the schools; finally the chairman invited me to have lunch with him at a restaurant. It was situated at the edge of the village, in the middle of a small forest. After the meal we went for a stroll. The path took us to a clearing in the woods, and we stood suddenly before a Buddhist temple. I was interested and indicated that I wanted to see it. The chairman said that he was too busy, that there was really too much to be done, and that if I would permit it, he would excuse himself. Obviously he had no desire to visit the temple, and, as I found out later, he didn't even want to enter the grounds.

The temple was well preserved and partly renovated. Sticks of incense were placed in a votive vessel before a statue of Buddha; they were still glowing and spread their peculiar Far Eastern odor through the hall. A peasant stood in an attitude of prayer before one of the lesser gods.

There was a cloister behind the temple, and I wanted to visit this as well; but my interpreter begged off. "The monks will be having their midday rest. Let's not disturb them." Through the windows, which were barred by wooden slats, I could see the monks sitting cross-legged on low benches, fanning themselves and talking. When

I pointed this out to my interpreter he still resisted, repeating, "Do not disturb."

Obviously, a visit to a Buddhist cloister had not been planned for visitors to a people's commune, and my interpreter was not sure just how to act. So we mounted the hill behind the cloister, which, as I realized, must play no small role in the lives of the believers. Small caves had been dug to hold numerous statues of Buddha, some of wood, some of stone. The feet of the faithful had worn wide paths over hundreds of years, and the pedestals of the statues showed how many thousands of hands had reached out to touch them.

In the cities I had inspected pagodas, temples, and cloisters, all currently in use. But this did not surprise me. What I found remarkable was that such a large temple and cloister should exist in a people's commune.

I had seen five Buddhist monks in their yellow robes boarding a plane in the Peking airport. They were Chinese, not a foreign delegation. And in Changchun, Buddhist nuns in their black veils had sat next to me in a movie house. The movie had dealt with the slogan, "Create technical innovations!"

One can go to church in Peking, Canton, or Shanghai; the portals of the churches are open; the Catholic service accords with the liturgy, which is held in Latin. The sermon I heard was in Chinese, but as no interpreter accompanied me into the church, I could not understand it.

There is religious freedom in China, according to Article 88 of the Chinese constitution. However, according to a pronouncement made by Mao Tse-tung in 1949, religious freedom is guaranteed only to the sects and their believers that conform to the laws of the state. The People's Republic of China has few laws. The state—that is, the Party—determines the law according to circumstances and necessities.

A high functionary of the Communist Youth Association explained this to me: "The battle against superstition and religion is one of our most important tasks. Because of our belief in materialism, we fight against superstition and religion with all our might."

That seemed to contradict what I had been told by a functionary of the research section of the Office for Religious Affairs in the State Council of Peking: "No one discriminates against religious setcs; no one combats them."

The youth official took up my objection. "The fight against religion and superstition is carried on outside the sects."

When I asked what the fight consisted of, he explained, "We try to convince people."

"Of what?"

"Of scientific materialism, of the fact that religion is superstition and superstition is nonsense. We explain to the people that belief in gods began only because certain natural phenomena could not be interpreted and because man is impotent in the face of natural catastrophes. Nowadays we control nature by technical means, and we have scientific explanations for the natural phenomena. Religion is superstition. But religion is also opium for the people. It has been used to exploit the people."

The functionaries of the Office for Religious Affairs kept reverting to this fight against religion. This is how they explained it: "Our constitution guarantees freedom of religion, but it also guarantees freedom of atheism. Both the religious sects and the atheists may proselytize in equal measure."

I asked what "equal measure" meant.

The answer came promptly: "The religious sects carry on their propaganda inside the church, the atheists outside the church."

In other words, the believers who go to church can be addressed by the religious sects. It is hardly necessary to convert them to religion. But everything outside the church belongs to the free field of the communist fight against religion. This is scarcely a fight with equal weapons.

I inquired about the size of the denominations in China. Buddhism is considered the largest, but the number of adherents is not known. The officials explained, "The Buddhists do not practice baptism and have no parish register. So the number of Buddhists cannot be ascertained. In round numbers, there are 400,000 to

500,000 Buddhist monks, nuns, and lamas in China. They pursue their spiritual life without interference."

At a communist mass rally in the Peking People's Hall, a few supposedly very prominent Buddhist priests sat next to high government officials. Their heads were shaved; they wore their yellow robes and acknowledged the applause with folded hands. It was they who most scathingly condemned "American imperialism."

Quite a few Buddhist delegations from abroad were in Peking while I was there. They visited the holy sites of their religion and conferred with church dignitaries. There were delegations from Indonesia, Pakistan, India, Nepal, Bhutan, Thailand, Burma, Cambodia, Laos, North Viet Nam, and other countries. They found the holy sites renovated and in excellent condition. The Chinese Office for Religious Affairs is responsible for carrying out these renovations.

Peking is fully conscious of the power of Buddhism, and Communist China wants to appear as a friend of the Buddhists in the other Asiatic countries. China in the role of "religious protector" is supposed to appeal especially in South Viet Nam, where only a short time ago Buddhist monks had been persecuted and had set themselves on fire in public as a demonstration against the government.

However, I was unable to find out whether the monasteries in the remoter provinces are really open and being renovated, and whether believing Buddhists everywhere in China are allowed to hold religious services. I am inclined to doubt whether foreign visitors could ascertain this.

For Chinese belonging to the race of Han, Buddhism is, as I mentioned in an earlier chapter, a transitory phenomenon. They incorporated elements from Buddhism into their complicated but never solid structure of belief, placed Buddha on an equal footing with other gods, used him to supplement their ancestor cult, and above all "Sinified" the Buddhist faith. But Buddhism may not play a very large role among the pure Chinese.

Even today, when entering a Chinese home one has to step over a sill twelve to sixteen inches high. "That is Chinese architecture,"

I was told. But these high doorsteps serve a special purpose: they keep out the evil spirits. Even if such a spirit managed to cross the high threshold, he would come up against a wall. Since it is assumed that the spirit is not very bright, he would think that the house had no other door, and leave. The people go around the wall into the house. This is hardly in keeping with a serious belief in Buddha.

In the main, Buddhism finds its strongest adherents among the national minorities, especially the Tibetans.

Other national minorities are believers in Islam. About ten of the more than fifty minority groups in China are Mohammedans. Their number is estimated at ten million. When I asked a functionary of the Office for Religious Affairs how many Chinese followed Islam, he answered, "A few dozen thousands."

More is known about the number of Christian communities. "Three million Catholics live in China. They are tended by, in round numbers, ten thousand monks, priests, and nuns. The other Christians are divided into more than sixty sects, and the ministers and lay priests may number between 700,000 and 800,000. All Christians in China belong to the Han race [that is, they are Chinese]."

He listed a series of principles formulated by the government for the treatment of Christians and religious faiths in general:

1. The government guarantees the freedom to belong to a religious congregation and to attend religious services.

2. The government protects churches, temples, and mosques.

3. Religious congregations are permitted to publish their own books and periodicals, to hold theological seminars, and to train priests.

4. Believers have the same rights as all other citizens of the state, and also the same duties.

How does that work out in the case of the Catholics?

Among all the religious faiths represented in China, they were under the most intense pressure from the communists. Foreign missionaries were locked up by the dozens, accused of counter-revolutionary activity, murdered or imprisoned for long periods, or, at the least, expelled from the country.

An equally harsh fate was suffered by many Chinese priests and bishops.

The faithful were forced to participate in "reorientation courses" and suffered at least mental torture. Then the government forced a break between the Chinese clergy and the Vatican. The Pope was branded as "a tool of the imperialists" and the Vatican as "a spy center." Some of the priests succumbed either to force or to psychological pressure and became "patriotic." Today they profess adherence to the communist regime, support certain propaganda activities of the government, and exert their influence on the faithful to "participate in the socialist reconstruction."

Altogether, according to information supplied by government officials, the Chinese Catholics are led by two archbishops and forty bishops. One of these archbishops has become a "patriot"—that is, a man relied upon by the communist government. The other, who did not follow suit, has been pushed into the background. Of the forty bishops, fewer than twenty were officiating at the time of the communist takeover. All the others were consecrated later by the "patriotic" archbishop, as indeed he was entitled to do. All of them, without exception, are "patriots." Together with the old bishops, the new "patriotic" bishops make up the episcopal conference where "patriots" are therefore in the majority and see that the wishes of the regime are carried out.

"Although the Vatican has changed somewhat, it remains the foe of the Chinese nation, an accomplice of imperialism," declared the functionaries. In my opinion, the first part of that statement suggests that some contact has been made between the Chinese Catholics and the Vatican.

I asked about the material condition of the Catholic Church. The church properties have been confiscated, but the state pays "a rental interest that exceeds the legal requirement." Hence the Catholic Church must receive an income from the state treasury. "Further sums accrue to the church from collections among the faithful and through the distribution and sale of periodicals and books," I was told. But there is only one Catholic periodical in China, which appears irregularly under the title *Carrier Pigeon*.

A similar Protestant periodical is called *Heavenly Wind*. The Buddhist publication appears more often and bears the title, *Buddhism in the Present Time*.

There is a Catholic publishing house in Shanghai, but it produces mainly bibles. Naturally, there is no religious instruction in the schools, and it may not be given in the churches.

I asked whether the priests received salaries from the state. They do not—the church is supposed to support itself. But priests, "like all citizens of the state," could call for financial aid from the government in time of need. There are also a number of lay priests "who live by the work of their hands."

I asked whether missionary activity continues and whether it is still possible to join a church. "Anyone can join the church, and anyone can leave the church. Both freedoms are guaranteed."

Further emphasis is placed on the assertion, "Religious freedom is a long-range policy. It will remain in force for many decades."

The Youth Association leader added, "We will not solve the problem of religion for at least another hundred years. We do not resort to force. It's a question of ideology, of strengthening the conscience of the masses."

But co-existence between the government and the various churches is not as peaceful as it may seem. Aside from the extensive atheistic propaganda and psychological pressure on the faithful, the government has other effective weapons. I became aware of this when I asked what functions were served by the research section of the Office for Religious Affairs.

"We are responsible for determining which churches are to be renovated and maintained. We have to concern ourselves with the financial needs of the priests and other functions."

Among the other functions is allocating the paper supply to the church publications—a very strong lever for the state.

At the end of my talks with the heads of the Office for Religious Affairs, they felt compelled to outline their position once more. "Our friends ask us why we tolerate religion. It is true that Marxism-Leninism stands in opposition to religion. We don't believe in it. That's one thing. How we treat religion is another thing. We have decided on a policy of religious freedom after a profound analysis of Marxism-Leninism. Marxism offers a scientific explanation of why religions come into existence, why they persist, and why they will automatically disappear with the development of the social order. We can wait for that development. It would be a mistake to hasten its arrival by force."

Naturally that depends on one's interpretation of "force." The period in which priests were persecuted and the faithful were exposed to severe pressures is apparently over. But it has borne fruit. Only "national churches" are left in China, churches that follow the wishes of the state and its dictates. Naked force is no longer necessary.

News of bloody religious persecution reaches us from only one province of present-day China: from Tibet. There the theocratic state on the roof of the world has been destroyed.

"Chairman" Dalai Lama

One morning my interpreter surprised me with the news that I was expected in an hour at the "House of Nationalities." I had not requested such a visit, so I supposed that the foreign ministry had its own reasons for inviting me.

The director of the house received me in an extravagant tearoom, but in our long conversation I learned only that the building had been constructed during the "Great Leap Forward," and that it served as a home, exhibition hall, and meeting place for China's national minorities. Here congresses were held to discuss and solve such problems as autonomy, education, agriculture, and industrialization.

As I have mentioned, China has several dozen different minority groups who, in return for unconditional submission to Chinese sovereignty and to communism, have been granted some autonomous rights—apparently to a much greater degree than they had before.

Although the manager invited me to look through the house, there was no real guided tour of the rooms or inspection of the facilities. But he did call my attention to the exhibit on Tibet. While the history and development of all the national minorities are depicted in the large exhibition halls, Tibet predominates.

A young man received us at the entrance to the hall that

housed the Tibetan exhibits. He himself was a Tibetan, and the manager asked him to tell his life story. He must have done so several times before, for he gave me a bare outline without any hesitation. "I was born the son of a serf near Lhasa. The land on which we lived belonged to the cloister of the lamas. At that time most of the land in Tibet belonged to the clergy or the secular nobility. Until the Liberation the soil was tilled by serfs. My father and mother had to work in the fields for twelve to fourteen hours a day without pay. We children were taken along to the fields on our mother's back while we were small; later on, at six, we had to work too. We had no school. Those who didn't work hard were punished. Blows were the order of the day. Almost every day of the week we had to watch one of the serfs being tortured. They were locked up in cages or chained to a block of wood for the least mistake. We had no homes of our own and lived in hovels and caves. We carried on our backs the sedan chairs of the lamas and the wooden chairs of the nobles. We traveled sixteen miles or more in this fashion, and sometimes we were beaten. We had a life worse than horses. That was my youth. It was a life without hope."

A new era seemed to dawn when the Chinese Army of Liberation marched into Lhasa in 1951. Not right away, because the Chinese troops had only come "to protect the Tibetans." They didn't try to interfere with their lives. "Only those who actually worked for the Chinese could hope for a better life. So one day I ran away to a Chinese military camp and asked if I could work there," he went on. "I was accepted. For the first time in my life I was treated as a human being. There I first learned about the communist idea, and the soldiers taught me the fundamentals of Marxism. We Tibetans were enthusiastic and tried to gather as many young countrymen around us as we could. Finally the Liberation Army gave us a school. We learned to read and write. I was more than happy when I learned to read the writings of Chairman Mao Tse-tung for myself. We repeatedly urged our Chinese comrades to do something for the liberation of our people. But the power of the lamas and the nobles remained unshaken."

He told much more about his life and finally described, with animation, how the lamas and nobles "hatched a plot" in 1959, and stirred up the Tibetans against the Chinese troops. These troops—who had come into the country only "to keep the Tibetans from being taken over by the imperialists"—were treacherously attacked. What could the Chinese comrades do but defend themselves against the "counter-revolution"? The Dalai Lama fled, and with him the leaders of the lama dictatorship and the feudal nobles. The land was parceled out among the serfs and poor peasants. Now, for the first time in centuries, the Tibetans were free, he explained.

His only regret was that the backwardness of his people kept them from collectivizing the land and establishing people's communes. Tibet was at the beginning of a new development, so it was inevitable that the soil would remain the property of individual peasants for many years, each one tilling his own fields. But the young people were impatient to establish production associations (kolkhozes) and reach the highest organized form of the people's commune as soon as possible. Many of the younger Tibetans were moving to the cities, where they would build industrial plants with the help of Chinese comrades. For the first time Lhasa, the capital, had its own electric power plant and an iron works. This young man had been chosen to study in Peking and now he was working at the "House of Nationalities." That was his story.

We then began our tour of the exhibits. First we looked at documents, old engravings, books, and deeds, all in glass cases. I wondered what they were supposed to prove.

One of the engravings showed a Tibetan delegation at the court of a Chinese emperor. "In those days the Tibetans came to Peking to plead with China to take over the protection of Tibet. They also asked the emperor of China to send scribes and administrators to Tibet so that the Tibetans could share in the great Chinese culture. The emperor acceded to their wishes, and since that time the Tibetans have been under the protection of China and have absorbed Chinese culture. When the imperialists say that Tibet was a free state which China annexed, this is not true. Our link with the Chinese has always been a very strong one, and only under Chinese protection were we able to lead an autonomous existence. The barbarians and imperialists were able to subjugate us only in periods when the Chinese were weak. Under the leadership of Chairman Mao Tse-tung, China is strong again, and Tibet is glad that China stands ready to protect and defend her." Again, my companion sounded as though he had said the same words many times before.

The documents on display were meant to prove his statements. Many were memoranda of negotiations between the Tibetans and the Chinese emperors, copies of Chinese-Tibetan treaties, and the protocols of Chinese administrators in Tibet itself. As all these documents were in either Chinese or Tibetan script (the latter, remarkably enough, came from India), I had to rely on my guide's translations.

The next cases contained documents showing how the "imperialists" had tried to subjugate Tibet. Several were in English. There were exchanges of correspondence between the Dalai Lama and British envoys, copies of supposed instructions to investigate Tibetan uprisings against the Chinese rule, "proof of the conspiracy against China." Some of the documents were as much as fifty years old. Others originated between 1956 and 1959. Among them were letters reportedly written to inflame public opinion and provoke intervention of the United States and the United Nations in Tibet.

Another collection of documents revealed that the Indians had made themselves "the tools of the imperialists," stirring up the Tibetans against China and instigating revolts in an attempt to bring Tibet under Indian influence.

The next hall had photographs showing how Chinese troops had found the Tibetan people, dressed in rags, living in caves, sleeping in places no better than stables. Others showed columns of serfs carrying lamas in wooden chairs. There were pieces of clothing with explanatory markers. "This clothing was worn by the serf So-and-So for sixty-one years. He had no other clothes." The clothing consisted of nothing more than patches sewed together and caps supposedly worn by three generations of serfs. The home of a family of serfs had been reconstructed here. This and all the other exhibits were meant to show the poverty and misery in which the Tibetan people existed before the Chinese troops came.

Naturally, another side was shown too. In the next room the pomp and magnificence of the priesthood were highlighted, with valuable ritual objects, gorgeous vestments, gold and silver artifacts. There were long lists of the serfs belonging to various cloisters or to noble families, and household account books showing how much income was enjoyed by the monastery or the noble family and how little they had spent on provisions for the serfs.

Then I entered a torture chamber in which dozens of instruments had been collected, along with old engravings, records of court proceedings and verdicts, extracts from archives—all intended to convince the visitor that torture had been used by Tibet's ruling classes until the 1950's.

In the middle of the room stood two large cages with holes in their tops. According to our guide, prisoners had been put in these cages with their heads sticking up through the holes. Then the cages were raised on poles. Only those who were as tall as the cage could stand up. Those who were shorter—and most of them were—hung by their heads. An old engraving showing this form of torture offered the necessary proof. The torturers also cut out their victims' tongues and gouged out their eyes. One of the engravings showed the heart torn out of a man's body. In front of the pictures, the instruments used were on display in glass cases.

Then we came to the most gruesome exhibit of all. A dozen human tongues, several hearts, glass containers filled with human eyes in alcohol, and among them a few dolls. "Those are no dolls," the guide said. "Those are children. That sort of thing often happened in Tibet. The children of serfs were killed and mummified, partly to punish the parents and partly to use in certain religious rituals."

The last room dealt with the Tibetan "counter-revolution." Pictures of the fighting between the Chinese troops and the Tibetans were shown. One of the most impressive showed a row of high lamas, advisers to the Dalai Lama, in their long robes, with hands crossed above their heads, being led from the palace of the Dalai Lama by heavily armed Chinese officers. "That was the staff of the counter-revolution," the guide explained. Other pictures showed

Tibetan volunteers behind machine-guns, rifles, pistols, bayonets, and other arms taken from the Tibetan insurgents.

At the end of my tour of inspection I realized why this visit to the "House of Nationalities" had been arranged in addition to the planned program. I had expressed a desire to visit Tibet—a desire which, as I have already explained, came to nothing because there was no available transportation. Here I had been offered a "substitute insight" into Tibetan conditions, albeit an insight through communist eyes. This is how Peking would like the world to see Tibet, the Chinese entry into that country, and the tragic events that followed on the roof of the world. We must assume that much of this serves propaganda purposes, but not all of it could have been invented.

The Tibetans were not always poor mountain people who consecrated their lives to Buddhism and asked no more than a devout life of prayer. The original Tibetans were one of the most warlike tribes of Asia. In the seventh century they were already a distinct people under strong military leadership, raiding and subjugating nearby provinces. Around that time a Tibetan fighting expedition is supposed to have invaded China, vanquished the Chinese army, and entered Peking as a conquering force.

But in the ninth century Buddhism was established as the official religion of the Tibetans, and its essential nature brought about the end of forays and conquests. Now the Tibetans themselves became the victims of aggression. The Mongol ruler, Kublai Khan, conquered them in 1247 and used the Tibetan highland as a military base for further Asiatic conquests. From this point he began his penetration of China, advancing as far as Peking. Tibetan troops were among his hordes. He conquered the Chinese capital and proclaimed himself emperor of China. From that time until the present, the destinies of China and Tibet have been interwoven. The Mongol rulers regarded Tibet as a province of their realm, which was also the Chinese realm. They apparently granted Tibet a high degree of autonomy and left the actual power in the hands of the Panchen Lama and the Dalai Lama.

Not the Panchen Lama but the Dalai Lama was the spiritual

head of Tibet. The Panchen Lama was the head of the secular government, although he too ranked high in the theocratic hierarchy. In the fourteenth century, at the latest, Tibet became a state controlled by the priesthood, inspired by religion in all spheres of life and based on religious precepts. Of the roughly 2,500,000 Tibetans, at least 300,000 were priests and monks. The Dalai Lama was considered a reincarnation of Buddha. For almost five hundred years, a coalition existed between the Panchen Lama and the Dalai Lama. The Dalai Lama gave orders to the monasteries and the priests, while the Panchen Lama conducted the affairs of government. All offices were held by both a secular and a religious official. But the final word on all matters was spoken by the priesthood. The lamas were in effect the superiors of their secular colleagues in all official positions. Again and again, friction developed between the Panchen Lama and the Dalai Lama. They frequently fought each other, and Tibetan history frequently describes the Panchen Lama or the Dalai Lama allying himself with some foreign power to act against his adversary. Chinese forces almost always played a part in these disputes. Dalai Lamas and Panchen Lamas fled into China and went into exile there.

After the Mongols, the Chinese rulers of the Ming Dynasty continued to rule over Tibet. Two high Chinese officials were always stationed in Tibet, although some were driven out and others put to death, which unleashed Chinese punitive expeditions. Nonetheless, Tibet managed to retain its established autonomy and there were periods when it shook off its dependence on China, but always when China was weak and wracked by war. Every strong Chinese emperor tried to reassert his country's rule over Tibet.

In 1792 Indian Gurkhas invaded Tibet but were bloodily beaten back by the Tibetans. It became necessary to seek help from China, so the Tibetans subjugated themselves to the Manchu Dynasty then in power. The Manchus were to protect Tibet thereafter.

China's sovereignty over Tibet failed in the nineteenth century, as China itself was being threatened by the European powers. In 1904 the first European expeditionary force entered Lhasa; an armed British mission started from India and concluded a trade treaty with the Tibetans. In 1906 the Chinese government was induced to recognize English influence in Tibet, in return for which Great Britain recognized Chinese sovereignty over that country. In 1907 an Anglo-Russian compact confirmed the sole right of the Chinese government to negotiate all matters pertaining to Tibet. Supported in its claims, China tried to solidify its suzerainty over Tibet militarily, and Chinese troops entered Lhasa.

After the fall of the Manchu Dynasty in 1911 the Chinese troops in Lhasa mutinied, bringing about a suspension of actual, effective Chinese control in this highland for a few years. The Tibetans declared themselves independent, while the new Chinese president, General Yüan Shih-kai, designated Tibet as a Chinese province. In 1913 the English arranged the so-called Conference of Simla, where it was determined that Tibet would have equal rights with China and England. But in 1914 Tibet recognized the suzerainty of China in exchange for a Chinese guarantee of autonomy. China received the right to nominate officials and to establish military garrisons in the eastern part of Tibet. And in 1922 the newly organized Communist Party of China declared as one of its objectives the firm incorporation of Tibet into the Chinese nation.

Furthermore, Chiang Kai-shek also clung to the suzerainty of China over Tibet, and he succeeded in having this claim confirmed repeatedly, especially by the United States. An attempt by the British to achieve autonomous status for Tibet during the Second World War was rebuffed by Washington. But with the collapse of the Chiang Kai-shek government in 1949, it looked as though Tibet might escape the grasp of the communists and remain an independent state.

The communists did not waste any time. During the expulsion of Chiang Kai-shek, the Panchen Lama fell into their hands. He had fled from Tibet and found refuge with Chiang Kai-shek. The Panchen Lama came to the same agreement with the communists that he had reached with Chiang Kai-shek: Chinese suzerainty over Tibet would be re-established and the leading position in the country would be restored to him.

In October, 1950, one year after the communist seizure of power in China, the Peking government announced that it had ordered the People's Liberation Army to "free [the Tibetans] from imperialist subjugation and to occupy China's western border." Peking's definition of "China's western border" was the western border of Tibet. In order to occupy it, they must occupy Tibet.

The Tibetan army, about ten thousand strong and relatively well armed by the British and the Indians, offered determined resistance but was overcome by 100,000 Chinese soldiers. Tibet's dream of independence was ended. The People's Liberation Army marched into Lhasa with red flags flying. There it came upon the Dalai Lama.

True to the example of the Chinese emperors, Mao Tse-tung did not want to depose the Dalai Lama and thus accept his ally, the Panchen Lama, as sole ruler of Tibet. Both lamas were brought to Peking, where in May, 1951, they signed "an agreement for the peaceful liberation of Tibet." This agreement provided that China would again assume responsibility for the defense and foreign policy of Tibet and, further, that it was entitled to maintain military garrisons there. Beyond that, Tibet's autonomy was guaranteed and the Dalai Lama and Panchen Lama were recognized as the spiritual and secular leaders of Tibet.

For a few years the Chinese proceeded cautiously. Their main concern was to establish reliable ties between China and Tibet. A road more than six hundred miles long was built to Lhasa. Simultaneously, construction of a railroad was begun. Several military and civil airports were built. The first telegraphic link with Lhasa and several other points was established by Peking. Tibet's Indian, Pakistani, and Afghan borders were occupied.

The Chinese Communists had not yet begun to interfere seriously with the religious, economic, and internal political life of Tibet. But they had begun to recruit workers for road and railway construction; and, according to a memorandum of the International Law Commission in Geneva, no less than 200,000 Tibetans had been forced into labor by the Chinese. The commission further announced that fifty thousand of these had died of hunger and exhaustion or had frozen to death. The Chinese were said to have begun arresting the abbots of the monasteries and killing some of them.

The first uprisings occurred in 1956 but were reportedly put down in a bloody battle. Now the Chinese undertook the ideological infiltration of Tibet. They knew where to find allies. The serfs were freed, Chinese laws for the equal rights of women were introduced, and schools were established for the young people. In the villages the Chinese founded people's councils (soviets; the Tibetan name for these is Minang Tsongdu). Through these people's councils the Chinese Party secretaries tried to convert the people to communism. Assemblies were held almost daily. But the people often arrived at the wrong conclusions in these assemblies, rejecting foreign domination and asking the Chinese to leave the country. Their obstinate belief in the Tibetan tradition made the villagers cling to their established customs and oppose Chinese legislation. The seeds of resistance against China were sown within the soviets. When Tibet stood on the brink of revolution in 1959, its resistance movement bore the singular name of Minang Tsongdu—"Soviet." The resistance had originated in the very soviets which the Chinese had established.

In March, 1959, the Dalai Lama, who had defied the Chinese, unlike the Panchen Lama, was asked to participate in a reception for the Chinese commander-in-chief in Tibet, General Chang Kuo-hua. The Dalai Lama's armed bodyguards were forbidden to accompany him. When this condition became known in Lhasa the word spread like wildfire from house to house: "They are going to arrest the Dalai Lama." Although there was no evidence to support this, the people of Lhasa surrounded the Dalai Lama's summer palace, demonstrated against the Chinese, and prevented the Dalai Lama from accepting the Chinese general's invitation. Upon this, Chinese troops marched up to the palace, Chinese artillery fired two shots, and the signal for the uprising was given. The Chinese troops found themselves under attack by the Tibetans. A bloody slaughter ensued. The Dalai Lama and his ministers and advisers fled from Lhasa. The Chinese, knowing nothing of this flight, ordered an aerial bombardment of the summer palace.

The bombs destroyed the summer palace, but the Dalai Lama was beyond their reach. He and his retinue fled across the Himalayas and reached the Indian border. Once in India, he appealed to the world and to the United Nations to help his people. At that time fighting was taking place everywhere in Tibet. The uprising was greater than the revolution in Hungary, but neither the world nor the United Nations could decide to help the Tibetans. According to all existing treaties, Tibet was an integral part of China, and so the Tibetan uprising was considered a matter of Chinese internal policy. Chiang Kai-shek was willing to render assistance with arms and airborne troops, but on condition that the Tibetans acknowledge the control of China. He was prepared to support an anticommunist uprising, but not an anti-Chinese one. If only for this reason, no Nationalist Chinese troops entered Tibet. In addition, Chiang lacked the necessary aircraft and bases. India, on the other hand, pleaded for a peaceful settlement, was prepared to recognize Chinese suzerainty over Tibet, and merely tried to mediate between the insurgents and the Chinese.

Reportedly, more than ten thousand Tibetans fell in the battle against the Chinese in Lhasa alone. In the next few years about 100,000 Tibetans are said to have followed the Dalai Lama into India. The International Law Commission in Geneva has released a report in which the extent of the fighting is described. According to this, tens of thousands of Tibetans lost their lives in battles with the Chinese, and it took China fully two years to subjugate Tibet. About 65,000 Tibetans are estimated by the Commission to have been executed after the uprising, many cloisters destroyed, and the monks killed or impressed into labor gangs. The Chinese are said to have decreed the deportation to China of all children between the ages of six and fifteen, and put them in boarding schools. The International Law Commission describes the actions of China in Tibet as "genocide." The entire hierarchy of lamas and nobles is said to have been wiped out.

It is certain that not much of the country's autonomy remained after the 1959 uprising. Even so, the Panchen Lama is now considered the head of the country, and he, like the Dalai Lama, remains a full member of the Tibetan government. Despite his flight, the Dalai Lama has not been officially deposed from his office as "chairman" (president) of Tibet. This is significant since the Dalai Lama may decide to return some day, which would no doubt ease the Chinese position in Tibet, especially if he were to present himself as an ally of China.

From China's policy in Tibet, it appears obvious that nationalistic motivations often take precedence over communistic reasons. The Chinese policy in Tibet is primarily nationalistic. The attempt to make common cause with the Tibetan theocracy, to keep the Panchen Lama and the incarnate Buddha as governors, to permit the Dalai Lama to continue as nominal head of an autonomous Tibetan government despite his opposition and subsequent exile—all these are indications of concern for the greater China. Communism merely goes along with it.

So far, land reform is still carried on, apparently out of fear that the people would renew their opposition if kolkhozes or even people's communes were introduced overnight. Colonization of Tibet is said to have been started on a grand scale, with hundreds of thousands of Chinese settling in the Tibetan highland in the last few years. The International Law Commission mentions claims that more than four million Chinese have been brought to Tibet, which would mean that there are now more Chinese than Tibetans. Is it to make certain that Tibet will never again escape Chinese domination?

As I was leaving Peking, a new film called *The Serfs* was being shown for the first time in the movie houses. It was meant to depict the oppression of the Tibetans before the Liberation. The principal actors were all Chinese.

26

The judge goes to the accused

We were in the appellate court for civil affairs. I entered a small courtroom. On a podium stood a desk adorned by two Soviet-type stars. Above, on the wall, hung a picture of Mao Tse-tung. Four people sat behind the desk: a woman judge who was presiding over the court, two assistant judges—one man and one woman—and a recording clerk. Their functions were listed on large white placards for the information of the accused and the spectators.

On a side wall hung another placard listing a few brief rules: children under eighteen were not admitted as spectators, the judge was responsible for maintaining quiet and order in the courtroom, and the parties involved could speak only after obtaining permission from the judge.

The procedure began without any formalities. No one rose when the judge entered the room. Plaintiff and defendant were called in by the bailiff. They took seats on two chairs in front of the judges without bowing or greeting the court. There were four benches for onlookers, and three other persons besides ourselves were there.

The case was a divorce hearing. An official of the health and welfare division of the Peking Railway Office was bringing an action for a divorce from his wife, a physician at the Peking hospital connected with the Railway Office. The plea had been rejected by a lower court.

The woman judge began the proceedings by introducing herself and her associates, and asked the couple whether they wanted to enter an objection about the composition of the court. Both said they accepted it. As in the West, the identification of the couple was read and confirmed. The plaintiff was then asked to state his reasons for wanting a divorce.

He claimed that his wife had neglected him for years, that their two children suffered from his wife's inability to get along with her mother-in-law, and that she had also become hostile toward his family. The wife denied it all. It was true that she had neglected her husband, but for the last year she had tried to remedy this. He had made it impossible for her to do so. He was selfish and stubborn and kept demanding that she confess to misdeeds she had never committed.

For nearly two hours the judges tried to get at the facts from the testimony of the husband and wife. Their family life was gone over in detail, and finally the crucial question was put to both of them: "Are you still in love?" He said "No." She said "Yes." He wanted the divorce, she did not.

Then came a second crucial question which must be understood in the light of China's past. The wife was asked, "Did you enter the marriage of your own free will?"

Until 1949 marriages were arranged by the parents, and the woman was not always asked whether she wanted to marry the man of her choice. But here the question was answered in the affirmative by both husband and wife. It had been a love marriage.

Now the husband was asked to leave the courtroom. The judges interrogated the wife. It became apparent that the court was better informed about the details of the couple's life than had been evident during the testimony. They knew that the wife had acted badly. She admitted it. And she was contrite. She delivered a perfect self-criticism.

The court indicated that it was satisfied and asked the wife to draw the logical conclusions from her self-criticism. She promised not to repeat her errors, which she had now recognized as such, and to try to atone for them. Again the judge asked her whether she still felt "true love" for her husband. She said emphatically that she did.

She was asked what she hoped for if the marriage continued. She believed that the marriage could become harmonious again and, above all, that the couple should devote themselves to bringing up their children.

The court withdrew to deliberate.

Next the husband was urged to try again to live with his wife. But he declined, pointing out that this advice had already been given by the lower court, and that it had been fruitless.

It was then pointed out that neither party had been guilty of adultery. In view of this circumstance, the court handed down the decision, for which the judges and plaintiff rose from their seats. The divorce was not granted.

Although this scene reveals very little about the legal system of China, it shows that the prescribed legal principles are strictly followed even in such non-political matters as divorce. In my subsequent conversation with the presiding judge of the court I learned that there are firmly established laws for only a few legal questions. There is no general legal code in present-day China.

This is in contrast to the old China, as well as the China of Chiang Kai-shek. In imperial China the administration of justice was scrupulously observed. China is regarded as one of the oldest constitutional states in the world. The emperors of the Han Dynasty created a separate ministry of justice two thousand years ago. The first record of a code of law dates from 536 B.C., and by the end of the fourth century B.C. a codification of criminal law was introduced by Li Ku'i. In the year 200 the Chinese legal code contained 26,272 paragraphs of more than seventeen million words. Some 960 volumes were required to accommodate this plethora of laws.

Only with the decline of the monarchy in the nineteenth century did jurisdiction also decay. The paragraphs remained, as did the courts; but as the central power of the government no longer reached into many regions of China, and as it was weakened in other areas by mismanagement and corruption, the law often became too flexible to guarantee justice.

Under Chiang Kai-shek's rule new laws were introduced to bring Western and especially Anglo-Saxon concepts of law to China. But soon the same situation arose as in the last decades of the monarchy, and the administration of justice, like the government, became weakened and corrupt.

Communist China has enacted few legal edicts. The constitution itself sets forth at some length the rights and duties of citizens. It is a modern and, at first glance, a democratic constitution. All citizens are equal before the law, and all their freedoms are guaranteed.

But all these paragraphs are necessarily limited by the fact that the state is ruled by the "dictatorship of the proletariat" and that the citizens must serve this dictatorship. This restricts personal freedom, and, furthermore, leaves it to the authorities to decide whether or not the citizen is transgressing against the dictatorship by his actions.

It is not possible to extend this simple but effective restriction to every sphere of life. Therefore the government has issued some edicts that have acquired the force of law. They concern "guidelines for the arrest of citizens," "guidelines for the expropriation of real estate," "guidelines for the preservation and dissolution of marriages," and "guidelines for the organization of the courts."

In addition, "education through labor" has been elevated to the status of a law. It is the aim of this law to "promote order and socialistic reconstruction in the country." In the opinion of the officials, anyone who disturbs the order, opposes it, or fails to contribute adequately to socialist reconstruction can be forced to perform useful labor. The official explanation is that this is aimed at tramps, professional beggars, loafers, drunks, and other antisocial elements, of which there were hundreds of thousands in China, if not millions. But some sections of the law do not apply only to these groups. The forced-labor law applies to anyone who "offends against work discipline, and who after being dismissed from his job cannot find any means of support."

Forced labor is also for those who "do not follow work instructions, object to being assigned to a difficult job, refuse to listen to anything at their place of work, come into conflict with official business, or do not improve despite repeated attempts to educate them."

Clearly this paragraph makes it possible for any individual who does not submit to the instructions of the Party secretaries, factory directors, and chairmen of communes, or who does not carry out their instructions to the letter, to be charged.

The majority of the Chinese—who are rightly known throughout the world for their diligence and willingness to work—have undoubtedly submitted to the decrees of the government and the Party. The slogans of the communists did not fall on deaf ears when they appealed to the Chinese people to help make China once more great, mighty, and the equal of other nations. Chinese nationalism is so strong, particularly in view of all that happened to China in the nineteenth and twentieth centuries, that the people voluntarily endured many sacrifices to reach this goal. Nevertheless, there must have been millions who did not readily submit to the harsh discipline and the exorbitant demands of the regime. That the Chinese people have been totally disciplined can best be explained by the law for "education through labor."

"Re-education through labor" can take place in prisons, camps, penal communes, on irrigation projects, railroads, and dams, and probably in mines; perhaps today mainly in the remote, inhospitable parts of the country. Chinese refugees have reported that in addition to hard labor and ideological training, physical punishment was the order of the day in prison; but only labor and ideological training were resorted to in camps and penal communes.

Camp inmates were divided into groups of six, led to practice criticism and self-criticism several times a week, and expected to vie with each other in "rethinking, repenting, and reforming." The degree to which they rethought was constantly under review, and it is interesting to note that conclusions were reached not by talking with the inmates but by observing them at work. American psychologists have confirmed this method. One who is not inwardly convinced that his punishment is justified, who continues to resist authority, is unable to do his work wholeheartedly, even if he wants to make a good impression for opportunistic reasons. But he who lets himself be educated, who realizes that his attitude has been detrimental "to the interests of the Chinese people," and who is ready to become a "new person," joining enthusiastically in the new regime, will also succeed in his work and will gradually be pardoned. At first he is permitted to work without surveillance. Later he may remain as a "freed man" in the penal colony and may be permitted to marry and establish a family.

Western experts who have investigated this system on the basis of testimonies offered by numerous refugees have come to the conclusion that the Chinese method probably brings anti-social persons back into society as healthy members, but that on the other hand it would break the resistance of political opponents, except a few with especially strong convictions.

This "re-education through labor" is also a part of what is called brainwashing. But it is employed not only against political opponents, but also against malingerers and people who object to the work tempo.

"Re-education through labor" apparently was quite rigorous during the first few years after the communist seizure of power. As citizens were required to denounce their neighbors for merely dirtying the street or trying to obtain personal advantages, let alone for becoming involved in political activity against the communist government, it seems likely that hundreds of thousands, if not millions, spent longer or shorter periods in the labor camps. This is openly admitted in China. In the opinion of the Chinese, re-education is not a negative thing but an "achievement of the socialist order of society" and an auxiliary means of "reforming people for their own good."

This also solves the riddle of how and why 700 million Chinese have abandoned many of their deeply ingrained habits in just a few years. It explains why one can leave money practically lying in the street and never see anyone pick it up except (and then only before witnesses) to take it to the police. In the hotels where I stayed the servants came after me with things I had thrown into the wastebasket, which they believed were still usable. For example, it was impossible to get rid of a pair of worn-out shoes. Wherever I threw them, they were promptly returned to me.

For these reasons, the Chinese police manage with a minimum of laws which apply to almost everything. This makes it possible for them to adjust their judgments to the changing requirements of the state—that is, to the current policy of the Communist Party.

The presiding judge of the court of appeals confirmed this interpretation. "The law has to serve the dictatorship of the proletariat, the interests of the proletariat and the state, just as do the police and the army. In the execution of its duties, justice has to start solely and exclusively from the basic premise."

I asked how this could be reconciled with the "equal rights for all" provided for in the constitution. The presiding judge said frankly, "The law in our country has to serve one class, the proletariat. This is represented by its dictatorship. As the dictatorship wants only the best for the proletariat, its guiding principles serve the rights of all citizens."

From this I concluded that citizens who are not proletarians are without rights, and that even proletarians could come into conflict with the government if they did not feel that the dictates of the government were useful to them.

The judge retorted, "That is not correct. For instance, it is in the interest of the dictatorship of the proletariat that non-proletarians, too, receive full rights. By observing this principle, we foster the dictatorship of the proletariat and, at the same time, all citizens have equal rights. Conversely, the proletarian must also be held accountable if he offends against the interests of the dictatorship of the proletariat. He is merely a single member of the proletarian class. As such he can transgress against the interests of his class."

I asked how law is administered in China. "The case you saw today is not typical. It gives the impression that justice is meted out in the courtroom. That seldom happens. Sentence is usually pronounced on the spot."

"Where and how?"

The judge explained how the law works. If a plaintiff appears or a denunciation is made, the court goes "to the site." It questions the plaintiff and the defendant in their living quarters, in the factory or people's commune where they work, or wherever they may be. The members of the family are also interrogated.

"Then the court listens to the people—the workers in the factory, the tenants of an apartment building, the street committee [which I have yet to describe], the friends of the accused, the labor union, the youth league, the women's organization, or the Party, if the accused is a member of any of those organizations."

In this way the court gets a "comprehensive survey of the facts." More than that, "it takes the total thought processes of the defendant into consideration in its deliberations. It examines his whole life, his behavior with others and at work." The court then passes a suitable sentence immediately, in the factory, in the people's commune, or at home.

"Its main concern is to re-educate the defendant, to make amends for his faults, and to remove any discord. For it is a people's soviet, presided over by judges from among the people. Therefore they are guided by what best serves the people," the judge explained.

"Isn't the court sometimes over-influenced by the testimony taken on the spot?" I asked.

"No. Since 1949 the consciousness of the masses has improved to such an extent that what they say carries a great deal of weight. The masses tell the truth. The masses are a collective entity, and the entity never errs. Above all, it always acts in the interest of the state."

Trial procedures cost nothing; neither the plaintiff nor the defendant pays any court costs. I asked whether, in view of this fact, the courts were not swamped with cases.

"Oh, no," said the presiding judge. "Relatively few complaints are handed in. People basically want nothing to do with the courts. They try to iron out their differences within the family or among their colleagues."

In other words, the people have remained faithful to the ancient system of meting out justice within the family, and they generally shy away from calling on the people's courts for help.

I asked if it were possible for the accused to defend himself.

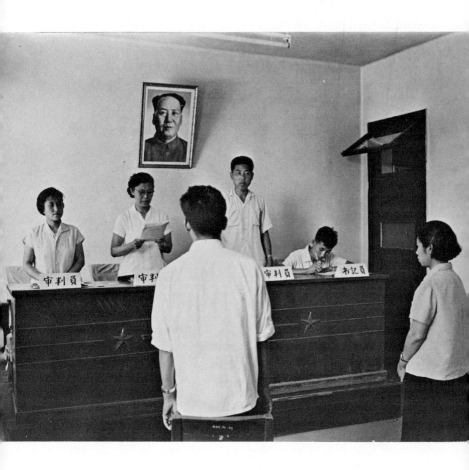

A court of appeals in Peking, where a decision in a divorce case
is being handed down. The lady judge is flanked by two jurors.

"That is the best thing he can do. It gives him his best chance, for his defense shows his thinking, and his thinking enables the judges to pass just sentence."

"Are there any lawyers?"

"Yes, they exist. But they cost money. That's why few defendants turn to a lawyer."

"As there are no private occupations in China, the lawyer has to be an employee of the state. Is it possible for him to defend the accused against the state?" I asked further.

"Attorneys are not employees of the state. They have an association, a society which is recognized as autonomous," the judge said.

So they form a sort of cooperative and, like all members of cooperatives, are dependent on the state because it pays them.

As there is hardly any possibility of interpreting the legal texts for the benefit of the accused, let alone finding a loophole in them, and as the judge's sentence is predetermined on the basis of the "testimony taken from the masses," I do not believe that a lawyer has much scope for action in China.

Nevertheless, the presiding judge tried to explain to me that "there are many possibilities for the defense of those accused." It turns out that they can also be defended by representatives of any mass organization—that is, the Party, the youth organization, the union, the women's organization, etc. One does not need legal training to do this.

Moreover, the judges need not have any legal training either. By virtue of a decree of the people's council on jurisdiction, any Chinese artisan can be appointed a judge after his twenty-third birthday, on condition that he has led an unblemished life. The appointment is announced by the people's council of the province.

However, the Chinese universities have graduate law schools. The people's councils prefer to have graduate lawyers as judges and states' attorneys. These graduates have been especially indoctrinated in the "guidelines of the state."

I inquired whether the court based its verdict on confession alone or whether it was required to seek corroboration through objective evidence. The presiding judge said that a confession alone was not sufficient evidence for a conviction. However, the testimony of the "masses" is regarded as objective evidence, at least in political offenses. There is a bill pending to provide for the punishment of political crimes: the decree for the suppression of counter-revolution. It is severe.

I asked whether the death sentence was often pronounced.

"Death sentences are pronounced in cases of murder, rape, and counter-revolutionary activities." But then the judge continued, "We avoid imposing the death sentence as much as possible. We lay much more stress on re-educating the person. Death sentences are meted out in cases where the indignation of the masses is too great. The judges cannot go against the will of the masses."

The indignation of the masses is undoubtedly great enough when the Party wants the death sentence inflicted; when this is not desired, the masses are probably lenient.

Since the aim of the sentence is the re-education of the individual, I asked if the sentence was given without specifying a time limit. After all, it is possible for one person to be re-educated in a relatively short time, while another needs more time. Such an argument, I found, was inadmissible. "The sentence always specifies a definite period of punishment. If the person is rehabilitated sooner, the prison administration can remit a part of his time. But it is usually not more than a quarter or a third of the sentence. There are also amnesties."

"How can the prison administration tell that a convict has been re-educated?"

"The educators in the prisons and the labor and training camps work with the convicts. They know their thinking. They note the results of the re-education, mainly in the work performed and the attitude of the prisoner toward his work."

There are no fixed limits on punishment for specific crimes. The sentence depends upon the "opinion of the masses," the circumstances, the attitude of the accused, and his previous conduct.

I was told that China does not have a particularly large police force. The total number of police, traffic officers, criminal investigators, secret service personnel, and special task forces is less than two million. This is quite possible. The authorities get their information from many sources which have no direct connection with the police apparatus. Above all, they get it from the "street committees."

Every street in a Chinese city or village has such a committee. Long streets have more than one. The street committee is an arm of the Party.

When I asked what these committees did, I was told that they work in two directions: they transmit the wishes and instructions of the authorities (and the Party) to the people, and they are charged with the responsibility for carrying the wishes and criticisms of the people to the authorities (and the Party). "They provide a close link between the people and the government," I was told.

This kind of "attention" also extends into the factories, people's communes, and other work places. Here functionaries of the Party, the union, and other organizations are mainly concerned with the "ideological consciousness of the masses." In effect, the politico-ideological training of the people is going on constantly.

It seems to be pursued intensely at times, more loosely at other times. According to reports, in previous years and particularly during the "Great Leap Forward," each free moment seems to have been used for the ideological indoctrination of the masses. I was able to see, during my stay in China, that the work forces of individual enterprises had to attend a meeting for criticism and self-criticism at least once a week.

When I asked about this I was told, "Political training is a voluntary matter; the workers themselves determine whether, when, and where and how often they want to assemble. The management of the factory [or the people's commune, the hospital, the college, etc.] has nothing to do with it."

There have been times when the communists required every individual to turn in a written self-accusation. Hundreds of these were said to have been posted on the walls of factories. I saw no evidence of that practice, and the feeling prevails in China that the government and Party are giving the people a breathing spell.

It is surely no more than a pause, for radio, television, and newspapers constantly feature appeals for an intensified class struggle. The effort to eliminate the middle class and everything that deviates from Party doctrine still goes on full blast. Future campaigns within the framework of the class struggle are to be expected. I got the impression that there were almost no gaps in the training and surveillance of the people of China.

Of course, this implies that the surveillance system is without loopholes. The authorities can rely on the street committees, the neighbors and colleagues. This explains why the courts are so well informed about the life and past history of defendants and why the judges conduct their trials "outside the courtroom," where the accused lives or works.

A few words about my own experience at this point will give at least a partial clue to the surveillance and control exercised over foreigners who visit China.

In no other country have I needed so many official papers as I did in China. They included an entry permit, an interior travel permit, a sojourn permit for each city, a permit to continue the trip, and an exit permit. In addition I received an identification as a journalist, to be shown if I ran into any difficulties. None of these documents was issued with any generosity. The dates for entry and expiration were specific, and not even a one-day delay would have been permitted unless I had requested a change beforehand.

For example, I could not have left Peking a day earlier or later than I did, and I had to take the plane or train for which my travel permit was valid. Likewise, it would have been impossible for me to make a change in my itinerary without prior authorization, or even to return to a city I had just left.

On the way from Nanking to Shanghai I mentioned to my interpreter, who was accompanying me, that I thought it would be a good idea to fly back to Peking from Shanghai so I could have another series of interviews there. He looked at me blankly. "You cannot go back, you have no permission."

I did get back to Peking, but it took a good deal of effort and a good deal of intervention before I got the necessary permits and the flight ticket.

For three days I was told that the return to Peking would simply come to nothing because the flights were booked solid. When the permit and flight ticket finally arrived, the plane was half empty. In my opinion, the lower-echelon officials were just being prudent; if the responsible office had not granted my travel request, the trip would have been impossible because the flights were fully booked—something known to happen in the West, too.

The exit permit was not issued until the end of my journey. During the greater part of my stay I had no real assurance that I would be let out of the country. I doubt that anyone in Peking ever had any idea of keeping me. All the same, it bothered me quite a bit that I had no exit permit, nor even a permit to get to the border, to say nothing of being allowed to cross it when I wanted to.

When entering or leaving, one has to state at exactly what point and by what means of transportation he plans to cross the Chinese border. Neither the entrance nor the exit can be made at a point not prearranged. This means that the authorities always know exactly when and where a foreigner crosses the border, his whereabouts in China, where he is going and how long he will stay in each place.

I soon realized that the authorities also knew what I was doing in each place, where I went and whom I saw. Of course it is hard to prove. As I said before, a foreigner is not allowed to choose his own hotel. It is picked out for him, and he learns its name only when he reaches the city.

At this point I want to emphasize that I am only describing my own experiences. I do not know whether tourists or businessmen, for example, are subject to the same controls as journalists.

I have no doubt that the interpreter provided to a foreigner in China supplies the authorities with a running commentary on his remarks and behavior. In my case it was quite obvious. A series of remarks I had made in "private" talks with the interpreter were picked up a few days later by other Chinese officials, although without any indication of their source. I soon learned to tell my interpreter things I wanted to get to the ears of the authorities. After a few days this little game became quite amusing.

So the interpreters make reports. But there are hours when you are alone. You can go for walks unaccompanied and generally do as you please so long as you don't break any laws. It wouldn't be necessary to answer the interpreter's questions the next day—but it would also be silly to refuse to answer, or to make up a story. Every floor of the hotel has its own hall porters who see you enter the stair-way or the elevator. You also pass a series of servants at the door of the hotel. They are always sitting behind their counters, doing noth-ing. If you take a cab or ricksha you are in the driver's company—and the same drivers are always on duty at the hotel.

If you stroll along by yourself you will soon attract attention, being a European; and if you do anything suspicious, of course it will be reported to the authorities. It would be impossible to enter a foreign embassy unnoticed. Policemen in their beautiful white uniforms and tropical helmets are posted in front of each embassy in pairs, as sentries. Through small telephone booths they can be in instant touch with their superiors.

The individual traveler may not notice this, or he may not resent it. This only became depressing to me when I visited other cities such as Anshan or Fushun or Changchun. There I was put up in well-furnished hotels, asked what I wanted for lunch and din-ner, and told when to go to the dining room. When I left my room at the appointed time a maid was at the door, to show me the way. She did not go with me, but at the next corner there was another maid, and so on from corridor to corridor, from one flight of stairs to the next, through the foyer of the hotel, and into the dining room. Once I counted five, and at another time six, maids who had been stationed there for my sole benefit. On the return trip the whole thing was repeated in reverse.

I tried several "breakouts." Politely but firmly, I was told that I was headed the wrong way. That soon became amusing, too.

Less amusing was the fact that except in Peking I nearly always had a large dining room to myself. I was by no means the only guest, but the others were all in another room. I could not only hear them, but on some of my breakouts I managed to get as far as the door and get a look at those happy throngs. They were all Chinese.

Even then I wasn't sure whether I had been isolated so that I would see and hear less or so that I would be undisturbed and un-observed during meals.

In Shanghai, where I was not the only European guest at the hotel, there was a different form of isolation. The beautiful restau-rant was on the top floor of the hotel, with rows of windows facing the harbor and the main thoroughfare. When I tried to sit near a window I was politely told that all the tables were reserved and that another table was being kept for me. It was in the middle of the rear wall, so that I was as far as possible from all the windows. I spent several days in that hotel and took all my meals in the restaurant. Only a few of the window tables were actually occupied. Most of them were empty all that time. But if I had sat there, I would have been able to see the dock installations and part of the harbor, and probably the ships arriving from other ports.

In China, I met English, Belgian, French, and Australian tourists who told me that in no other country had they been so well treated as in China. Their programs were conducted without friction, departures for sightseeing trips to historic cultural sites were always prompt, they returned on time to find a fabulous meal waiting, the service was quick and courteous and the hotels comfortable. There was no sign of any surveillance.

I am quite ready to believe that all they told me was true. In their eyes the guides, interpreters, waiters, and hotel servants had no other function than their counterparts in the rest of the world. And the tourists wanted only what they wanted in other places. They came with a group, wanted to stay with the group, and the prearranged program was what they expected. Why shouldn't everything be comfortable and free of friction?

On the other hand, I must admit that, at my request and therefore with official permission, I was shown a surprising number of things in China: industrial installations, people's communes, housing developments, universities, hospitals, etc. It was a great deal more than I had been shown in other countries that are ruled by dictatorships. Further, the directors and functionaries gave me, in my opinion, rather candid and complete information. There was no lack of interesting and revealing contacts. But I felt that all this was being done on special orders, and that a journalist can work successfully in China only as long as the authorities wish.

27

What people read in China

In one respect there is complete conformity between China, the Soviet Union, and other communist countries: the press. In a communist country nothing is more monotonous than a newsstand, and the Chinese newsstands are perhaps the most monotonous of the lot. Not because, as a European, the tourist can't read the papers; on the contrary, the strange print gives the impression that they are quite lively. But one soon comes to recognize the same monotony that prevails, in say, *Pravda* or *Neues Deutschland* or *Rude Pravo*. The articles are interminable, seldom broken by a subhead, and full of ideological phrases and flowery terms which strike the Western visitor as too abstract, too ornamental, or too far removed from reality. News—that is, reports on important events—is almost always missing. At best, you get an ideological interpretation of what has happened, and it is difficult to reconstruct the actual event.

I was amazed at the apparent ease with which Chinese journalists seem to bring all these abstract ideological essays home to the reader. The Chinese script consists of ideographs. Most of the signs stand for concrete objects, and abstract ideas can be reproduced only through combinations of them. Until recently, Marxist concepts were strange not only to the Chinese but also to their written language. What signs could one use for "dialectical materialism" or "socialist realism"?

"That presents no problem to us," a Chinese official told me. At first I was inclined to think that Marxist terminology, already highly developed in the European languages, had simply been incorporated into Chinese; that communism had introduced numerous foreign words into the Chinese language. Far from it. The Chinese language has incorporated few foreign words, and for a good reason. Because the European languages are based on the Latin alphabet, it is relatively easy to adapt foreign expressions. This is impossible with Chinese pictography. Each sign represents a syllable or a word rather than a letter, so words from European languages cannot be reproduced letter by letter. One can only try to find Chinese words that correspond phonetically to European syllables, and even that is difficult. Almost any Chinese word can be pronounced in four different tones, or melodies, each signifying something entirely different. If the Chinese tried to transfer words from the European languages into their own, they would have to use Chinese words that would halfway correspond in sound to the European pronunciation; but the words have, of course, their own original Chinese meaning, and the foreign words thus taken into the language would correspond to some Chinese concept. It would be impossible to choose similar sounding Chinese words and string them together to achieve a phonetic imitation of the foreign word; the Chinese words used would have to make the same sense as the foreign word.

The first foreign words the Chinese had to assimilate were designations for the people from strange lands who had landed on their shores. They tried to imitate the sounds of England, France, America, Germany, Russia, and yet give them a Chinese meaning. From the word "America" they took the sound of the Chinese words "Mei-guo," meaning "Beautiful Country." So the Americans became "people from the Beautiful Country." For "France" they found Chinese words signifying "Country and Law," "Fa-guo." In the same way, England became "Intelligent Country," Germany "Virtuous Country," and, as a neologism of our century, the Soviet Union was "Awakening Country."

I asked who invented these words. "Our translators. They are the first to encounter foreign words, and they have to translate them into Chinese. They look for designations the Chinese can adapt easily, that retain part of the phonetic value of the foreign word and yet can be easily reproduced in our language and in our script."

He mentioned a few examples, among them the word "communism." It is represented by a Chinese word combination meaning "common property"—everything belongs to everybody. The word "tractor" underwent a similar transformation; it was partly preserved phonetically in a phrase composed of the words "pull" and "machine." Other modern concepts were reproduced by combinations of old established expressions. Electricity received the Chinese designation for "lightning"; "film" became "electrical shadow play," and department stores—something new for the Chinese—to this day are called "large houses with a hundred wares."

The largest Chinese lexicon contains sixty thousand different characters. Many of them convey a single concept, and many have been eliminated in the course of the writing reform carried on by the communists. Other characters were simplified so they would be easier to write. In the beginning, each written character stood for a word. But as the language developed it became necessary to use two or more characters to express new words. Today, it is taken for granted that an intellectual has a command of five thousand to six thousand characters. Chinese elementary schools try to teach the pupils approximately three thousand characters. Those who know 3,500 characters can read about 95 per cent of a current Chinese newspaper.

Newspaper printing plants have six thousand different characters at their disposal; but so far no workable typesetting machine has been invented that can handle so many characters. For that reason, all Chinese newspapers have to be set by hand; that is, the compositors have to take the characters by hand from the type fonts and assemble them into words and sentences. As early as 1928, the Chinese government under Chiang Kai-shek tried to introduce the Latin alphabet to supplement the Chinese written characters. This reform failed, although it was later tried again. After they seized power, the communists tackled this problem energetically, requiring all Chinese words to be reproduced by Latin letters. In 1949 about 90 per cent of the Chinese population were still classified as illiterate, since it takes about six years to learn sufficient characters to read a newspaper. This meant that nearly 600 million people had to be taught to read and write.

But the communists were unable to achieve complete success with this program, although today the street signs in all Chinese cities bear both Latin and Chinese letters. All important printed matter, books and newspapers, is almost entirely printed in Chinese characters. There are supposed to be some newspapers printed in Latin characters, but I was unable to find one. Furthermore, it is emphasized that the Chinese characters must be preserved under all circumstances, as an expression of Chinese individuality and thought. Compared with Latin letters, each Chinese character is a miniature work of art. Even the most aggressive communist phrases take on the appearance of abstract paintings when written in Chinese characters.

But the script is the least problem to be faced by present-day Chinese journalists.

"The press in our country is an instrument of the class struggle in the hands of the working class. It has to represent solidly the viewpoint of the proletariat or, in other words, to guard the interests of the overwhelming majority of the population. It has to fight the forces of aggression and imperialism, led by the United States, and to expose them. In addition it has to support the struggle of the oppressed peoples, and to tie their friendly relationships together in the spirit of proletarian internationalism." That was the answer the chairman of the press guild in Shanghai gave to my question about the aims of the Chinese press.

This indicates what can be expected of the contents of a Chinese newspaper. Just the same, I wanted to know what the sixty Chinese daily papers wrote about.

This is the picture that emerges:

1. About international events, the Chinese press publishes only what is handed out by the official government press agency, Hsiuhua (New China). "We have unlimited faith in the reliability and truthfulness of this agency," my informant said.

2. Domestic political reports, especially the speeches of high government and Party functionaries, descriptions of mass meetings,

etc., are also supplied to the newspapers by the government and Party.

3. The successes of "socialist reconstruction" are reported. "This reconstruction gives us a lot of material. It shows how the backwardness of the country is being overcome, how the people are gaining control over their country, how enthusiastically they are going about it, and what a high moral level is being maintained," the Chinese editor said. This news category consists mainly of descriptions of exemplary work performances in factories, people's communes, and the remote regions. "The heroes of labor" are honored and presented as models to the rest of the people.

4. Reports on literature, art, science, and sports; new editions of books, especially the works of Mao Tse-tung; the revolutionary transformation of the Peking opera; the plots of movies; scientific discoveries and inventions.

5. It is the task of the press to raise the "revolutionary awareness" of the people. To this end, it publishes reports of the activities of "Chiang Kai-shek agents," of the "crimes of imperialism," and occasionally of sabotage and "counter-revolutionary acts."

"In short, it is our task to instill a new morality in the people and to give them examples from which they can learn," said the chairman of the union. Incidentally, he was on the staff of the Shanghai daily, *Liberation*.

Then he revealed that 80 per cent of the content of his paper, as of Chinese newspapers generally, was edited not by the press agencies or the editors but by the readers themselves. Readers supplied the newspapers with "worthwhile and important reports."

I immediately asked what kind of material these reports contained. He gave me a few examples. "Right now it is very hot. The people can't get to sleep until late at night. They don't even like to go indoors. So they sit on benches in the park and talk. A fourteen-year-old Young Pioneer writes us that on the benches and the sidewalks there is a lot of talk about superstitions and about dirty things. He challenges the public to talk about more important things. We might talk about how things were before the Liberation, how well off we are today, what tasks the socialist reconstruction demands of us, and what we have achieved.

"This Young Pioneer's letter was printed prominently in *Liberation*. But that was not the end of the matter, by any means. It pulled an enormous reader response. Many agreed with the young boy, supported his ideas, and gave further examples of what should be talked about on these hot evenings. We printed a number of their letters, and this moved other Chinese newspapers to take up their suggestions and to start a campaign of their own. Thus, a young reader started a wave of newspaper reports all over China."

That is not all. A thousand letters came in from readers who promised "the newspapers and the people" that they would keep their conversation "clean" and "true to the rules."

"That's what you use to fill the pages of your paper?" I asked.

"Yes, of course; it's interesting and necessary. But we also publish news and reports with which we don't agree," my informant said.

But this doesn't contradict the rules. He went on: "For instance, the speeches and accusations made against China by the revisionists in the Soviet Union. They talk against us, but we print every word. Our newspapers are very courageous in this respect; they trust the ability of the people to recognize lies and to unmask them. We leave it to the people to condemn such opinions."

This unmasking occurs promptly. Thousands of letters to the editors express their readers' indignation over "the expressions of the revisionists" and refute them. These contributions are printed in page after page of the newspaper. Finally the newspaper itself takes an editorial stand on the matter, explains why the readers are right, and condemns the "revisionists."

It was the combined editorial staffs of two newspapers, the *Peking People's Daily* and the *Red Flag,* who composed the lengthy and famous replies to the open letter of the Communist Party of the Soviet Union and carried the Chinese attack on "the leadership of the CPSU."

I asked whether the papers carried any local news. This was affirmed at once. Work achievements in the local factories, local heroes of labor, and cultural events are reported.

"What about fires, crimes, violence, thefts, and so on?"

"In the old-time Shanghai newspapers [that is, before the communist takeover] there were stories of murder, suicide, and rape, as well as so-called society news," I was told. "Our people don't want to read about such things. Nevertheless, we sometimes publish this type of news. What matters is not that we report something, but *how* we report it."

"What do you mean?"

"If there is a fire, the event itself is of secondary importance. What matters is how the people fought the fire, how they risked their lives and made sacrifices. That means the story is educational."

He cited other examples. "There are no objective reports on crimes. That is, we don't describe the crime and the circumstances under which it was committed. We report that the criminal is sorry for his deed, that he acknowledges his fault, and the moral conclusions that can be drawn from it. There was a young worker who was interested only in amusements, so he couldn't concentrate on his work. This caused great damage in the factory. He recognized his fault, and other workers, as well as the Party, helped him see his errors and start a new life. We report things like that."

I asked how this was reported. "The young worker himself wrote his life story for us." And the union representative summarized the aim of such reporting: "We help readers to understand these phenomena, raise their consciousness, and point out the achievements necessary for socialist reconstruction. It is not our aim to direct the attention of readers to bad conditions and irregular behavior."

On the other hand, sports are extensively covered, but only in papers that are not organs of the national or local Communist Party. For example, Shanghai has an evening paper devoted to sports reports. In contrast to the purely ideological dailies, it prints criticisms of movies and plays—even if all of them are favorable.

Photographs are also published in Chinese newspapers. Most of them show government and Party functionaries or foreign guests at receptions. There are also pictures of mass demonstrations.

I did find one thing in Chinese newspapers that is missing in other communist countries: the comic strip. I had always thought it an invention of the West. If so, the communists have successfully taken it over. Well-drawn cartoons tell stories of the Long March, the "Anti-Japanese War," and the "War of Liberation," also the establishment of the people's communes, the struggle against the counter-revolutionaries, the new life of Chinese women, and the experiences of the Communist Youth Association.

The effect of these comic strips is powerful, especially on readers who have not mastered many written characters. On Chinese trains and in waiting rooms, dozens of booklets containing these illustrated stories are on display. They are an effective means of ideologically influencing not only children but adults, with whom they are quite popular. Hundreds of such booklets are available in the bookstores.

Naturally, I wondered whether Chinese readers had an opportunity to see foreign newspapers. In the hotels and some waiting rooms I had found the official organs of the New Zealand, Australian, North Vietnamese, North Korean, and, above all, the Albanian communist parties. But there were no non-communist newspapers from abroad, nor even the communist papers from the European "brother nations." Neither *Pravda* nor *Izvestia* can be bought in China nowadays.

But I was assured that the venerable library of Peking subscribed to almost all Western daily and weekly newspapers and that they could be read there. "They are available mainly in the interests of science," I was told.

I asked whether an average citizen could read them. "No one is interested in reading lies and defamations about China," was the reply.

I was obstinate. "But if someone wanted to read, say, the American dailies, could he read them here?"

The answer was contemptuous. "If there is someone who absolutely must read the American papers, he could read them there."

Broadcasting in China is hardly different from newspaper work, so far as newscasts, commentaries, and announcements are concerned. I came to realize that significantly more talk than music or entertainment was broadcast. As I mentioned in an earlier chapter, broadcasting has been a principal means of influencing the Chinese masses, since the sixty newspapers—whose circulation figures no one seemed able to give me—reach only a fraction of the people compared to the centrally controlled loudspeakers set up in the cities and the people's communes.

Television, the most effective propaganda medium, has not yet been developed very highly in China. Although the larger cities have their own television stations, few programs are transmitted. For example, in Shanghai a television program is shown on alternate days, and it lasts from two to three hours. Transmissions are more frequent in Peking, but they are confined to news reports, scenes of political rallies, scenes from receptions given by Party and government officials (usually a few days after the event), and movies. At present the individual stations are not linked into a network, so there is no way to broadcast an event over a nationwide hookup.

Another fact that limits the effectiveness of television is that there are very few sets. Those that exist are located mostly in the palaces of culture and Party offices.

The press, radio, television, movies, and theater are so completely at the service of the Party and its ideology that I wondered whether the people were not often bored, whether the constant stream of propaganda didn't get on their nerves.

But sound non-communists who know China denied this. "Don't forget that to the Chinese the most important thing is survival—his cup of rice. That wouldn't be enough to make a Westerner happy, but it's different in China."

So I decided to take a close look at the food situation of the Chinese people.

28

The cup of rice

China still buys between two and three million tons of wheat a year from Canada and Australia. Outside China, this has led to the belief that the food shortage there is as serious as ever, and that the government has not been, and perhaps never will be, able to solve China's foremost problem—how to feed 700 million people.

When I talked with Chinese economists and politicians, they pointed out emphatically that China's wheat purchases abroad did not mean a food shortage. "We produce more than 180 million tons of rice and wheat a year," the eminent economist Yung told me in Peking. "By comparison, what do two or three million tons of Canadian and Australian wheat amount to? We buy wheat, and we export rice. We also re-export wheat to Algeria, Cuba, and Albania. We raise more than 110 million hogs a year. Look at our trade agreement with the Soviet Union—a good share of our export to Russia is pork."

But unquestionably China had to depend upon wheat imports in the years of the great natural catastrophes, 1960 and 1961. Food supplies then were strictly rationed. Since that time, there seem to have been some good harvests. At any rate, the markets are well supplied with vegetables and meat, not only in the cities but in the country and in small industrial centers. Nowhere did I see people standing in line to buy food. Coupons are still required for certain wheat products, but the rations seem to be adequate. And enough vegetables and meat are available to keep the rationing of wheat products from lowering the standard of nourishment. In fact, wherever I went and whatever the time of day, I saw stalls full of vegetables, fowl, and meat.

Apparently the system of distribution is far better organized than in other communist states. The large cities have innumerable small markets, one at almost every major intersection. Deliveries of vegetables and meat are made in the traditional Chinese manner, on two-wheeled hand carts.

Large central markets have also been established. Like the buses and trains, they are always kept clean and swept to teach the people the importance of sanitation. Salesmen and saleswomen must observe all the rules of hygiene; they often wear masks covering the mouth and nose, as well as sleeve protectors and gloves, and they handle the food with tongs. Hands that take money may not touch food. At times the women vendors perform incredible feats, taking money and making change with the left hand so that the right hand will not come in contact with the coins. In a central market in Shanghai, at a hundred degrees in the shade, I couldn't see a single fly on the meat hanging in the open air—a result of the anti-fly campaign.

All the wares offered here are listed on large boards with the lowest and highest prices for that day. For people who are confused by these huge boards, listing a hundred or so items, or for those who can't read, information is presented in another way. In the middle of the market are glass cases displaying the items on sale— vegetables, fruit, meat—modeled in wax. The lowest and highest prices for the day are also marked on these displays.

The customers were concerned not only with prices but, as I could see, with what was available; that too could be determined from looking at the wax models.

Behind the showcases stands a "scale of justice," where each buyer can have his purchases weighed. If he has been given too little, the employees behind the scale make an adjustment. A small discrepancy is made up by one or two onions; a larger one by a cash refund. But the "scale of justice" works both ways. If the customer

Produce in a market in Shanghai.

has been undercharged he has to make up the difference. There isn't exactly a run on the "scale of justice," but it is pretty well patronized.

Certain sections of the market offer services designed to ease the customers' work. For a small charge fowl are killed, picked, and dressed; eggs are tested for freshness by holding them up to the peephole of a small lantern; and meat is cooked over large oil drums.

Most remarkable are the stalls where hundreds of plates are set out, each holding all the ingredients for a special Chinese dish: small pieces of meat, fish, seafood, pre-cut vegetables and the like, in portions for one, two, or four persons. Here you can buy all the ingredients for a meal without having to go from stall to stall for the separate items.

But these stands are less frequented, since the prices are somewhat higher than they would be if the ingredients were bought separately.

The Chinese, if he is not well off, is a very frugal eater. The cup of rice that can nourish him for a whole day is proverbial—and rightly so. But even the humblest Chinese peasant or worker loves a good meal if he can afford it.

Chinese cooking is famous for its flavor and variety, and a big Chinese meal may consist of ten to twenty courses. From soups of sharks' fins and swallows' nests through all the varieties known to Europe and America, the repertory of a Chinese chef extends to baked chicks or duck eggs that have been buried for months in lime and thus been transformed into delicious aspic (the famed "rotten eggs").

Since the country is so large, each region has its own way of preparing food, the most famous being the Cantonese, Shanghai, and Peking methods. They differ from each other at least as much as do Swedish, French, and American cooking.

Peking is famous for "Peking duck"—about twenty dishes that can be prepared from the different parts of a duck, including the webbed feet and the brain. The cook's art consists of transforming all these parts into delicacies of a unique taste.

Canton is famous for its "dragon and tiger meat." It is best not to ask for an explanation of these terms. The dishes are delicious, but if the European knew what was being placed before him he might decline. As dragons no longer exist, they have been replaced by snakes, and as tigers are getting scarce, cats have been substituted. Even monkey meat is eaten with gusto.

The foreign traveler does not get far with the Chinese if he rejects "rotten eggs," snakes, cats, or monkeys with the comment that these are not food for human beings. His host will explain at some length that there is hardly any difference between, say, a snake and a partridge, since both feed on insects. And that a cat is certainly a cleaner animal than a pig.

On the other hand, the Chinese do not tolerate the "rotten milk" eaten in Western countries—that is, cheese, which is unknown in China. "And what about the mold that grows on some of your cheeses?" was the retort in many a discussion of food.

Naturally, the daily food prepared in Chinese homes is not so delicate or varied. But even on my visits to peasants in their communes and workers in their quarters I saw three or four vegetables and rice dishes on the table. Meat is served only once or twice a week, and then it is usually pork, which is plentiful and relatively cheap. Beef is very scarce, because there is little grazing land and cattle are too valuable as draft animals.

Hot water is usually the only drink served with meals. In most provinces it is necessary to sterilize water by boiling it, since the rice paddies are fertilized by manure and the water that spreads over them could contaminate the wells. So the Chinese have been drinking hot water for thousands of years.

Incidentally, this is how tea was discovered: the leaves fell into hot water and made it more palatable. Green tea and jasmine tea are used to flavor the hot water, which is drunk without sugar. Other beverages, such as lemonade and beer, are seldom cooled. Pouring cold liquids into a warm body is abhorrent to the Chinese.

Iceboxes for cooling beverages are found only in the hotels where foreigners stay. The ice is brought in by peasants, who cut it from frozen rivers and lakes in the winter and store it deep in the earth until summer.

There are four kinds of beer in China, most of them quite good. The best is Tsingtao beer. Until the First World War Tsingtao was a German colony, and first-rate breweries were established under

German guidance. The Germans left long ago, but the Chinese brewers have passed on the secret of good beer from generation to generation.

The culture of grapes for wine is also carried on in China on a large scale. In the grocery stores you see more wines made from grapes than from rice. Also displayed are the Chinese champagnes and the famous Mao Dai, a liquor made from rice. The Chinese make brandy and whiskey, too, although these fall far below Western standards.

But China is not a land of milk and honey. One must not forget the low living standard of the general population when one sees the well-stocked markets and the excellent food served in the restaurants. What seems a normal food supply to the European is luxury to the Chinese; "normal" prices are out of his reach. The same is true of the varied menus in the restaurants, which are only for the highest income groups and for foreigners. The average Chinese cannot afford them.

I wondered whether the government's efforts to create its own atomic stockpile were carried on at the expense of the people's living standard. That is a hard question to answer in a nation so backward in its economy. In an industrialized Western nation the poor quality of textiles and consumer goods, the shortage of cars, trucks, and tractors, the low degree of mechanization would all be sure signs of inordinately high expenditures for armaments. But "guns for butter" is a Western measuring stick. In China, where textiles are of poor quality anyway, where trucks, tractors, and cars are scarce, it is hard to say how much of this low standard is due to armaments or sheer backwardness. Presumably Chinese industry would have developed more rapidly if a good part of the nation's cash reserve, foreign exchange, raw materials, and labor force had not been diverted to arms production. But as there are no statistics, and as the standard of living in present-day China cannot be compared with that of the past, it is impossible to make a concrete statement about these matters.

One thing is certain: China maintains the world's largest standing army, roughly three million men. At great sacrifice it produces its own jet fighters of the Soviet MIG type, and is said to have the fourth largest fighter plane force in the world. It makes its own tanks and guns from Soviet designs in a Soviet-installed factory. And it has the secret of atomic weapons. It has assembled and exploded two nuclear devices since October, 1964. This presupposes the existence of a very large and very valuable industrial complex. To achieve political and military equality, then, China's leaders must have channeled a large part of the country's economic reserves into the manufacture of armaments.

29

Mushroom cloud over China

In northeast China, the biggest industrial section of the country, large tablets hang at the gates of factories. Inscriptions in several colors repeat the Party slogans and set forth the factory's production figures. But some of those I saw also showed the figure of a Chinese soldier. He was holding a rifle with fixed bayonet, on which was skewered American reconnaissance planes of the U-2 type. On each plane a date was printed, the date on which—as the Chinese claim—they shot down these American "spy planes" over Chinese territory.

When I asked whether the planes had been manned by American or Chinese Nationalist crews, no one could answer. But everyone I talked to insisted that American planes have penetrated Chinese air space again and again, and "it's understandable that a large number have been shot down."

I doubt that Chinese air defense has really brought down any U-2 planes. The Soviets have succeeded only once, although it is true that American flights over the Soviet Union were discontinued after that. China, which presumably has no powerful anti-aircraft rockets and is said to have no jet planes capable of reaching the altitude at which the U-2 operates, would find it even more difficult to bring them down.

But there is no doubt that U-2 flights manned by Americans or Chinese Nationalists have been made over Chinese territory. American spy-satellites also keep a photographic eye on China from outer space.

So it is easy to understand how the U.S. Secretary of State, Dean Rusk, could predict the first Chinese atomic explosion seventeen days in advance. It is also easy to understand how the Americans knew the exact magnitude and composition of the device exploded.

At some time in the past, the Soviets delivered two, if not three, atomic reactors to the Chinese. They were meant for peaceful purposes, but the Chinese have presumably managed to convert them for other uses. It is rumored that the famous Italian nuclear physicist, Pontecorvo, who defected to Russia, worked in China as a Soviet expert.

The Western nuclear physicists who revealed atomic secrets to the East and who were prepared to develop atomic weapons for the East bloc were for the most part idealists. Hence it is not inconceivable that a man like Pontecorvo would divulge more information to the Chinese than the Soviet leaders wanted him to. Some of those physicists decided to make military atomic secrets available to nations that might become targets of the existing atomic powers at some future date. Putting these vulnerable countries in possession of atomic weapons, they reasoned, might lessen the possibility of attack and thus increase the possibility of world peace. So China's first atomic bomb may well have been constructed according to Pontecorvo's specific directions.

The world's nuclear experts have several theories about the Chinese atom bomb. Since 1956 the world has known that China is working on the development of atomic weapons. A thorough examination of available Chinese publications and reports of political speeches shows that China has the technical as well as the human resources necessary to produce atomic weapons. There are enough trained physicists and engineers, both uranium and thorium are present in Sinkiang Province, and a program for increasing the nation's hydroelectric installations, which would enable them to use atomic reactors, was begun.

The logical place for the nation's atomic armament industry is in Sinkiang, where materials are available and the Soviets are rumored to have built the largest atomic reactor in China. Nevertheless, American reconnaissance planes have for a long time been unable to locate China's nuclear plants. This lack of proof that large installations exist had given rise to the theory that China—despite its atomic explosions—does not in fact have an extensive atomic industry.

At first there was a simple explanation: the Soviets could have released to China, for peaceful purposes, small quantities of enriched uranium that would have been adequate for an atomic bomb. In that case we need not assume the existence of a Chinese atomic armament complex, nor need we expect another explosion for a long time, since the Chinese cannot produce further atomic weapons.

This theory sounded reasonable, but it was not quite logical because the Soviet Union, like the United States, had always guarded against the possibility that someone might misuse its fissionable material. The United States has never delivered more than about thirteen pounds of enriched uranium to friendly nations, and at least fifty-five pounds are required to produce one atom bomb. In the West it is believed that the Soviet Union has been even more cautious about deliveries of uranium to other socialist countries.

There remained the barely credible possibility that the Chinese have an uncontrollable source of enriched uranium—a black market, as it were. But no black market could supply more than the minutest amount of this material.

When the radioactive cloud from the first Chinese bomb explosion began to spread in the stratosphere, American scientists brought down samples of the radioactive dust and analyzed them. They concluded that the Chinese had made their bomb from uranium isotope U-235. Both the United States and the Soviet Union had hoped that it would prove to be a plutonium bomb, one of the so-called "dirty bombs" that produce a great deal of fallout and hence cannot be used as a tactical weapon. Although plutonium bombs belong to the so-called "advanced" group developed after the U-235 type, they can be made without the help of large power plants or production facilities. The first French atomic bombs were of this type. Production of a U-235 bomb, on the other hand, is proof of a very large industrial and armament capacity.

The theory has been advanced by some physicists that China has developed an entirely new process for making atomic bombs. In theory, there are several possible ways of splitting the atom which would require less electrical energy and smaller installations than those now utilized by the United States and the Soviet Union. However, Western physicists have not been able to put these theories into practice.

Could the Chinese have developed a simpler process for making this type of atomic weapon? All through their history they have proved that they can produce their own inventions and perfect their own processes. True, it seems unlikely that they should have developed a new nuclear process where a vast army of Western scientists, with unlimited resources at their disposal, have failed. But the slight possibility that they might have developed their own separation process has given rise to a certain unease among informed circles in the Western world. We still do not know how large China's atomic resources are. The explosion of a plutonium bomb would have revealed the stage of nuclear physics arrived at by the Chinese; the radioactive dust of such a bomb, brought down from the stratosphere, would have made it possible to draw several conclusions. As it is, scientists must wait for further Chinese atomic explosions before they can be sure of the separation processes employed or the extent of China's atomic stockpile. Meanwhile, to the West the idea that China might be able to produce atomic bombs more cheaply and rapidly than Western nations can is disquieting to scientists and military leaders alike.

In China I repeatedly asked officials and government leaders about their position on atomic weapons. The answer was always brief and always the same: of course China is engaged in atomic research, and will eventually have all the atomic secrets, but it is important not to overestimate the atom bomb. The bomb is not as frightening as is commonly supposed, nor as decisive, in the last analysis. Even the best weapons are useless unless a people strengthened by a firm ideology stands behind them; no people can win with weapons alone.

When China exploded its first atomic bomb I recalled a conversation I had had with an open-minded but patriotic Chinese. He thought it was a "great misfortune" that the West, by which he meant the United States and Europe, possessed atomic weapons. He tried to make me see that such weapons should not be in the hands of "immature people."

I asked him to explain, and we talked for several hours. This is the gist of his viewpoint: Mankind does not really need technology, which contributes nothing toward making people happier. "Mature people," who can understand the world, past, present, and future, and fit their knowledge into a comprehensive pattern, know this. Only "immature people," in the spiritual sense, try to attain good fortune and happiness by new inventions, by technological and industrial expansion. In China, where happiness and harmony have been the goals for thousands of years, it has always been self-evident that technology must impair harmony and, as a result, happiness. Therefore human effort, spiritual or material, should not be dedicated to technological advancement.

"We invented gunpowder. We knew it could be used as a weapon. We have used it as a weapon at times. But we soon stopped. We invented rockets many years before the Europeans discovered them. We have used rockets as weapons, but our spiritual maturity kept us from developing them for that purpose. To be sure, we did not take the world around us into consideration. We saw only our world," he said.

What about the atomic bomb?

"I believe that if we had invented the atomic bomb, we would never have used it. We would have let it rest just as we let gunpowder and rockets rest. I believe that we might even have built the atomic bomb, but we would never have tried to see whether it worked. We would have known it would work, and we would have been able to calculate its effect. It would never have occurred to us to prove it."

Then, in unmistakable tones, he blamed the Americans for not only testing the atomic bomb but putting it to use at the end of the Second World War.

Why did he go into all this?

I think it was because the Chinese do not have atomic weapons, because they resent the atomic superiority of the Russians and Americans, and because the Chinese feel impotent in the face of their atomic inferiority—a case of sour grapes.

But something else was involved: the pride of the Chinese, who regard themselves as a superior people; the old conviction that China is a culturally and spiritually superior nation and that other peoples are barbarians by contrast; the embarrassment of having to admit the superiority of those very "barbarians" because they possess nuclear weapons.

In the meantime China has exploded its first atomic bombs. My Chinese friend's opinion has therefore been disproved—his assertion that if China had possessed the secrets of the atom she would not have demonstrated their practical use. The Chinese atomic scientists, like the Chinese military, are apparently very much interested in knowing the potential of their atomic weapons.

Certainly one of China's greatest problems is to overcome its technological backwardness. And in this respect the Chinese whom I have just quoted was quite right. For hundreds and thousands of years the people of China took no interest in the practical exploitation of their inventions or the development of their technology. The human being was the universal measure. When technology was brought to China by foreigners, the people were all the more disgusted by it.

The foreign experts who built industrial plants and technical installations in China were astonished to find that even intelligent Chinese were often hostile toward technology. Although the political leaders recognized the importance of industrial development, and realized that every great nation must have a progressive technology, the people themselves had great difficulty in coming to terms with this concept. The Chinese have been inspired again and again by individual human achievements and by group accomplishments, but the mechanical achievements praised in the official newspapers and magazines still seem to them somehow artificial.

Chinese newspapers reported spontaneous demonstrations when Radio Peking announced the explosion of the first atomic bomb. People were said to have run through the streets, gathered in large numbers, and cheered the communist government. And yet the government communiqué verifying the first successful test began with the significant sentence, "We are of the opinion that the atomic bomb, which was created by human hands, will also be abolished by human hands."

That may have been florid propaganda, thrown in to emphasize the peaceful intentions of the Chinese government and allay the suspicions of not only the other Asiatic nations, but the Africans and South Americans. But possibly also it was aimed at the Chinese people themselves. Just as gunpowder and rockets were invented and then not used, it would be consistent with the Chinese national character to build atomic bombs only to abolish them.

But the Chinese government has no such intention. On the contrary, we can assume that a good share of the national product —that is, economic reserve—is going into atomic armaments and will continue to do so. Those who govern China know very well the degree to which their international status, both military and political, depends upon atomic armaments. That status needs to be improved—regrettably, because China is still a poor and backward country and ought to be making every effort to improve the living standards of her people. But China is not alone in allowing power politics to take precedence over the needs of the people. This is a sign of the times and can be seen in both large and small countries.

At that, the military value of the Chinese atomic bomb is still questionable. Possession of a few experimental bombs does not confer the status of an atomic power on any nation. That calls for a stockpile not only of atom bombs but of all kinds of other nuclear weapons. In addition, it is necessary to have the means of delivering them to a potential enemy—suitable carriers, specially designed planes, and missiles.

Considering the industrial installations I saw in China, I question whether the nation will be ready for several years, or even decades, to produce suitable carriers and an arsenal of atomic weapons. Its only large planes are the jet fighters previously mentioned. All the civilian planes are of Soviet or English origin. None of them are jets. The Russians have delivered two-engine Ilyushin 14's and four-engine turboprop Ilyushin 18's. China also bought a series of four-engine turboprop Vickers Viscounts from the British.

At the time of my visit, English engineers were arriving in Peking to restore some of these planes to working condition. In Hong Kong I heard that when they saw them they threw up their hands in despair. The Chinese, trying to get along without foreign help as long as possible, had tried to care for the planes "out of their own strength." As they apparently didn't understand the mechanism, they decided to dismantle a few of these expensive planes and use the parts for repairing the rest. The English have a phrase for that— "machine cannibalism."

This suggests that the Chinese do not yet have the technical ability necessary to maintain such complex apparatus. But it would be a mistake to count on that. The Chinese have already forged ahead in other areas to an amazing degree. We must take into consideration the possibility that some day they will be able to produce atomic carriers. Obviously, the government would willingly sacrifice a great deal to achieve this; the construction of the atom bomb proves it.

Whether China will become an atomic power in the near future, then, depends on several things, but the possibility must be taken seriously. Also, the political value of the bomb must not be under-estimated. The mere fact that the Chinese, more or less "out of their own strength," were able to discover atomic secrets strengthens the domestic position of the communist government. From now on, even more Chinese will look upon communism as the only salvation for their country.

The atomic explosion not only strengthened the communist regime within China but made certain that its Asian neighbors, and even the Africans and South Americans, would admire or fear the Chinese even more than before. Both fear and admiration have the same result—respect. Increased respect for China automatically weakens the position of the West in Asia, as well as in the other developing areas of the world. Naturally, it also weakens the position of the Soviet Union, assuming that the Moscow-Peking conflict will continue.

We can also expect that the clamor to accept China in the United Nations will grow louder, for other countries feel uncomfort-able when they are at odds with an atomic power which they cannot even face in discussion. And China is not only a potential atomic power, it also has a huge population. China, however, seems less disposed to apply tor membership in the United Nations. Fortified by a new "atomic self-confidence," it now demands more than just acceptance in the face of widespread opposition—an acceptance that might put its delegates next to those of the Nationalist Chinese from Formosa. Red China wants to be considered the equal of the United States and the Soviet Union and to be generally acknowledged as the third great world power. It demands recognition of its wishes in the Far Eastern sphere.

China has already proved how uncomfortable it can make its neighbors—in South Viet Nam, in Laos, in the Congo, in East Africa, in Latin America, and in relations with India and the Soviet Union. It has already threatened to found a "Counter-UN," and wants to play a leading role in the association of emerging nations as well as in world communism.

Therefore it seems important to understand China's position in relation to the rest of the world.

30

The fettered giant

Marshal Chen Yi received me in a small palace in the former French sector of Shanghai. He is today Vice Premier and Foreign Minister of the People's Republic of China. After a formal welcome, he begged me to be seated in one of the upholstered chairs in the reception room. Tea was served, followed by ice cream. Marshal Chen Yi opened the talk informally by speaking of Shanghai, where he had once been mayor. Then he switched to questions of foreign policy. "Formosa, Hong Kong, and Macao are enclaves of the imperialists in our country. They are parts of our country, and they will be liberated," he declared.

But the next moment he showed that he was a realist. It did not matter whether the liberation came now or fifteen years from now. "Time will solve these problems," he said.

This would suggest that China does not feel threatened by Formosa, or even by the presence of the U.S. Seventh Fleet in the Formosa Strait. But one fundamental fact emerges from all I was told by the marshal and other competent sources: China feels encircled. It is very much aware of its own size, of its huge population, of its tradition and history. It can rid itself only with great difficulty of the concept that, now as before, it is the "Middle Kingdom." And it is even less willing to accept the idea of playing a subordinate role in world politics.

That has been China's fate until today, due to the fact that the country has had no atomic weapons, no missiles, no long-range bombers, nor even an adequate fleet. Without these instruments of power, China is a fettered giant. It cannot "liberate" its Taiwan Province (Formosa). The Chinese must sit and watch the aircraft carriers of the U.S. Seventh Fleet cruise up and down their coast. They have not been able to place a safety belt between their country and its enemies—and "enemies" is a term understood in Peking as applying primarily to the United States.

China apparently compares its situation with that of the Soviet Union and of the United States. The Soviet Union is bordered on the west by a neutral Finland, a neutral Austria, and a chain of countries with close military and ideological ties: Poland, East Germany, Czechoslovakia, Hungary, Rumania, and Bulgaria. And even Yugoslavia and Albania are not military allies of the West.

The United States has extended the limits of its "contacts with the enemy" even farther. In Europe there is NATO; in Asia Minor, the Middle East Pact; in Asia, SEATO; in the Pacific, Formosa, Japan, Okinawa, the Philippines, Australia, and Hawaii as bases and allies.

Thus, the two great atomic powers have broad safety zones. China's line of defense runs through China itself (the Formosa Strait). To the east and west it has only two minor satellites, North Korea and North Viet Nam. And the southern half of each of these countries is an ally of the United States.

This is the world situation as it looks from Peking. For a long time China probably hoped for help from the Soviet Union—help in overcoming the new government's impotence, in arming it with long-range missiles and bombers and finally atomic weapons. The fact that Moscow did not offer this help is one of the basic reasons for the split between China and the Soviet Union. In a sense, Chinese politicians feel that Moscow shares the responsibility for the fact that American warships cruise along the coast of China.

The Soviet Union's refusal to deliver modern weapons angered the Chinese. They felt they had fallen into a kind of colonial dependency upon Moscow. But although China had received economic aid from the "mother country," the Soviet Union had not enabled the

Chinese to defend themselves effectively. Chinese rebellion against the Soviet Union is therefore similar to the rebellion of a colonial country determined to loosen its ties with the mother country.

What the Soviets, until the fall of Khrushchev, called the "Chinese power chauvinism"—fancy speeches about the country's strength and its right to equal consideration with other world powers—can be found in other Asian countries and to a high degree in Africa and Latin America. But, in contrast with some of these countries, China is really large—in terms of population, the largest nation in the world.

In one respect, China is also capable of striking, even if it will have no atomic weapons for some time to come. It has the world's largest ground forces. More than three million soldiers make up the standing army, and every man, woman, and half-grown adolescent is a member of the people's militia, ready to fight in a guerrilla war. That army has proved itself superior to the United States armed forces under certain specific conditions: in impassable terrain, jungles and swamps, stormy seas, and bad flying weather.

The explanations given me by government officials made me realize that Peking is not taking refuge in illusion. Peking knows that large-scale warfare, conducted with atomic weapons, is beyond its power today and for many years to come. On the other hand, it knows that any attack with conventional weapons, on home territory, can probably be repelled. An occupation of China by foreign troops is regarded as utterly impossible. A country as large as all Europe, with 700 million inhabitants, cannot be occupied.

So there are two considerations: the Chinese cannot launch an attack if it would mean unleashing an atomic war, but they do feel secure in spite of being "encircled."

Apart from the question of Formosa, there seems to be no reason why China should not seek peaceful co-existence with the United States. However, a number of things make this impossible. First, there is the attempt of the communist government to secure a better starting position before coming to any "peaceful conclusion." That is, China would like to create a buffer zone around its own borders, just as the Soviet Union and the United States have done—a buffer zone of nations at least amicably disposed toward China. Southeast

Asia, including South Viet Nam, Laos, Cambodia, Burma, and Thailand, would be a suitable objective. But it would also be reassuring to see Japan, the Philippines, Indonesia, and India assume a neutral attitude, if not actually a friendly one.

At the same time, the communist leaders seem to feel obliged to remove every stigma of "colonial dishonor" ever perpetrated on China. Just as Hitler wanted to nullify the Versailles Treaty, the Chinese leaders want to re-establish their ancient borders. They want to create a "Greater China."

The Chinese-Indian border conflict sprang from precisely this desire. Before the British takeover of India, the disputed regions had been nominally Chinese. Peking reasons that they were taken from China by a colonial power and explains China's participation in the border conflict not as an attack on Indian territory but as a "belated attack on English colonial rule, which India has tried to perpetuate."

Naturally, the Chinese hotly deny that they attacked India. Marshal Chen Yi stressed this in his talk with me. They merely "fought back after the Indians had launched a large-scale offensive against them."

But the Indian-Chinese border conflict proved that Peking has not lost all sense of reality. The Chinese knew just how far they could go without provoking a large-scale war and risking atomic retaliation. Thus, they try to achieve their major goal only within reason (or, as it is termed in China, the "concrete condition") : to re-establish traditional borders and surround their country with a buffer zone of satellites or neutral nations.

At the time of its greatest expansion, China controlled these buffer states. Korea was under Chinese suzerainty, the territory corresponding to North Viet Nam had been subjugated by China and was paying tribute to the Chinese emperors, and so were present-day Nepal and Burma. These countries were not torn away from Chinese domination until the nineteenth century, when the European powers and Japan appeared on the scene.

I was assured that Peking wants only a neutral Southeast Asia today. "We know that anything more would be unacceptable to the Americans. But we cannot accept anything less than true neutrality.

It is impossible for South Viet Nam to remain a staging area for imperialism against China."

But the otherwise realistic Chinese politicians are blind to one important argument: the neutrality of southeast Asia would have been assured long ago, as one of President Kennedy's cherished goals, if the communist guerrilla warfare in this area had ceased. In Western eyes, it was communist aggression that prevented the neutralization of Southeast Asia.

And it is this guerrilla warfare that keeps the United States from putting any further faith in Peking's assertion that the Chinese want nothing more than neutrality in the area. More probably, it seems, the Chinese are playing Stalin's devious game: demand neutrality, then continue the communist attacks until the neutral government is toppled and replaced by a satellite government. There is no way to predict when or where this will end.

I had had many serious talks with American politicians on this subject, and now, discussing it with the Chinese, came to the conclusion that neither side is able to put itself in the other's place. The Americans, after their experiences with the insidious communist advance in Europe, Asia, and Latin America, still reason that no further concessions of any kind must be made to the communists. Hence, they must make an all-out effort whenever they clash with communism—as in Laos and South Viet Nam. Berlin, Greece, and Korea are perfect examples. Washington believes this to be the only correct and effective policy.

What is partly overlooked are the differing conditions within the disputed countries. Viet Nam and Laos cannot be compared with Greece, let alone Berlin. The Asiatic countries have not yet initiated urgently needed social and economic reforms; they are still feudal, in some cases even slave, states. If they cannot achieve their revolutionary goals by evolutionary means, they must go through their own democratic and national revolutions, just like the United States and the nations of Western Europe.

So far, the United States has not been very successful in persuading anti-communist governments in Southeast Asia to adopt evolutionary means, and apparently it is afraid to put much pressure on these governments for fear of weakening their fight against communism. The result is a vicious circle. Communism would have less chance of gaining ground if there were no real goals for it to attain in these countries.

The dilemma of the United States in Southeast Asia is much like that in Latin America. With communism already pounding on the gates, the Americans must ally themselves with anti-communist forces even though these are non-democratic. In Latin America, where this process has not advanced too far, the United States is trying to further democratic and social evolution through the Alliance for Progress. In Southeast Asia it seems to be too late for that.

Whether these countries can be defended by military power, in view of their internal situation, is open to question.

Nevertheless, the United States has to try to save Southeast Asia. If the communist advance were to succeed, if the Americans should suffer a military defeat, the effect on the world would be catastrophic. The remaining Asiatic nations would no longer feel secure and would probably try to negotiate with Red China. The withdrawal of Indonesia from the United Nations was a serious indication of a new Asiatic orientation. Hence the determination with which the United States clings to its position in this area. The Chinese view of the West as a "paper tiger" must not be confirmed, even though doubts have arisen in Washington as to the advisability of the government's Viet Nam policy. It remains to be seen whether Americans can find a political solution in South Viet Nam (a "social revolution") to make military victory possible.

The motives of the Americans are misjudged in China. The Chinese firmly believe their own propaganda, which attributes imperialistic designs to the United States and insists that the Americans want to encircle China so the communist rule can be smashed and China again be subjugated.

The thesis of the Soviets, that peaceful co-existence is possible, is rejected disdainfully by the Chinese—not because Peking is incapable of correctly evaluating power politics, but because the ideologists in Peking believe that such co-existence would also result in the destruction of communist power. The communist state would be weakened by the adoption of middle-class standards; its material well-being and the corruption of its ideals could bring only degeneration.

After a scant fifteen years of communist rule, with an unstable economy, Peking does not feel secure enough to risk such "dangers." It offers only one strategy: the Chinese must cling to the idea that the West is imperialistic; that the United States, as the strongest Western power, is the arch-imperialist; and that American actions, no matter what they may be, are to be deeply distrusted.

Thus a high wall of suspicion has been thrown up between China and the United States, to which both sides have contributed. But Foreign Minister Chen Yi seemed to be sober and realistic: the country is too weak and too tired to seek exhausting disputes with the United States.

Yet the Chinese politicians have again and again forestalled any possibility of an understanding between the two nations. Their ideology is their motive power, all the more so because they have used it as their main weapon in their conflict with Moscow: the concept of the world revolution, as against peaceful co-existence.

This forces the Chinese to support revolutions in all parts of the world, to pursue the struggle against the West far from their home territory. The Congo is a typical example.

I had an experience in Peking that confirmed this attitude. The Foreign Ministry had invited me to visit the "Grand Hall of the People" at three o'clock one afternoon for a "mass demonstration against imperialist aggression in Viet Nam." The huge room, which seats ten thousand, was already packed when I got there.

Most of the participants were students and soldiers. Apparently they were the people most quickly and easily assembled for such a purpose. There were spoken choruses and songs, and finally the meeting was officially opened.

Leading the honored guests, Chou En-lai, the Premier, stepped onto the stage. He was followed by other highly placed Chinese politicians, foreign delegates, and envoys from friendly countries: Albania, North Viet Nam, and North Korea. One speaker followed another—Chinese, North Vietnamese, South Vietnamese, Laotian —all vigorously applauded.

The applause increased to hurricane proportions when an African stepped from his seat of honor and walked to the microphone. He was the delegate from the Congo; that is, from the pro-Chinese forces fighting in the Congo. Every one of his sentences was punctuated by round after round of applause. When he finished, the listeners went wild with enthusiasm. Chou En-lai sprang up, came forward and embraced the African, kissing him on both cheeks. Twenty of the prominent guests did the same, each time accompanied by wild applause.

The meeting had been called to demonstrate against the "imperialistic aggression in Viet Nam." But the hero of the day was the delegate from the Congo.

At the end of the demonstration, which lasted several hours, a girl from the Communist Youth Association went up to the podium and read a resolution. Seemingly endless, it contained the usual protests against imperialism, a demand for the withdrawal of American troops from South Viet Nam, and a plea for the "liberation" of that country.

In closing, she emphasized that all imperialists were only paper tigers and that the struggling peoples of the world would vanquish imperialism in the end. The forces of progress would be victorious everywhere on earth.

In Peking they think they know the secret that will bring about this victory. Mao Tse-tung's analysis of the social forces in the world holds the prescription for world revolution. It is not necessary, as Marx, Lenin, and Stalin believed, to wait for the bourgeois revolution and the development of a national industry. China has demonstrated to the world that the socialist revolution is possible even in an undeveloped country without a proletariat, and that a nation can change directly from colonial status to a "people's democracy."

Since two thirds of the world consists of developing countries, and since two thirds of their peoples are just emerging from colonial rule (in the Chinese scheme of things, they are still under neo-colonialism), Mao Tse-tung's way may be the only possible one for them to follow.

The claims of the communist leaders in Peking to the leadership of world communism are also based on this premise. In their opinion, the Soviet Union has betrayed two-thirds of the human race by subscribing to peaceful co-existence with the West. China feels obligated to help "all subjugated peoples in their struggle against colonialism, neo-colonialism, and imperialism." As a nation, China has no desire to wage war on the West, but Peking believes that the world revolution must be continued and that China's task is to further it.

But the Chinese overlook one thing. If the Soviet Union, as well as China, adopted this policy, war would probably ensue. If Moscow failed to give continuing evidence that it stands for peaceful co-existence, the world situation would become more tense, the front against communism would close ranks, and the West would take more rigorous action.

In other words, only Moscow makes it possible for Peking to maintain its stand against the West. However, there is a wide gap between China's policy of world revolution and its ability to put its policy into effect. Despite great sacrifices, China is not able to offer much help to the peoples it claims as followers. It can outfit a few rebels with arms and make a play for the good will of Asiatic and African governments that are already established. But most of them would no doubt bestow their favors on any nation that filled their people's stomachs, and they are already being fed by the United States and the Soviet Union.

The Chinese find this outrageous. In their opinion, these governments are entering into neo-colonial relationships with their eyes wide open. China calls out to them: "Do not give in to this temptation, or you will never be free! Do as we have done—use your own strength."

Again, Peking overlooks a few things. Neither the Africans nor the Latin Americans possess the Chinese mentality, and most Asiatics cannot compete with the Chinese in diligence or in the ability to subordinate themselves to a cause. They have not been centrally governed for four thousand years as have the Chinese.

Only time will bring this difference home to Peking, as it did to Moscow. But China has already learned one lesson: it is not easy to strive for a vast world objective when so much remains to be done at home.

31

Can you eat steel plates?

I met Mr. Yung Lung-kuei in the International Club of Peking. Mr. Yung is a professor of economics, vice-president of the Second Asiatic Economic Seminar, vice-president of the Chinese Council for the Advancement of International Trade, and holds several other high positions. In a five-hour talk he tried to tell me what had been happening to the Chinese economy between 1949 and 1964.

He divided this time into several periods, the first of which, from 1949 to 1952, he called the "reconstruction." It is at once apparent how closely economics and politics are related in China, for he said that two tasks had been accomplished during this time:

1. "We had to make up for the failures of the democratic revolution. The special privileges granted to imperialists were abrogated, mixed Chinese and foreign companies were dissolved, the compradors [economic collaborators] were removed. Simultaneously, we carried out land reform. The big landowners were dispossessed, and the poor peasants and workers were given their own plots of land. Big capital was confiscated, and democratic reforms were put into effect."

2. "We made an all-out attempt to bring agricultural and industrial production to the same level as before the Liberation, to stabilize prices and prevent inflation. Production had suffered

severely because of the fighting, and land reform caused another setback."

According to Professor Yung, it took the government only three and a half years to accomplish all this. Then came the First Five-Year Plan, from 1953 to 1957. "It was carried out under unusual circumstances, and we exceeded the goals we had set," he said.

This plan had several objectives: the land that had been handed over to the peasants was collectivized, production cooperatives of the lower type and later of the higher type were set up, and near the end of 1957 all arable soil was organized into 750,000 kolkhozes—that is, collective farms. Artisans too lost their private status. "Six million of them were organized into cooperatives."

The same fate overtook business. "Seventy thousand private companies became semi-official state companies." That is, the state took them over, in many cases keeping the former owners as managers, paying them salaries and interest on their former capital.

But the greatest achievement of the First Five-Year Plan was in industry. "We laid the foundation for industry. Roughly a thousand large and middle-size plants were built and apparatus installed."

According to Yung, approximately three billion yuan (approximately $1.2 billion) over and above normal expenditures were spent to expand heavy industry.

He leaned back in his easy chair and recalled 1957. He said it was a year of "proud figures." "We were already producing more than five and a half million tons of steel. Industrial production had risen by 18 per cent in five years. Agriculture was producing 4½ per cent more than before the Liberation."

His face was earnest as he mentioned the period of the Second Five-Year Plan, theoretically covering the years from 1958 to 1962. Mr. Yung no longer cited numbers, nor did he mention the achievements of the Second Five-Year Plan. He talked about the privations of that time and the reverses the people suffered. "Two unexpected blows were dealt us. Incredible natural catastrophes plagued us. And then the Soviet Union tore up its pacts, withdrew its experts, and stopped deliveries."

Asked about the natural catastrophes, he said, "In some areas the drought lasted eighteen months. In others it rained for two hundred days. One coastal region was devastated by twenty typhoons. In three years, harvests from more than 210 million acres were ruined. That is equivalent to all the arable land in China."

He described the departure of the Soviets. "In July, 1960, all Soviet specialists were withdrawn without notice within a period of thirty days. There were more than 1,500 of them, and they took all their plans and blueprints and, in several cases, irreplaceable spare parts. Today, the Soviets reproach us for blaming our failures on their departure, but actually it hit us hard. Suddenly we had to shift for ourselves. Second-class industries were abandoned because we had to concentrate on the most important ones, calling in instructors who should have been training a new generation of workers but instead had to run the plants. Half-finished factories stood idle because the Soviet machinery was no longer supplied. As you can imagine, the Second Five-Year Plan was terribly disrupted, both by the natural catastrophes and by the departure of the Soviets."

Mr. Yung forgot to mention a third disruptive factor, the "Great Leap Forward." Within its framework, the 750,000 kolkhozes were converted into seventy thousand communes, and the machines were overworked until they broke down. Naturally, these large-scale changes in agriculture and industry resulted in serious setbacks.

Mr. Yung indirectly admitted this. "We were entering virgin territory with the 'Great Leap.' We lacked experience, so we had to experiment. We had jumped in without being able to swim, and so we had to swallow a lot of water. But we learned how to swim."

However, he thought that the achievements of the "Great Leap" outweighed its failures. Describing the period after the catastrophes and the departure of the Soviet experts, he said, "We were determined to overcome our difficulties by ourselves. We could rely on the exertions of an entire people. Since 1961 we have followed a policy of recovery."

This effort is still going on. The Peking government has endeavored to stabilize agriculture and industrial production, while letting the people and the Party cadres recover from the over-exertions of 1959 to 1961. The results were not evident for two years, Mr. Yung said. "We were not able to see a general improvement in the economy until 1964. In that year things were on the upturn. Today we can say that we have overcome our temporary difficulties. We still have problems, but we understand them, and we know we can overcome them."

In the discussion that followed I realized that the entire economic policy of the country had been turned upside down since 1961.

"Formerly, we followed the advice of the Soviets," Mr. Yung explained. "They told us that heavy industry came first in importance in a socialist country. We acted accordingly. Then we began to wonder. We asked ourselves what roles industry and agriculture should play over a long period. Upon investigation we decided that agriculture and light industry must back up heavy industry and must be developed along with it."

During that time the Party offered a new slogan, "Walking on both legs." This meant the equal development of heavy industry and agriculture, but it meant more than that. Obviously, it would be impossible to bring industry and agriculture up to modern standards overnight, or even in the near future. If the plans for the people's communes had called for tractors and machinery to work the fertile soil more efficiently than could be done by using hand plows and manual labor on small fields, it was also easy to see that the tractors and machines would be lacking for a long time. China does not make more than twenty thousand tractors a year, and the picture isn't much brighter where trucks and farm machinery are concerned.

So "walking on both legs" had a second meaning—to use traditional methods along with modern ones. In practice, this meant keeping or re-opening small handicraft production centers and, in the people's communes, using old methods of working the land instead of waiting for tractors and modern machinery.

This method of "walking on both legs" is still in operation. But the equal emphasis on agriculture and industry that was affirmed in 1961 lasted just a year. In 1962 a new directive was issued: "Agriculture is the basis and industry the leading force for the development of the people's economy." These words are in line with Marx, who gave industry preferential treatment. But in practice the new slogan stood for something quite different.

Mr. Yung explained to me in great detail that it is impossible to build heavy industry "out of one's own strength," without capital. Capital has to come from somewhere. In China, it has to come from agriculture, which therefore has to be developed to the point where it provides a surplus. The sale of this surplus gives the state the necessary capital for industrial development.

But it is not that simple. The state has to buy the harvest from the communes—that is, from the peasants. Thus, money goes into the hands of the peasants. Now the state has two possible ways of getting this money back: by taxing the communes (14 to 16 per cent of their gross income) and by supplying the farmers with consumer goods. The peasants buy the products of light industry in state-owned department stores, and so their money finds its way back to the state.

Two facts are noteworthy. Industry is owned by the state, so it is not subject to taxation, which would simply mean taking money out of one pocket and putting it in the other. Also, it is not necessary to tax the workers, whose wages are given them at the discretion of the state and can be set as low as is feasible to begin with. This obviates bookkeeping. So the state gets its urgently needed capital mainly from the peasants. But it cannot take everything away from them through taxes; both peasants and workers must have access to consumer goods. So the people's wages flow back into the state treasury.

But consumer goods can be supplied only when light industry is highly developed. This has been done in China, and continues to be done. Today China walks on three legs rather than two: agriculture, light industry, and heavy industry. Agriculture has preferential status, then light industry (it seems to me), while heavy industry has to wait for capital.

This confirms the Marxist thesis that socialism cannot be created out of nothing. It is possible only where strong industrialization already exists. Politically, the Communist Party has achieved victory in China. Economically, it has yet to accomplish what a bourgeois capitalist society should have done over a period of decades, if not centuries.

This is what the Soviet ideologists meant when they accused the Chinese Party leaders of having abandoned industrialization, thus committing a mortal sin against Marxism. Mr. Yung vehemently denied this. "Industrialization remains our objective. But the question is how to achieve it. To survive, we must all work in agriculture. Whoever thinks he can do without agriculture must perish. Agriculture brings the accumulation of capital and the raw materials for industry. It thus fills two requirements for the industrialization of our country, and it is the basis of our economy. We must bend all our efforts to achieve progress in agriculture after two thousand years of backwardness. And we must ask our Soviet friends, 'Can you eat steel plates?' "

Then Mr. Yung said something very important. "If we had followed the Soviet road to heavy industry, we would have had to pay a high price—unlimited inflation. If we make capital investments without producing an agricultural surplus, if we take money from the peasants without giving them consumer goods, the presses would be printing currency day and night. You have surely noticed that there is no inflation here. Both wages and prices have remained stable. I call that a healthy financial situation."

In the Soviet Union under Stalin, the growth of heavy industry was paid for by inflationary measures. So I asked Mr. Yung whether his thesis was not meant as an indirect criticism of Stalin's economic policy. He denied it. "Stalin did the only right thing. Don't forget the time in which he lived. The Soviet Union was the only socialist country on earth. It was surrounded by a host of enemies, by imperialists and fascists. The Soviet Union would have been destroyed had it not built up its heavy industry, even at great sacrifice. Only the fact that heavy industry was already established saved the Soviet Union in the Second World War. This vindicated Stalin. We live in a different time, when there are many socialist countries and imperialism is becoming weak. We can use other methods."

Here it should be added, of course, that despite Russia's backwardness in 1917 her industrial development then was better than China's in 1949. But it is understandable that the professor did not mention this.

From all this two questions emerge: Where does China stand today, economically as well as politically? What is its place in the world?

The small leap backward

According to the Chinese, the Soviet ideologist Suslov predicted in 1961 that the Chinese economy would break down within six months. Did Moscow really believe this? The Western observers with whom I talked in Hong Kong upon my return from China declared unanimously that in 1961 they had expected the Chinese economy to collapse within a few months. That was how hard China was hit by the disastrous policy of the "Great Leap Forward," by the withdrawal of Soviet experts, by the cessation of deliveries from the Soviets, and by natural catastrophes.

Chinese politicians nowadays are proud to have overcome all these reverses "out of our own strength." But what exactly was "our own strength" from 1961 to 1964? Was it not primarily a slackening of the reins? The Second Five-Year Plan, which should have run from 1957 to 1962, was promptly called off. In each factory and each commune only the possible was being done, without strict rules and without planning. The one thing which the state apparently managed to keep under control was the rationing of foodstuffs, textiles, and shoes. But this measure merely assured a marginal existence for the Chinese.

It was then that the border gates at Hong Kong were raised on the Chinese side, so that anyone who wanted to leave China could do so. Hundreds of thousands fled to the British colony to escape the rigors of life in their own country.

China has recovered slowly, very slowly, from this economic setback.

Government and Party, so improvident in 1959 with the "Great Leap Forward," remembered their former tactics—tactics that had led to victory after victory for twenty-five years: listen to the people, recognize their misery, and act accordingly, whether or not the action coincides with the ideological line of the moment. The weak must make concessions, must evade the forces of the enemy, must lick their wounds, as Mao had taught.

And this is what happened. In the people's communes, which had been turned overnight into virtual labor camps for peasants, most of the directives were rescinded. The central administration of the communes was relaxed, and the means of production were turned over to the smallest work units, the production groups. The peasants were put to work on their original fields.

Despite intense ideological disputes with the Soviet Union, in which China vehemently attacked the Soviet kolkhozes because they permit peasants to keep a piece of ground for themselves, the Chinese peasants were now allowed to have their own plots.

Taxes were considerably reduced. A commune need not pay a higher tax if it brought in a bumper crop, so that the peasants could increase their income through greater exertion. Although the Chinese politicians had rejected this type of incentive in their differences with Moscow, they now actually approved it.

Directives were issued to build up light industries. The necessary machines could be built by the Chinese themselves, so there was no need to depend on Soviet deliveries or Soviet experts.

Today one sees in Chinese cities something that is missing in the Soviet Union—huge posters advertising fountain pens and ballpoints, sewing machines, bicycles, radios in every size, shoes, stockings, paints and inks, kitchen utensils, and all sorts of implements. In the movies, just as in the West, advertisements are shown before the newsreel.

Heavy industry must be developed slowly. Its first task was to raise quality and provide a larger selection. But the lifeblood of the nation runs between agriculture and light industry. As a result, there is a wider variety of consumer goods in Chinese department stores than in most of the communist states in Europe. In terms of purchasing power, prices are high, and by our standards quality is poor, but even so, these goods provide a material incentive. Peasants and workers try to earn money because there are things to buy. We might almost say that the Chinese leaders have taken refuge in the economic principles of capitalism, at least for the present, to lead the country back to stability.

These principles are working, too. Agricultural production in 1964 was again large enough to feed 700 million people.

Other measures were also adopted, in addition to those in the economic sphere. Like the peasants and workers—indeed, the entire nation—the Party cadres were granted a respite. In the last two years there has not been one campaign to push the people to greater efforts. On the contrary, the "creative pause" has been given a big propaganda play and is attributed to Mao Tse-tung. No one is supposed to overexert himself; everyone is to have enough rest so he may do his best during working hours.

In all factories the demand for quality is given the same weight as that for quantity. Thrift is preached. The slogans of the "Great Leap Forward" have been reversed.

From reading the Chinese newspapers, seeing the newsreels, listening to political speeches, one gets an impression that nothing has changed since 1959. The Party line is followed faithfully, and everything seems as rigid as before. Yet in reality it is quite different.

I saw proof of this at the mass demonstrations in the Peking "People's Palace" that were called to protest "imperialist aggression" in Viet Nam. The ten thousand participants had to wait half an hour before the demonstration, which featured the usual battery of threats and bellicose accusations. During that waiting period, shouting choruses began among the demonstrators. I naturally assumed that the people were repeating political slogans and demanding the destruction of imperialism.

The choruses were then translated for me, and this was their context: The students in the orchestra section insisted, "The girls in the balcony should sing a song!" The girls replied in chorus, "The students in the orchestra should sing a song!" Then, "The soldiers should sing a song!" The soldiers didn't have to be asked twice. A conductor jumped up, baton in hand, and they sang. In chorus, the girls and students thanked them. Then the soldiers called out, "We did what you wanted—now you sing a song."

And so it continued, back and forth. What had sounded so threatening was really a popular amusement. But the newspapers the next day implied that the people of China had risen to smite the imperialists.

I have already mentioned that I was in Peking at a time when the newspapers were printing long admonitions to the people not to discuss love, superstition, and religion during their evening strolls in the park. To read these articles and the letters that commented on them was to be reminded of the heavy hand of government control. But walking in the parks, hearing the singing and laughter and animated talk between boys and girls, I had the feeling that there was little talk about building the socialist state.

When I went through the people's communes, accompanied by the chairman and Party secretary, I didn't notice any increased work tempo or any show of special respect when these dignitaries appeared. The leisurely work pace was unchanged. I got the same impression in the factories. Invariably a number of machines were standing idle, waiting to be repaired, but even the workers at the other machines didn't seem particularly industrious.

Family life, which had been seriously disrupted by the "Great Leap Forward," seemed to have been re-established everywhere. The giant park in Peking's Summer Palace was thronged with people on Sundays, tens of thousands of parents and children. The children were dressed with great care, the girls with their hair curled, the boys in clean shirts.

A few amateur painters were at work in quiet corners of the park; people were singing alone and in groups; pictures were being taken. A few people even carried portable radios. Thousands were enjoying the bathing beach, the girls in pretty, modern suits (no bikinis). Under the trees at the edge of the lake, parents were playing with their children.

Another reason why the government has re-established family

life and family solidarity is that the state can provide old age benefits and care for the sick only to a limited degree. Children still have to care for their aged parents. But that works only when the children respect the parents, when the natural love between them has not been destroyed. And so today respect and love for one's parents are urged in the schools and in the Communist Youth Association.

Naturally, the class struggle must go on. Not only that—efforts are being made to intensify it. But since China wants no popular unrest now, the fight has gradually been shifted to the ideological plane. Obviously, a purely ideological effort isn't too effective, so it is grossly exaggerated in order to get results.

Everywhere in China I tried to find out what had happened to the infamous city communes, which were reported to have imposed even more severe hardships than the people's communes had at the beginning. The residents of each street had been forced into production units. Housewives were supposed to report for work at dawn, apartments were tidied up by a cleaning brigade, children were relegated to kindergartens and boarding schools.

All my questions were quickly shoved aside. "These were experiments. We never got beyond the experimental stage," Professor Yung said. "The city communes involved too many problems. Above all, the problems of property ownership got too complicated."

A few scattered city communes are said to exist in Peking and Shanghai, for experimental purposes. I was not able to inspect them, but it seems unlikely that they have remained as originally planned.

And so China presents the picture of a great nation catching its breath. The creative pause has lasted four years now, which troubles some foreign observers. The government is suspected of preparing another great blow, a second "Great Leap Forward" or something of that sort. I saw no indication of any such thing. But the situation can change overnight.

What, then, has the Chinese Communist government accomplished in the fifteen years of its existence?

Unlike all the governments that preceded it, it has fed its people. Even in the years of terrible natural catastrophes, the people had enough food to survive. They might have been hungry, but not many starved to death.

But the costs of survival were great. Even if Chinese economists emphasize that the wheat imports were relatively small compared with domestic production, they still cost China a third, if not half, of its foreign currency reserves. To prime the pump of agriculture, the government spent another third of its foreign exchange reserves on artificial fertilizer from abroad. This has severely limited the purchasing power of China's industrial sector.

Heavy machinery is no longer delivered to China by the Soviet Union, either as foreign aid or against Soviet purchases of pork, wheat, or soybeans. The major installations China needs must be bought in Japan and West Europe and paid for in cash. As the foreign exchange reserves have been depleted, China's industrial imports are only about as large as Switzerland's.

Despite all this, China is a desirable trading partner in the eyes of many Western industrialists. They are banking on the future. This gigantic country, with a population of 700 million, will need a lot of merchandise some day. The first to establish themselves as business partners will reap the benefits.

That is one consideration. Another, more immediate, is that when China buys, it buys complete industrial installations—whole factories down to the last nut and bolt. Whoever gets that purchase order is doing big business.

While I was in Peking, industrialists from the German Federal Republic closed a deal with the Chinese government for a complete plant to produce polypropylene and another to produce nylon thread. In both cases the transactions involved millions of dollars.

The French, English, Italians, Belgians, and Danes were also engaged in such negotiations. The Chinese pay in letters of credit, which are payable on sight in England or Switzerland.

China is one of the few countries in the world to be almost free of foreign debts. Even her debt to the Soviet Union is said to be almost paid up. The Chinese also fulfill their trade agreements punctually, according to experts.

I asked Professor Yung where China gets her foreign exchange reserves. "From profits on export exchanges, as does every other country," he said. "And from invisible incomes." These invisible incomes are derived for the most part from Chinese living abroad.

In round figures, about 12 million Chinese living in various parts of Asia, and also in the United States, South and East Africa, Latin America, and Europe, are contributing to the development of the mother country. Many of them are enormously wealthy. Here we have the phenomenon of capitalist Chinese who, partly under pressure and partly voluntarily, support the Chinese communist government—and not always without self-interest. The investments they make in the mother country are well repaid by the Peking government in interest and dividends, and the government bonds they buy are likewise interest-bearing.

But their personal ties to the homeland are probably more important than the profit motive. Most Chinese living abroad have numerous relatives in China, whom they support with money. The relatives are paid in local currency, and the government gets the foreign exchange. Hence, the government has a special interest in furthering good relations between the Chinese who live abroad and their relatives and friends at home. The relatives, by registering with the government, may acquire the right not only to receive money orders from abroad but to make their purchases in special shops where merchandise of better quality is offered. They are said to get marriage permits more easily than those who have no relatives abroad. Overseas Chinese are invited to send delegates to the People's Congress, and, further, their interests receive official government attention.

So the cooperation between the communist regime and the capitalist overseas Chinese is close, one important reason being that the many Chinese abroad are uncertain whether they will be allowed to remain in their host countries for the rest of their lives. Chinese colonies, especially in Asia and the Pacific, have repeatedly been under attack. There have been demonstrations against the Chinese, whose ability and diligence have made them successful—and thus targets for the envious natives. Under these circumstances, the Chinese abroad want to keep the door to the mother country open. And the government takes this into account. With the foreign currency it builds settlements in which the foreign Chinese can reserve apartments or houses for the future.

But these overseas Chinese have other reasons for helping the mother country. They are, strange as it may seem, quite proud of their homeland, even though it is a communist state. In the last 150 years, China has never been as unified and as strong as it is today. It is an old dream of the Chinese to see their nation great and powerful. To them, its form of government is a minor factor.

Dynasties and regimes have come and gone in China. Many have been terrible. But the generations that followed never measured a dynasty by the amount of sacrifice it demanded, only by its achievements. Above all, governments are judged by China's ability to "save face" in its relations with the rest of the world. Beyond a doubt, China's strong position today impresses the Chinese living abroad, or at least a good many of them.

This posture also impresses the mainland Chinese. At the beginning of the communist regime many intellectuals, bourgeois democrats, and industrialists made their services available to the new government. In their eyes, this new government had rid the country of the colonial enclaves set up in China by foreign powers, had established Chinese sovereignty and carried out the essential land reforms promised so many times by other regimes.

Later they were to be bitterly disappointed—when the terror, the compulsion, and persecution started, when the land reform was nullified by collectivization and the peasant became a forced laborer. Many are still disillusioned. The government has tried, through its recent relaxed policies, to win back their sympathies and ameliorate their discontent. And it is, despite communism, a *Chinese* government.

There are exiled Chinese who, sharply condemning the cruelty and severity of the regime, still add, "Perhaps it had to be done."

The communist government has done only what democratic governments in Europe and the United States have achieved without cruelty and harshness: It has taught its people to read, write, and count. It has condemned self-interest and laid upon its people the responsibility for the common welfare. It has done away with unemployment. It has made one of the world's cleanest countries out of one of the world's dirtiest. It has guaranteed a minimum existence for its people and has laid the foundations for industrialization.

All this could have been—and, indeed, would have been—done by a democratic government. But none has ever existed in China. The errors of Chiang Kai-shek's military dictatorship, its corruption and nepotistic mismanagement, its organizational failures, its lack of modern reform, enabled communism to develop in China.

Communism has brought much blood and tears to the Chinese people, but not economic misery. The Chinese, now as before, are not well off. Like their fathers and grandfathers, they must struggle for a minimum of food and clothing. But for the first time in 150 years they are assured of that minimum.

It is not enough to point to high prices and poor quality of consumer goods, uncertain justice, spying and surveillance, and decide that these constitute a total evaluation of the present Chinese system. If one did so, it would be easy to indulge in the sort of wishful thinking that blinded Western eyes to what was going on in the Soviet Union and, later, Cuba. We cannot assume that this regime will collapse or that it is unpopular with the masses. This may have been true during certain periods, but not all the time; and this must be understood in the West.

China's foreign policy is another matter. Does it really differ essentially from the foreign policy charted by Lenin and Stalin? Not very much. Lenin and Stalin, too, professed to be for peaceful co-existence, with the significant reservation that the Soviet state must further the cause of world revolution. We do not know at this time whether the Soviet Union has generally abandoned that goal or merely let it drop into the background for tactical reasons. Nonetheless, the Soviet Union has become more or less the partner of the West. Internally, also, the Soviet Union and the East bloc countries are undergoing an economic and a resultant political development that is welcomed by the West.

Can we say today where China will stand in thirty years? By that time the Chinese communist government, if it survives, will be as old as the Soviet Union is today.

We look with concern at the power of 700 million people. This population, which may reach the billion mark in the not distant

Wherever a foreigner appears in China, he is usually applauded—
an illustration of "education in the spirit of proletarian
internationalism" and friendship among nations.

future, exerts a pressure that markedly differentiates China from the Soviet Union, and creates a different kind of danger—the "Yellow Peril" that our parents and grandfathers used to talk about.

China has done very little to allay the concern of the West and of its own neighbor states in regard to the "Yellow Peril." On the contrary, in the last few years it has repeatedly rattled its saber. The Chinese have fought in Korea, occupied Tibet, and penetrated into Indian territory. Their government has called for the re-establishment of the old borders; that is, it envisions territorial expansion to the south, west, and north, including the Soviet Union. Above all, China supports the guerrilla warfare in Viet Nam and is the chief obstacle to peace negotiations between the United States and North Viet Nam.

I do not think this can be attributed to China's population pressures. We know that the Soviet Union, with no excess of population, tried to restore the borders of czarist Russia in Poland, Rumania, and some of the Baltic states. It also took care to bring its neighboring states in Europe under its political and economic influence. So it is probably too early to tell whether China's expansive pressure is due to the needs of its population or is simply the expression of a claim to national power.

Another aspect of this aggressive spirit stems from the Chinese government's Leninist-Stalinist concept of revolution. This concept, however, involves no specific plans, makes no provisions for Chinese expansion, and includes no territorial demands by China. All that it envisions is that as many countries as possible, and finally all the countries of the world, should be governed by communism. If the Chinese form of communism were to prevail in such a world system, that would be good enough for Peking; and so China does all it can to support and further its own brand of communist revolution.

Chinese leaders are supposed to have declared that an atomic war would be welcome because it would lead to the destruction of the West and end in the victory of communism. But the Chinese politicians with whom I talked assured me repeatedly that Peking follows a policy of peaceful co-existence, but—in contrast to Moscow—it simultaneously supports revolutions and "wars of liberation" all over the world. That the one precludes the other is now understood in Moscow. Peking does not yet seem to know it.

Thus China has been brought into sharp conflict with the West, its neighbors, and the Soviet Union.

In addition, China now has atomic weapons. On the one hand, this fact makes the Chinese more dangerous. But, provided the Chinese leaders could be brought to realize that they have much to gain through negotiations, China, because it has become stronger, could become more conciliatory without losing face.

For the sake of world peace, and above all for the sake of the Chinese people, this is to be hoped for.

For the Chinese are a peace-loving people. Today they are still very poor. Their economy is backward. Almost half of this huge country, the size of Europe, is sparsely inhabited and underdeveloped.

A Chinese government whose only concern was the welfare of its own people could find within its own borders a rich field for action, for a thousand years of peace.

33

Good-bye to the "other" world

I am sitting in the waiting room of the Peking airport. My plane for Canton leaves in half an hour. China's civil aviation does not operate at night, so there is great activity every morning. Flights go out at ten-minute intervals, connecting the provincial cities of this huge country.

I take a look at the other waiting passengers who are leaving Peking on business. Most of them are officials, as I can tell from their clothes and bearing. Others might be technicians or engineers, needed in the more remote provinces for some special project. Among them are a few women. The luggage of these travelers consists mostly of old-fashioned suitcases, many made of fiber or cardboard, sometimes tied with string. Some carry their precious belongings in baskets. Since it is summer most of them wear no coats, only shirts and unpressed trousers. Their feet are thrust into plastic sandals.

The doors to the customs room are thrown open, and I see something I have not seen for many weeks: a group of about thirty Europeans walks out onto the field, accompanied by four European stewardesses. The girls are wearing light gray uniforms, nylon hose, and high-heeled shoes. Their caps sit jauntily on their well-groomed hair, and each is carrying a shoulder bag with long leather handles. I look at the passengers—well-cut suits, white shirts, ties, raincoats, hats, leather luggage. I really feel like running toward this group of travelers, greeting them, talking with them. I feel a common bond with them. Because they are Europeans? Yes—but most of all because I believe they would understand me, would know what I was talking about. They and I know and belong to that other world —the European world, the West.

These travelers pass me quickly. I look out on the landing field at the plane toward which they are heading. It is the largest on the field, but so far away, almost on the runway, that I hadn't noticed it before. It is a jet. In all these weeks I had never once seen a civilian jet in a Chinese airport. The markings on the plane explain everything: CCCP in cyrillic letters (USSR). Are they Russians? Yes, most of them are. Others are businessmen and diplomats from other countries, taking the shortest and quickest way home, via Moscow. Obviously they don't want to disembark in Moscow in the clothes they have been wearing during their stay in Peking; anyone who wears a suit coat and tie here will certainly be conspicuous. I myself am standing here in a tropical shirt and linen trousers, because my exit permit is made out for Hong Kong. Day after tomorrow I too will put on a tie again.

Out on the field, one of the Russian stewardesses is giving the sign to remove the gangway to the Aeroflot plane when my flight is announced. Along with several Chinese I start to cross the field.

Two worlds, then, have met briefly in the Peking airport. Only someone who has become accustomed to the Chinese would realize how different those two worlds are, how much separates them— more than just clothes or skin color. "About half a century" goes through my mind, as I think of the changes in technology and living standards. But I correct myself immediately: "Or rather, four thousand years."

The flight from Peking to Canton takes nine hours. Before getting on the plane I am asked once more whether I want to eat Chinese or European style. There are four stopovers on the Peking-Canton flight, and in each airport restaurant I find that a table has been set specially for me, with knives and forks instead of chopsticks. With the meal the waiter also brings a complaint book and invites me to "practice criticism." The complaint book contains a request in

Chinese, Russian, and English, inviting the guest to write down all that displeases him and offer suggestions for improvements. It calls attention to the fact that a servant who has been criticized must turn in a report on the matters mentioned within three days, and that his supervisors will write to the complainant within ten days. Here again is China's struggle for discipline—probably the only way a communist government can exert that control which in the West takes care of itself through competition and material incentive.

I try vainly to see whether the others, the Chinese passengers, are as well taken care of as I am. I am not led into a separate dining room; perhaps there is none. Instead, my table is shut off from the others by a screen. So I look at the beautiful intaglio work on the screen, showing a dragon with many decorative details.

At the Canton airport I see a familiar face—my former Cantonese interpreter. He seems glad to see me. "How would you like to dine on dragon and tiger meat tonight?" he asks. "Only if you come along." His face lengthens. Hesitantly, he replies, "I think I shall have much work to do in my office tonight. Please forgive me for not accepting your invitation to dine."

Here it is again, the screen between human being and human being.

From previous experience, I know that interpreters are not allowed to take any meals with foreigners. They may not accept an invitation, any more than a tip. Without accepting his excuse, I say, "Fine. We'll do without the dinner and take a stroll through the city." Under these circumstances, it turns out that he really has nothing pressing to do at the office.

So on my last evening in China, we mingle once more in the teeming Chinese street life. We squeeze in among hundreds of people on the narrow sidewalks, cross streets in a zigzag course, dodge bicycles and tricycle rickshas, stick our noses into dozens of minute shops. Small groups of people are standing everywhere, discussing and gesticulating just as if it were still possible to haggle over prices in present-day China.

"Life here is different from that of Peking," the interpreter says. "This is the South. People have a different temperament."

We stroll along the banks of the Pearl River. Darkness has

fallen. Out there on the sampans the people have already lit their fires. Hundreds of lights are reflected in the water. People sit packed close together, talking, on the high walls of the quai. Thousands of cicadas are chirping in the trees above us. Over it all is a clear, star-sprinkled tropical sky. At this moment it is easy to forget that I am in a communist country, in a state that is making the rest of the world uneasy, a state whose ideology and military preparedness are felt as a threat.

We too take a seat on the quai. From the small plastic case he always carries my interpreter takes a fan. He opens it, hesitates, and then holds it out to me. It is an old fan, damaged in a few places but carefully mended, covered with Chinese characters.

"This was a present from my aunt when I was born. She put it in my cradle," he says. "She did the calligraphy herself. Isn't it pretty? I'll read it and translate it for you." His fingers move along the characters. They are wise maxims about life, in verse. "Always act as you wish others to act toward you," the advice of Confucius.

When he has translated all the verses my interpreter says, "Don't forget that this fan belongs to another time. But we do understand these poems even nowadays."

Early the next morning we are off to the railroad station.

There it is again, the pullman car for the travelers to Hong Kong. As the train pulls out a communist fighting song pours out of the loudspeakers on the platform. The railroad personnel salute with their red flags. "Zeitye, zeitye!" "Farewell!" my interpreter calls, waving.

Slowly the train pulls out of the station. Two posters pass in front of my window. "Welcome, Visitors, to the Permanent Industrial Exhibition of Canton" is printed on one of them. On the other are Chinese characters I have come to know well: "Proletarians of all countries, unite against the common enemy." What a strange contrast to the English "Welcome"!

And now there are rice paddies to the right and left of the tracks. They disappear, and we go through narrow valleys, climb many-terraced hills and mountains. Here and there are water buffaloes yoked to plows and people hitched to carts. Others are threshing the ripe rice by hand on small wooden benches. The villages that looked so strange to me when I entered the country now seem quite familiar—flat, straw-covered roofs with the towers of granaries between. Now and then a small stream, a canal, a dam, a water wheel. A detachment of militia marches single file over a small bridge—peasants who for this day have put on uniforms and shouldered rifles. The eternal and the new in China.

This time there are no other Europeans in the pullman car. Next to me sits a Chinese who plays with two nuts, letting them roll between his fingers. He has been visiting relatives in Shanghai; his home is in Hong Kong. Opposite are three Africans who have been visiting Peking at the invitation of some official agency. They are from the Congo.

The fans in the ceiling of the car make a whirring sound. The loudspeaker is on, and between melodies from Peking operas, announcements follow announcements. A socialist competition for greater neatness and cleanliness is in progress among the conductors of the individual coaches. A policeman is stationed at the door that connects us with the next car. He wears blue trousers, a white jacket, and a large pistol in his belt.

After a three-hour journey we reach the border. Before us stretches the long customs building. And there's the border interpreter again. He separates the passengers skillfully and once again conducts me into a tea salon.

Once again I fill out all the forms I filled out when I came in. Then we go to the small room where I must open my bags. The formalities are soon over, with no difficulties whatever.

And here is the interpreter. "Do you wish to eat here or to cross the border right away?"

Suddenly I recognize the feeling that has come over me. "No, thank you. I'll go at once."

I don't even wait for my baggage. It will be sent after me. I push my way toward the bridge, across the bridge. I must show my exit permit just once more, to the last Chinese sentry. He takes it, reads it through carefully, and slowly hands it back to me.

Five steps, then another uniformed man confronts me. This one wears khaki with the blue hat of the British border police: "Yes, sir . . ."

Index